As a "problem" to be solved,
a phenomenon to be explained,
a difficulty to be interpreted, the
Wrong Number
is stubbornly inaccessible
to the ordinary sciences, logic, or any
other forms of rational inquiry.
Its Art and Mystery belong wholly to the
realms of the non-rational, the irrational,
the surrational. To the extent that
the Wrong Number is a "problem," then,
it is a problem that can be "solved"
only by uncompromisingly
*poetic* means.

In the loose ends of everything,
we are trying to find
the beginning of something.

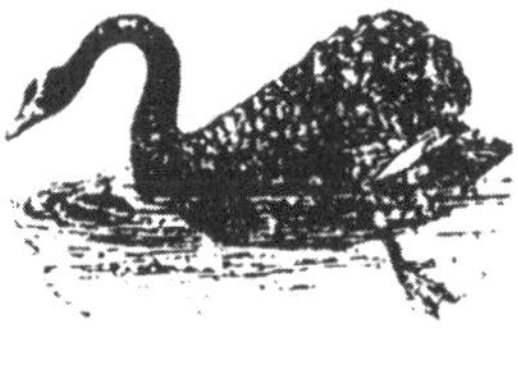

Surrealist Editions

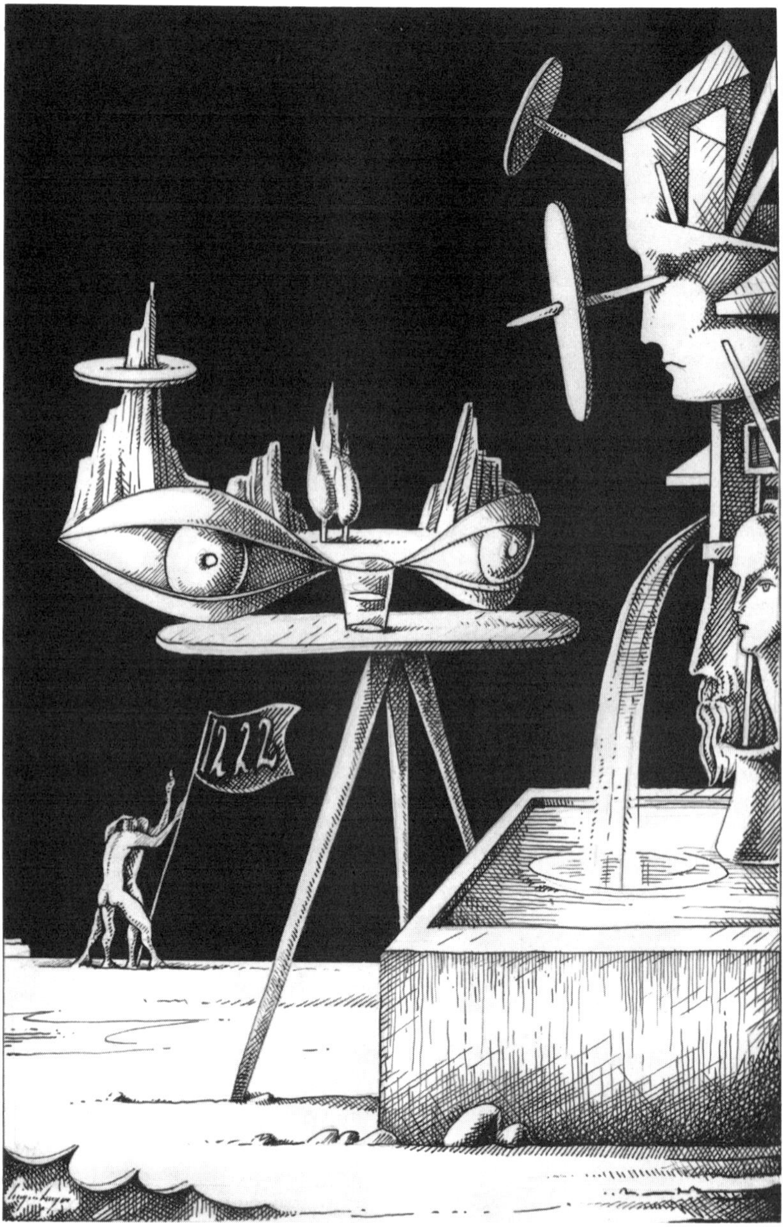
1222

Franklin Rosemont

# *An Open Entrance to the Shut Palace of* WRONG NUMBERS

*Drawings by*
Artur do Cruzeiro Seixas

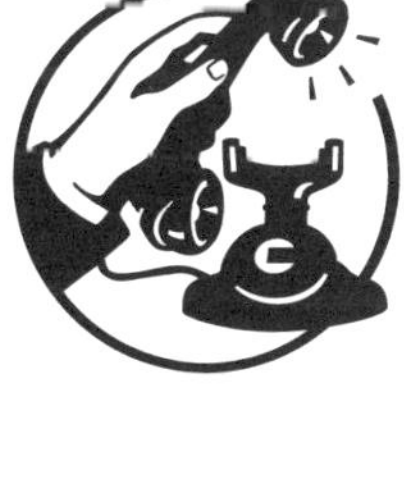

CHICAGO
SURREALIST EDITIONS
2003

*Cover drawing by*
*Artur do Cruzeiro Seixas*



ISBN 0-941194-34-5

First Edition

*Author's Note*

This is not a work of fiction.
Personally unacquainted as I am with the callers of Wrong Numbers cited in this book,
I have used their real names throughout—
assuming that the names they gave me were real.
Any similarity between these real individuals and characters in fiction
is strictly coincidental.

Surrealist Editions and Black Swan Press
are imprints of the
Surrealist Movement in the United States.

*For a complete list, write:*

BLACK SWAN PRESS
P.O. Box 6424
Evanston, IL 60204

*or visit the Surrealist Movement's website:*
www.surrealism-usa.org

# Foreword

Once this book began to write itself—or, more accurately, as soon as I realized that the first dozen or so pages were in fact rushing full speed ahead into something that would probably turn into a book—I was sometimes beset by the doubts that sooner or later cloud the minds of all chroniclers of heretofore unchronicled adventures in the unknown. Could it be, I wondered, that I was on the wrong track—that this was the wrong book, on the wrong subject, written at the wrong historic moment, in the wrong country, by the wrong person, with the wrong attitude, and for the wrong reasons?

That I persisted despite these doubts owes something to the venerable science of Flippism ("Heads, I write ten more pages; tails, I quit for a week"), but even more to my respect for what André Breton, in his *States-General* (1943), called "the art, so unjustly disparaged, of burning the candle at both ends." I was also reassured by the thought that, no matter how wrongheaded it turned out to be, a book so utterly lacking in "commercial potential"—as everyone insisted was the case—couldn't possibly be *all* wrong.

And now that it's done, or at least quasi-definitively unconcluded, I see that the dark cloud had a silver lining all along. Precisely *because* of its cover-to-cover wrongheadedness and absolute indifference to the monster of "marketability," this book can hardly fail to fall into the *wrong hands*—that is to say, the hands of the *wrong readers,* who are, of course, the best of all possible readers: the very ones who are most likely to make the wildest, most imaginative and creative wrong turns of their own, and therefore the most far-reaching discoveries.

Many surrealist comrades and co-conspirators helped shape some of the arguments developed in these pages, in most cases without even knowing it, and without ever referring to telephones or wrong numbers. Why did Philip Lamantia urge me to look into the works of Fabre d'Olivet at that particular moment? Why did David Gascoyne decide to send me, unannounced, "at the Winter Solstice 1995/96," a copy of Louis-Claude de Saint-Martin's *Le Crocodile*? And how did Gherasim Luca come to send me his *Théatre de Bouche* just as I was starting on the last section of this book?

I am especially grateful to Artur do Cruzeiro Seixas, of Lisbon, who, after reading an early draft of the opening section, sent me original cover art and drawings for the entire book.

Special thanks to Jen Besemer and Paul Garon, of the Chicago Surrealist Group, for reading and commenting on the text. And for other assistance of various kinds, a hearty *merci beaucoup* also to Eric Benveniste in Paris; Justin O'Brien in Chicago; Thomas Carey of the San Francisco History Center at the city's Main Library; and Myrna Bell Rochester in Palo Alto.

F.R.

Chicago, *May Day, 2003*

This book is dedicated to
PENELOPE
for all and everything,
as always,
and much more besides,
in the spirit (once again) of
our friend Eiranaeus Philalethes,
who wrote:
"Join heaven to earth
in the fire of love,
and you will see
in the middle of the firmament,
the Bird of Hermes."

# CONTENTS

Among the very few Americans welcomed into the Surrealist Group in Paris by André Breton himself (Paris, 1966), **Franklin Rosemont** later that year with his wife Penelope co-founded the first indigenous Surrealist Group in the United States, in Chicago. He has published several volumes of poetry, most recently *Lamps Hurled at the Stunning Algebra of Ants* (with drawings by Karol Baron), and *Penelope: A Poem* (with drawings by Jacques Lacomblez). His other works include *What Is Surrealism? Selected Writings of André Breton* (Monad Press), *Surrealism and Its Popular Accomplices* (City Lights), and several books on revolutionary history, including *Haymarket Scrapbook* (with Dave Roediger, 1986), *Juice Is Stranger Than Friction: Selected Writings of T-Bone Slim* (1992), and *Joe Hill: The IWW and the Making of a Revolutionary Workingclass Counterculture* (2003), all published by Charles H. Kerr in Chicago. Editor of four volumes of the international anthology, *Arsenal / Surrealist Subversion*, he has collaborated extensively on surrealist publications throughout the world, organized several important surrealist exhibitions, and currently edits the University of Texas Press "Surrealist Revolution Series."

Long recognized as Portugal's premier surrealist painter and graphic artist as well as one of the movement's finest poets, **Artur do Cruzeiro Seixas** was born in Amadora in 1920. His interest in surrealism began around 1943; five years later he was a militant member of the Surrealist Group in Lisbon. For fourteen years starting around 1950 he lived in Africa; in 1953 he organized the first sub-Saharan surrealist exhibition on that continent in Luanda, Angola.

Many of Cruzeiro Seixas's drawings have been reproduced in portfolios and albums, including *Local Onde o Mar Naufragou* (2001), and his poems have been collected in such books as *Eu Falo em Chamas* (1986). Among the important monographs on his work are *Cruzeiro Seixas* (Lisbon, 1989) with texts by Natalia Correia, André Coyné, Eugenio F. Granell, Edouard Jaguer, Antonio Maria Lisboa, José Pierre, and Franklin Rosemont; and most recently, the catalog *Cruzeiro Seixas: Other Forms of Dancing, Flying, Dreaming, and Wandering* (Fundación Eugenio Granell, 2001; available in the U.S. from Black Swan Press), with essays by André Coyné, Edouard Jaguer, Paco Lopez-Barxas, Franklin Rosemont, and Luis de Moura Sobral.

In addition to his numerous solo shows, Cruzeiro Seixas has participated in many collective surrealist exhibitions, including the 1976 World Surrealist Exhibition in Chicago, and "Totems Without Taboos," also in Chicago—the first U.S. exhibition devoted exclusively to the Exquisite Corpse game (1993). He has also collaborated on several publications of the Surrealist Movement in the United States.

# 1.

# THE STRANGEST WAY OF TALKING TO STRANGERS

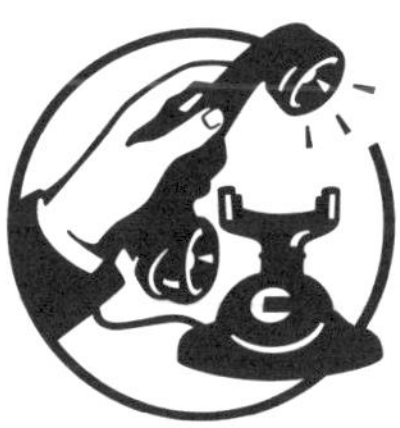

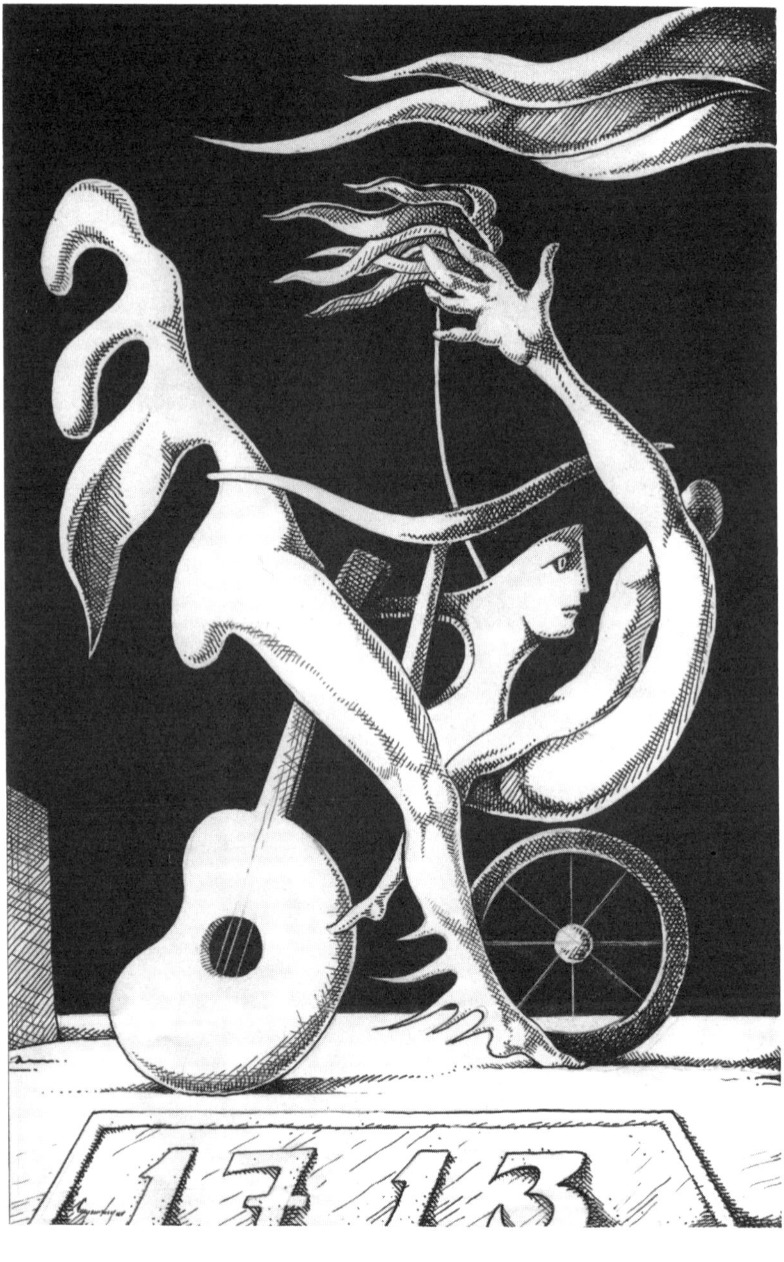
1713

## INSTEAD OF AN INTRODUCTION

Call me the *if* in drifting.

Where I come from, mountains are worth climbing even if they're not there.

I think in spirals, and mince no silences.

The way I look at it, just about all work is at cross-purposes, and I have never had any trouble finding better things to do.

What matters right now is that you don't know me and I don't know you. Who are we, and what do we want? In all probability, we've never met. We are, in two words, complete strangers. Our paths may have crossed somewhere sometime, but nothing is less certain, and neither of us knows anything about it. And yet, here we are, confronting each other in the pages of a book—of all things!

As for me, what can I say?

When I talk in my sleep, I know what I am sleeping about.

When in Rome, I prefer to do as the Zuni do.

Birds, I might add, understand me perfectly, and *vice versa*.

"The more poetic something is," according to Novalis, "the more *real* it is." Nearly a century and a half before I was born, he took the words right out of my mouth.

Windows and paintings are at their best when they invite us to tear down walls.

"History" tells us the Black Hawk War ended in 1832. Why, then, do I see it, hear it, and feel it raging on all sides?

In these woods, aren't we all babes?

I am fond of the definition of hurricane: *a violent tropical cyclone with winds moving at seventy-three or more miles per hour, often accompanied by torrential rains*. Somehow, it reminds me of my childhood.

My recipe for a good life: Love madly, live poetry passionately, go for long walks, get plenty of sleep, learn to see and to listen, remember that "in wilderness lies the preservation of the Earth" (Thoreau), and don't forget to read the poets.

I've never met a mountain, a tree, or a bird that I didn't like.

Wouldn't the game of chess be less boring if all the knights were Don Quixotes?

Falling in love on a Ferris Wheel is the finest of all possible postscripts to Hegel's *Logic*.

The laziness of poets is its own reward.

At times it seems that the only things that really count for me are the things that most people say don't count at all.

The words I like best are transparent, high-flying, and full of defiance. Their daredeviltry, which is also mine, appears to be all the difference between me and all those who, for whatever reason, are not me.

My preferred philosophers: Chuang Tzu, Spinoza, Diderot, Hegel. Beyond philosophy: Isidore Ducasse, Comte de Lautréamont, Thelonious Monk—and Bugs Bunny. All for one and one for all!

In the loose ends of everything, we are trying to find the beginning of something.

*Now*, for example. If you ask, "What happens next?" I shall have to answer truthfully: "I don't know."

After all, I'm a stranger here myself.

And you?

## The Theory of Passional Distraction

In the long run, aren't the moments commonly called "odd" the ones that really make a difference? The others—life's "even" moments—elide into hopeless sameness, a glob of gray on gray in the gray frame of a dimly-remembered past and a cold pre-forgotten future. The odd ones, however, stand out, for good or ill, and come back to haunt us, to invade our dreams, to provoke laughter, or in a thousand ways to make us wonder about the possible and the impossible, a new society, a different life.

In this book I propose to examine but one category of "odd moment": the Wrong Number. As a "problem" to be solved, a phenomenon to be explained, a difficulty to be interpreted, the Wrong Number is stubbornly inaccessible to the ordinary sciences, logic, or any other forms of rational inquiry. Its Art and Mystery belong wholly to the realms of the non-rational, the irrational, the surrational. To the extent that the Wrong Number is a "problem," then, it is a problem that can be "solved" only by uncompromisingly *poetic* means.

By poetry, I most emphatically do not mean those obsequious trivialities that are given center-stage during the disgusting government-sponsored hoax known as "National Poetry Month." By poetry I mean nothing less than life's *fundamental experience*: a kind of magic, infinitely *vital* and incessantly transformative. Such a *force*, which changes each of us and all of us as well as the world we live in, has little in common with the "literary."

I propose a rigorous definition:

*Poetry is an amorous conspiracy of the left eye's* this-is-it *and the right eye's* now-or-never *giving voice to the all-or-nothing possibilities of a future truly worthy of Desire with a capital D.*

Of course, I just took these words right out of my mouth.

But that is precisely the point, where poetry is concerned, and it cannot be urged too strongly that poetry, as an activity of mind, is concerned with everything and more. To dream with one's whole body is to live life in a way that is much larger than what is usually called life. Poetry accepts no limits; it does not even limit itself to mere limitlessness. To reduce poetry to anything less than all this would be, for all practical purposes, to deny its reason for being. And to deny poetry is to say yes to misery and to miserabilism.

A key concept in surrealism's critical vocabulary, *miserabilism* embodies all ideologies that rationalize misery. André Breton defined it as "the depreciation of reality in place of its exaltation." A direct offshoot of fascism *and* Stalinism, with "as many variations as there are categories of misery," the word miserabilism sums up the reality of contemporary capitalism—the capitalism of the World Trade Organization, the International Monetary Fund, the World Bank, Disneyland, the fast-food empires, the prison industry, and all the other plunderers and polluters of our planet.

In the miserabilist world order—*i.e.*, the existing state of society—most people live so little, and so pusillanimously, that it is often hard to recognize it as living at all. In such conditions, authentic poetry is always and everywhere a *disturbing* factor, an eruption of unanticipated and "irrational" challenges to the legitimacy of things-as-they-are. In a diseased social order oppressed by rules, poetry is the exception that breaks the rules.

All routine behavior—and "work" above all—impedes the delights of carefree wandering, which alone can lead to something worthwhile. What I call Passional Distraction—with a tip of the hat to Charles Fourier—seems to me the most fruitful way of interrupting and disrupting the miserabilist routines of life and urging people in the direction of the Marvelous, real pleasure and self-discovery, which are, after all, the major tasks of poetic action in our time. Serving as a kind of lever, Passional Distraction helps poetry sabotage the habitual, humdrum, boring, mundane and monotonous, as it moves us into the unique and the unexpected: a double defiance of the Reality Principle. Shaking up the reified relations between individual ego, society, and material reality, such defiance permits each and everyone to follow through the various automatisms and partial automatisms that allow the mind's eyes, and the body's eyes, and all the other sensory organs to plunge into the very heart of the real: the *surreality* in which all things are always new.

Ever more urgent, the intervention of poetry in daily life requires the diversionary use of "irrelevant" accidents provoked by the instability and malfunctioning of the existing order itself. One of the greatest pleasures (and therefore duties) of poets today is to liberate the overlooked, the ignored and suppressed, and therefore to bypass and, whenever possible, to *short-circuit* the ideological untruths passed off as the "official" (*i.e.*, ruling and manipulative) versions of "reality."

In essence, poetry is an activity in which people do their best, and *know* they are doing their best, precisely when they *don't* know what they are doing. Passional Distraction is but another name for effective poetic intervention on the perennially contested terrain indicated by Gauguin's ever-troubling questions: *Where do we come from? Where are we? Where are we going?.*

This free-floating inattentiveness, which dullards are wont to confuse with the murky incoherence of the scatterbrained, is in truth awareness raised to a vastly higher power. Dialectically resolving the most improbable contradictions, Passional Distraction reaches a point at which it becomes a particularly acute kind of concentration. I agree with F. W. H. Myers who, in his classic *Human Personality* (1903)—the first comprehensive survey of the manifold forms of what he called the "subliminal self"—argued that distraction could be *integrative* as well as disintegrative. In the aimless stroll, the automatistic trance, the hypnagogic revery, and the sudden occurrence of objective chance, Passional Distraction has again and again proved its mettle as a means of knowledge.

I do not extol delirium for its own sake, but rather for the great good it now and then allows each and every one of us to accomplish without effort. Thanks to the tried and true method of *riveted inattention*, distraction itself can be situated in the service of revelation and, as we shall see, of revolution as well.

# Voices at the End of the Line

The telephone rings. A voice unfamiliar to you asks for a person you do not know. Long-established convention offers you a choice of two standard and interchangeable replies:

"I'm sorry, but there's no one here by that name."

Or: "Sorry, you have the wrong number."

This is one of the commonest and most characteristic experiences of our time, and of the entire past century, and like so many other common and characteristic experiences it is regarded variously as confusing, disorienting, embarrassing, irritating or infuriating. For the overwhelming majority, Wrong Numbers are a small but bothersome invasion of what they are pleased to call their privacy; a regrettably unpreventable and unpunishable disturbance of the peace.

It was during the spring of 1976, in the weeks preceding the May 1st opening of the World Surrealist Exhibition at the Gallery Black Swan, that I began to wonder: Isn't it possible that all these Wrong Numbers might add up to something? Now and then through the years I had taken note of a few particularly unusual Wrong Numbers, but now a more systematic effort seemed called for. Largely because of the exhibition, the number of telephone calls I received in this period was dramatically greater than had been the case six months earlier, or would be six months later. The quantity of Wrong Numbers naturally rose as well, but out of proportion to the total number of calls. Neither before nor since have so many Wrong Numbers impinged upon my consciousness in so short a span of time.

In the spirit of disinterested inquiry I began to keep a kind of log of all the Wrong Numbers that came my way. In no time at all the experience involved a number of curious incidents as well as coincidences that were even more curious, and what started out as a short-term experiment evolved into a long-range project. Several years later, despite lapses and the lack of any sort of plan, I found myself still keeping something of a record of Wrong Numbers.

My original aim was simply to record, for each Wrong Number, the date and time of the call; the caller's sex, age, accent, and other distinctive characteristics; the name of the person asked for; and any other significant details. The project, however—such as it was—proceeded in a much less orderly fashion. Most of my notes were hastily scribbled on scraps of paper that I happened to find near the phone, and more than a few of them undoubtedly wound up in the wastebasket. Many notes were not dated. Some later proved almost impossible to read (most of these were records of calls received in the wee hours, and were jotted down in the dark). There were times when I felt too tired to write up a call in detail, and sometimes I was diverted by the doorbell, or another phone call, and kept no record at all. With few exceptions, only Wrong Numbers that seemed especially "strong" or enticing were transferred from scrap to notebook. There are large gaps. Over the years many notes, probably most of them, were lost.

It did not take long, however, for the list of Wrong Numbers to fill up several notebook pages. Occasionally I received two or three in one day; and sometimes two or three in quick succession from the same person. In these latter calls, the number had in fact been dialed correctly, but the caller was looking for someone who did not live there—evidently someone to whom that same number had been previously assigned.

Now and then I tried to engage a caller in conversation, but with little success.

Some callers were trying to reach restaurants, grocery stores, hardware stores, or other places of business. One caller repeated the number he had dialed and it was in fact my own, but it turned out he was trying to call the same number in another city (Cleveland, I think). In later years I received several similar calls from individuals who were actually calling New York, whose area code differs from Chicago's by only one digit. For several weeks in 1978 I received call after call for a local news bureau; the callers, all from out of town, were clearly in great haste, and often excited: "Hi, put Ed on, will you? This is Joe. I've got the story on that explosion in Detroit."

Another caller opened with "Hi, is Fred there?" Before I got past saying no he continued: "How about Carl, or Max, or Louis?" This time I was able to say "Sorry, there's nobody here but me" before he went on: "Geez, business must be slow, huh? Isn't *anybody* there?"

"Nobody you're looking for," I replied. "You've reached a Wrong Number."

"Huh?" he said, dumfounded. "This isn't the bar?"

I was impressed how quickly my Wrong Numbers ran the gamut of emotions, tone of voice, volume and mood. Shouters, whisperers, stammerers, baritones, sopranos, asthmatics, the hard of hearing, men with colds, teenagers with radios blaring, children goofing off, young women with Eastern European accents, and old women with dogs barking in the background all misdialed their way to my ear.

A sultry-voiced woman who did not give her name responded to my "Hello" by asking, seductively: "What are you doin' tonight?" I replied that I had nothing planned, and asked: "What did you have in mind?" Alas, she slammed down the phone when she learned that my name was not Reggie.

On the third of April 1978 a very young child, who was perhaps playing with the phone, started off with the words "Hello, what does O mean?" It took a few seconds for me to guess that she was wondering how to get the assistance of the Operator. I told her: "O just means zero. You dial O to get the Operator," but she replied: "What does zero mean? What does Operator mean?"

Some weeks later a vehement young man called and asked for Ernestine. "Sorry, there's no one named Ernestine here," said I, and hung up. I do not seem to have made a note of what I was doing at the time, but clearly I was occupied with something or other, or I would not have been so perfunctory. Five seconds later the phone rang again.

"Look, I need to talk to Ernestine," said the same voice. "It's very important."

"But there is no one named Ernestine here," I repeated. "You have reached what is called a Wrong Number."

My caller remonstrated further. I urged him to look up Ernestine's number just to make sure, but he wanted no advice from me. Altogether I think he called five times, perhaps six, the last time threatening me with physical violence if I did not let him speak to Ernestine at once. At long last I managed to convince him that he would be making a serious mistake by going to Ernestine's place and beating somebody up, thinking it was me.

What a movie we could have made!

Only once was I actually acquainted with the person a caller asked for. But I did not know the caller, and the caller did not know me. The caller, moreover, had no reason to think the person she sought could be reached at my number; she had, as she realized only while talking with me, misdialed the number she had before her, and reached my number by mistake, so that the call was an authentic Wrong Number.

There were times when almost all the calls coming in seemed to be Wrong Numbers—calls for Jeannie, Rhonda, Hélène, Perry, Maurice, Ford, Kathy, Sandy, Margie, Consuelo, Diane, Denise, Yvette, Caroline, Luis, Cleo, Nancy, Alberto, Carlos, Phil, Dulcea, and Mrs Savenelli (I am not sure of the spelling of these last two names), and many, many others. Only our voices met, and only fleetingly—but as Heraclitus would say, even those who take part in Wrong Numbers are workers and collaborators in what goes on in the universe.

Week after week, year after year, the strange procession continued: tough guys, sexy ladies, giggling tots, morose oldsters, hungry individuals in search of won-ton soup, excited male and female voices speaking in languages I do not understand, eager seekers of fresh fruit and vegetables, junkies trying to track down someone or other, mature women who might have been librarians, pompous folks whose speech was heavy with italics and bold face, men with faint voices and bad coughs, potential purchasers of new lawnmowers, sports fans eager to get to a game, vacationers just returned to the city, people wanting to "place an ad," patients with questions for their doctors, tired applicants for employment, boyfriends and girlfriends trying to reach their lovers, reporters in a hurry to get a story on the wire, fast talkers, mumblers, whiners, cacklers, drawlers, and at least one fellow with a bad case of hiccups.

And all of them, by some crazy chance, calling *me*.

Are Wrong Numbers a second life?

## The Interpretation of Interruptions

Early on in the course of this journey into the unknown I was forcibly struck by the similarities between the Wrong Number and auditory hallucination, specifically as the latter relates to the still much-mystified phenomenon known as poetic inspiration.

Any sudden ringing of the phone inevitably arouses one's sense of anticipation, but in a Wrong Number it is an unknown voice that speaks, and it utters the unexpected. The recipient of a Wrong Number finds himself/herself to be an unwelcome intruder between two unknowns. The voice that calls and the name it pronounces remain forever faceless and formless for the one who answers. Despite their brevity, therefore, Wrong Numbers are moments of acute derealization.

Fortunately for those who place a high value on their mental balance, the mysterious strangers who dial Wrong Numbers are always in a terrible hurry. They have time only for a few curt words before they dissolve, with a click, back into the silent gloom from whence they came. Were the experience to be prolonged beyond a few seconds, and one's ability to hang up the phone suspended, many might find it unendurable.

The Wrong Number is an essentially *irrational* experience, and all the more disturbingly so because it is also *concrete*. I do not know whose voice it is, but I am confident that it is a real human voice, and

I would recognize it if I heard it again. The voice is clearly addressing *me*, as an individual—notwithstanding the fact that the consciousness behind the voice expects and sometimes believes that "I" am another—and asks for a particular person by name. And although I have no idea who this sought-for person is, I do not doubt that such a person actually exists. Because of the purely aleatory character of Wrong Numbers, however, this person and the caller are related to me roughly in the way that elements in a dream are related to elements in another dream.

For various social and psychological reasons (to be discussed in subsequent chapters), very few Wrong Numbers—perhaps as little as one percent—are considered wondrous, sensational, mind-boggling, or even as good as a night at the movies. In my own experience, however, many are at least striking and memorable, either because they evoke particular names, persons, places, or incidents; or because they echo or expand upon something I had read or dreamed or thought about; or because they involve humor.

Some Wrong Numbers awaken nostalgia. Late in the evening of February 14, 1998—Valentine's Day—two different callers asked for Charlene. I was immediately reminded of a Charlene from childhood; we were in fifth grade together. Although we were hardly even acquainted, for several weeks we were both mercilessly teased by our classmates for having kissed each other—once!—at somebody's birthday party.

Now and then a Wrong Number assumes an almost *oracular* tone. This is especially true when the caller, sure that she/he has reached the right number, dispenses with the usual preliminaries. Some hint darkly at unforeseen events ("Hey, what time are you guys going to the game?") or momentous transformations in the course of one's life ("Well, buddy, I guess this is your lucky day!"). Others are levers of objective chance, as when a caller asks for Cathy or Emily at the very moment you happen to be reading *Wuthering Heights*, or asks for Rudy when you're listening to Thelonious Monk's "Little Rootie Tootie."

At the 1976 World Surrealist Exhibition, Penelope arranged the "Domain of Robin Hood," a dense forest of green gloves. During that same period we were amused by a large graffiti—"R. Hood"—spray-painted on a fence on Belden Avenue near our house; it was almost certainly gang-related, but still reminiscent of the old-time Sherwood Forest gang. In the weeks preceding the exhibition, and all during it, Penelope had reread her many Robin Hood books, and was in fact reading a new version of the outlaw's saga when, a few weeks later, a caller asked "Is Robin there?" Sadly, when I asked "Robin who?" the only response was a *click*.

On May 19, 1997, completing her book *Surrealist Women: An International Anthology*, Penelope noted that Ludmila Savitzky—whose name appears in the "Inquiry on Suicide" in *La Révolution Surréaliste* No. 2 (1925)—was an early French translator of James Joyce. Shortly afterward, a woman caller asked: "May I speak to Joyce, honey?"

Trivial in themselves, perhaps, such "coincidental" calls acquire a disquieting momentum when one follows another, and another, and yet another. Wrong Numbers come in endless variety, and are rarely regarded as monotonous. Always, however—and by definition—they are regarded as *interruptions*. They break into our lives unsolicited, and brusquely interfere with the things we are thinking or doing. And this interference does not necessarily end with the words "Sorry, wrong number," and the replacement of the receiver on the hook. For the unknown caller's voice and the name it has uttered have planted themselves irrevocably in the depths of our consciousness, and are quite capable of blossoming forth into our waking or dreaming thoughts at any time. At the very least they clash and collide with whatever it was that happened to occupy our thoughts before the phone rang, diverting our attention elsewhere. Independently of our will, the Wrong Number is also capable of establishing connections with the full range of one's conscious and unconscious preoccupations. They trespass into books and articles we happen to be reading, and into films or performances we have just seen, or are about to see. They may intrude on items in the news, conversations with friends, the morning mail, or any number of other incidents in the course of daily life. No detail from one's recent or distant experience is immune to their contamination.

For the most part, these minute, isolated bits and tatters of thought seem to constitute nothing more than a handful of mental confetti. Only rarely does one become aware of recurrences, coincidences, patterns, series. However, because of its sudden, unexpected and unsettling character, the Wrong Number is especially likely to stimulate such awareness. An experience in listening strong enough or unusual enough to remain in or near the forefront of one's consciousness, and which sometimes *organizes* other thoughts and images that come to mind, the Wrong Number is an example of the persistence of the auditory imagination.

Of course they also have ways of summoning free associations of their own, leading us down psychic sidestreets we hardly knew existed, and on occasion even into territories wholly unexplored. They may rise and fall in a matter of seconds, but their staying-power commands respect. Besides, even in geological time—one of the best of times, and surely among the very few worth talking about—a matter of seconds is nothing to sneeze at.

## Truth Through Error

The imaginative, revelatory, creative, and exploratory use of so-called mistakes is an important part of the cultural heritage of the East, West, and elsewhere. That mistakes are the greatest teachers is a fixture of folklore. However, in the strait-jacketed existence euphemistically known as daily life, in which the miserabilist mystique of the work-buy-die lie remains in force, such wisdom is rarely applied. Despite the long and impressive list of inventions and discoveries founded on miscalculations, faulty memories, chance collisions, freakish accidents, outright blunders, and other causes beyond the call of reason or logic, the unparalleled fruitfulness of error is by and large disparaged and denied.

The idea that so-called errors should be pursued rather than eradicated is one of the many elements that joins Hegel's dialectic to Blake's, for in this occulted realm, the most varied exoteric and esoteric thinkers tend to agree. Meister Eckhart's bold assertion, "We rarely find that people achieve great things without first going astray," supports the equally audacious statement of the alchemist Eiranaeus Philalethes, in *The Metamorphosis of Metals*, that "The greatest philosophers have learned most by their mistakes," which in turn complements William Ellery Channing's observation that error is nothing less than "the discipline through which we advance." Similarly, the well-known passage from the *Sho-do-ka*, quoted by Nyogen Senzaki in his *Buddhism and Zen*: "Wrong is not always wrong, nor right always right. If you cling to fixed ideas, a tenth of an inch's difference will set you ten thousand miles away," corresponds to Louis Claude de Saint-Martin's insight that "The measure of an error is at the same time the measure of its corresponding truth."

Hegel, in his *Phenomenology*, challenges us directly: "Should we not be concerned as to whether [the] fear of error is not just the error itself?" and "Should we not turn around and mistrust this very mistrust?" In Hegel's view, "the truth is the whole," but also—as his notorious love of homonyms and word-play suggests—*in the holes*. Any "truth" that rejects the myriad mistakes and missteps along the way is merely an ideological half-truth, or less: a truth without a body, a veritable *sieve* of self-deception.

Unequivocal, too, is the five-word declaration of the great jazz bass-player Charles Mingus: "There are no wrong notes."

In his 1955 book, *The Scrolls from the Dead Sea*, Edmund Wilson reflected on mistakes from the historiographical angle:

> The errors in sacred texts and the ignorant misreadings of them [are] really the constructive element in the history of civilization, since the religious ideas that have had most success have mainly been founded upon them.

In the sciences, the arts, and the affairs of ordinary life, error in its infinite richness has never ceased to light the way. Not surprisingly, its brightest manifestations tend to appear in poetry, albeit often in works that are not generally regarded in a poetic light. The most appealing and *effective* example I have found of advancing knowledge via error is Margaret Fuller's beautiful book, *Summer on the Lakes in 1843*—in many respects the most unrestrained and far-reaching work of American Transcendentalism. In this deliriously digressive philosophical travelogue, replete with poems, botanical and ornithological observations, imaginary dialogues, reflections on animal magnetism, and vigorous social criticism (especially regarding the ill treatment of Native Americans), Fuller's avowed determination "to establish truth by error" is clearly rooted in the impassioned desire that her restless subjectivity would "beat with the living heart of the world." Profoundly alert to the "unwritten poetry" of so-called "common life," she regarded the prairie wilderness of the Midwest (then known as the Old Northwest) as a land of marvels in which it was "as pleasant to lose your way as to find it." At every turn, in an adventure jam-packed with turns, her only compass was her unremitting expectation of the unexpected. In writing the book, Fuller clearly rejected the inhibiting conventions of thematic unity, continuity, and other merely literary values, and focused on the sense of wonder and surprise. Halfway through her story, she detours for twenty-four pages to discuss Justinus Kerner's biography of Frederika Hauffe, the "Seeress of Prevorst," whose peculiar case later attracted F. W. H. Myers and others. Overpowering new sensations of wilderness seem to have led Fuller to take a closer look at the inner wilderness as well. She who recognized Charles Brockden Brown (author of *Wieland, or the Transformation* and *Edgar Huntly, or Memoirs of a Sleep-Walker*) as a "born Hegelian" was no stranger to dialectics herself. An expanding awareness of the creative interpenetration of conscious and unconscious, reason and imagination, marked practically every step of her Midwestern journey—truly a voyage of discovery *and* self-discovery.

The result, typically dismissed as a "hodgepodge" by prosaic critics, is for me one of the most admirably unfinished and open-ended books of all time.

The Wrong Number, alas, has remained a mistake from which very few have even tried to learn anything. Of the poetic spirit's open roads, it appears to be one of the least taken, and is commonly derided as a cul-de-sac.

People who are afraid of barking up wrong trees will never discover the right tree. More importantly, they will never discover that there is no such thing as a wrong tree.

For my part, I like the watchword of Hoene Wronski—the post-Hegelian philosopher/adventurer who inspired Balzac's *Quest for the Absolute*: "The very act of seeking demonstrates our capacity for finding."

## Writing on the Telephone

Searching high, low, and in between for clues, hints, suggestions, rumors—*anything* that might shed a ray of light on the mysteries of Wrong Numbers—I inevitably stumbled into numerous dead-ends and detours. Once, in a far-from-pleasant mood combining lethargy, boredom, frustration, and a decidedly pessimistic humor, I undertook a side-trip into the obscure domain known as the "literature of the telephone." For several listless and exhausting weeks I read, voluminously albeit haphazardly, everything I was able to find (around the house, at second-hand bookstores, at nearby libraries) pertaining to the subject of telephony. I read histories, biographies, encyclopedia entries, journal articles, and even consulted a few technical works.

Much of this material was unbelievably dull, superficial, and repetitive—and none of it mentioned Wrong Numbers. Here and there, however, I found a book or article of real interest, such as Robert Hopper's charming 1992 sociological study, *Telephone Conversation*, and a few others that at least contained curious bits of telephone lore.

Best of all, however, was a splendid article by the distinguished historian/biographer Frances Winwar, in which she argued (convincingly, in my view) that the true inventor of the telephone was not Alexander Graham Bell, as is still widely believed in the U.S., but rather by an Italian immigrant, Antonio Meucci (1808–1882). According to this well-documented study—published in the September/October 1976 issue of the Chicago-based magazine, *La Parola del Popolo*—Bell was a child of two in Edinburgh when "Meucci first heard the sound of the human voice transmitted by electricity in 1849."

Meucci is an altogether fascinating character. Active in the Italian revolutionary cause, he was a close friend of Giuseppe Garibaldi, who in fact lived at Meucci's house in Staten Island during his American years. Among his thirty-odd other inventions was a type of hygrometer that is still in wide use today.

Meucci originally named his telephone the *telegrafo parlante* (speaking telegraph), and later shortened it to the more euphonious *teletrofono*. Written up at length in the New York *Eco d'Italia* in 1850, his invention was also featured in well-attended public demonstrations. For several years, as Winwar tells it, the Meucci Telephone Company provided "highly satisfactory service to some two hundred subscribers in Elizabeth, New Jersey." Between 1850 and 1862 he designed no less than thirty different models of the phone. Too poor to afford a patent, he later—after a series of personal calamities including a ruinous fire and declining health—sold the prototypes to a telegraph company whose directors in turn gave them to Bell, who then patented Meuci's invention as his own.

Frances Winwar's pioneering defense of Meucci has since been fully vindicated by other historians, most notably Basilio Catania, whose research has drawn extensively on Meucci's diagrams and other rare documents in the National Archives. The evidence for Meucci has proved so strong that the U.S. Congress, on the 15th of June 2002, officially acknowledged him as the true inventor of the telephone.

Thus Alexander Graham Bell, celebrated for six generations as *the* inventor of the phone, has been definitively exposed as an impostor. As has happened so often throughout the history of class society, the *wrong person* got the credit, the fame, and the money that rightly belonged to someone else. We know now that for more than a century, all that we were told about the history of the phone—the "standard literature on the subject"—was based on lies. Much more is involved here than the obvious fact that the history of the telephone needs to be rewritten. The very meaning of "telephony," and the role of the phone in our society are also called into question. The huge contrast between the prosperous, well-connected, boastful Bell and the quiet, unassuming Meucci, an unswerving radical, fluent only in Italian, and destitute in his later years, is quite revealing in this regard, for their conflicting personalities are reflected in their divergent views on the telephone.

For Meucci, the telephone was fundamentally democratic, almost anarchic—an instrument to facilitate communication among friends and family, to bring people together, to expand humankind's spirit of solidarity and cooperation. For Bell, it was above all an instrument of commerce and power—a device that was not only highly profitable, but also served to strengthen government, bureaucracy, and in a broader sense, all forms of social obedience and conformity. Bell's authoritarian model prevailed, of course, and what was commonly called the "Telephone Company" soon became the largest and most powerful monopoly in U.S. history.

With Alexander Graham Bell's fall from grace, most of what has passed for "telephone history" can no longer be regarded as non-fiction. Fortunately for the avowed writers of fiction who have introduced the telephone into their work, very few ever bothered to introduce Bell along with it. How the phone insinuated itself into the short story and the novel, first as prop and later as "character," would no doubt make an interesting study. In Mark Twain's *A Connecticut Yankee in King Arthur's Court* (1889), for example, the telephone is basically a gimmick: We are ushered into "the den of a medieval hermit turned into a telephone office," and the cast includes a baby named "Hello-Central"—a greeting that dates from the telephone industry's own infancy. One of the earliest stories in which the phone itself is a central character, playing a vital role, was Elizabeth Stuart Phelps's "The Chief Operator,"a turn-of-the-century tale of torrential rain, a broken dam, a devastating flood, featuring as heroine a switchboard operator, a young widow who sacrifices her life that others might live.

Telephones and telephone talk figure significantly in the work of writers as different as Villiers de l'Isle-Adam, James Joyce, Franz Kafka, Upton Sinclair, Ring Lardner, Claude McKay, Dashiell Hammett, Dorothy Parker, Harry Stephen Keeler, Nelson Algren, Chester Himes, Craig Rice, David Goodis, Lionel White, Jack Kerouac, Barbara Neely, and thousands of others, but it is a topic too remote from Wrong Numbers to consider here. The same is true of the telephone in poetry. Jones Very, Guillaume Apollinaire, Carl Sandburg, Robert Frost, Benjamin Péret, Langston Hughes, Kenneth Fearing, Diane di Prima, Joyce Mansour, Jayne Cortez, and Paul Garon are just a few of the poets who have brought phones into one or more of their poems. Rarely, however, have any of them raised, even elliptically, the burning question of Wrong Numbers. Nancy Cunard, by way of exception, in a little-known poem titled "Between Time and Etc.," seems to me to have captured something of the fugitive irrationality and desperate hope that certain solitary states of mind share with the Wrong Numbers of the world:

*One hand on the telephone . . . .*
*Everywhere the*
*Ephemeridae of nights, alone and not alone. . . .*
*Are we the real?*

Telephones are also conspicuous in popular poetry, most radiantly in Blues and Jazz songs. Elmore James's "Talk to Me, Baby" is a Blues classic:

*I talked to my baby*
*on the telephone.*
*She say, "Stop what you're doin'*
*and come on home."*

Tin Pan Alley also had plenty of telephone tunes; Irving Berlin's "All alone by the telephone" was one of the key clichés of the Roaring Twenties. A study of songs about phones and other electrical and electronic devices, from the late nineteenth century through R&B and Rock to Reggae and Hip-Hop, could tell us a lot about the society we live in. Even the barest sketch of such a project, however, would take us too far from the present object of our inquiry.

Popular literature abounds in phones, and has also proved to be a fertile field for Wrong Numbers. Some of the most illuminating writings on the "telephone experience" are the hilarious skits from the old Bob & Ray show on radio—such as "Lucky Phone Call" (in the book *Write If You Get Work*), and "Speaking Out" and "Phone Call to Anywhere" (in *The New! Improved! Bob & Ray Book*). Apart from a couple of *Daffy Duck* comics from the 1950s and '60s, nothing else in the literature equals the raw power of Bob & Ray's revelation of the telephone as an instrument for the communication of explosive poetic humor, conversational zaniness, and all-out pandemonium. Although not specifically concerned with misdialed numbers, these inspired classics of anti-rational dialogue, spotlighting the endless possibilities of telephonic funny stuff, have a lot in common with Wrong Numbers.

The mystery thriller appears to be the literary genre in which telephones—and Wrong Numbers—figure most prominently and often, sometimes as a major theme or recurring sub-theme. Dan Marlowe's *Doom Service*, a 1960 "paperback original" centered on corruption in the "fight game," oddly ignores the Wrong Number, but includes no less than forty-six mentions of telephones in its 160 pages—about one every third page—not counting references to "picking up the receiver" or "putting in a call." In this as in many other mysteries, the phone is no mere decorative prop, but a disturbing "object" or brooding presence.

The story that made the Wrong Number famous, or rather infamous, was Lucille Fletcher's 1948 radio-drama, *Sorry, Wrong Number*—the suspenseful tale of a woman who, by chance, as the result of a faulty phone connection, overhears what turns out to be a plot to murder her. An instant hit, it was replayed again and again on radio, expanded (with the collaboration of Allan Ullman) into a best-selling novel, and made into a major feature film (starring Barbara Stanwyck), which in turn has been shown repeatedly on TV. It has also been released as an LP recording, and in audio- and videocassette. Largely under its influence, the Wrong Number became a staple of *noir* films, and fiction as well, although for the most part it was simply a momentary device to add a touch of eerieness or to intrude, suddenly but more or less irrelevantly, on a prolonged silence. In Thomas B. Dewey's *Don't Cry for Long* (1964), the narrator anxiously awaits a call from a young woman he met the night before:

> I looked at my watch. . . .
> She promised to call, I kept telling myself. . . .
> She will call. . . .
> Maybe.
> I finished the coffee and ate a couple of dry rolls. [She] still hadn't called. . . .
> The thing rang at eleven-thirty and I grabbed it the way you grab a plate as it falls off the table.
> A wrong number.

Here, as usual in films and fiction, the Wrong Number is reduced to its traditional role as irritation, and hope deferred.

Alfred Bester's "Out of This World" (in *The Dark Side of the Earth*, 1964), is an interesting exception. In this science fiction tale, what *seems* to be a Wrong Number is actually something much more complicated. As one of the callers explains to the other toward the end: "We're on different time-tracks. . . . We're in alternative worlds. . . . The telephone lines between our alternate worlds have gotten crossed." When the crossed lines are repaired, a budding romantic dalliance ends abruptly.

A handful of oddities aside, the "literature of the telephone" was practically of no use in my exploration. The great bulk of this literature completely ignores Wrong Numbers, and the mentions of them in fiction tend to be condescending, negative, even hostile. Symptomatic of the "official" attitude on the matter is the fact that "Wrong Number" is not even a referenced subject in the Dewey Decimal or Library of Congress Cataloging systems.

My disappointing peregrination through this literature was long over when I chanced upon a felicitous little book titled *Hello. . .Wrong Number* by Marilyn Sachs. Penelope found this 97-page novel in August 2001, on one of our long walks; it was near the top of the "Free Box" outside a second-hand bookstore in Evanston. "Here's a book for you," she said, and handed me what I soon realized was a true marvel of marvels: a book unequivocally sympathetic to Wrong Numbers.

A winsome love story told entirely in telephone conversations, *Hello. . .Wrong Number* is a veritable refutation and negation of *Sorry, Wrong Number.* Unlike the latter, Sachs's book is uninterruptedly playful, eros-affirmative, free of "stranger/danger" paranoia, and openly receptive to the wonders of chance. As a front cover blurb says, the Wrong Number that starts the story "turned out to be the best mistake she ever made!" Fittingly, too, for a book that calmly breaks so many conventions, *Hello. . .Wrong Number* is a book for children (ages 9–13). And like so many books for children, it contains a strong message for us all.

If the literature on the subject of telephony proved of little help to me in my expedition to the Land of Wrong Numbers, I did find a wealth of material in literature *off* the subject. Indeed, the further away from the subject a book turned out to be, the more likely it was to contain precious information. The most helpful books of all—the ones that provided the deepest insights, contributed the boldest perspectives, and did most to expand my awareness of the depth and scope of the many questions involved—included several that were published years or even centuries before the birth of Antonio Meucci, and among more recent works, many that contained not so much as a single reference to phones.

What this book owes to the many poets and thinkers who, without ever having heard of such a thing as a Wrong Number, have nonetheless illuminated its place and role in and beyond our history and culture, will become obvious as the story unfolds.

# THE LONELINESS OF THE LONG-DISTANCE ANSWERING-MACHINE: A NOTE ON TECHNOLOGY

One of the many typically dreary experiences of daily life in miserabilist society is telephoning a friend several thousand miles away and having to listen to a long recorded message explain that no one is there. I find this almost as depressing as the canned laughter that is still used on TV comedies to let the audience know when and how long they are supposed to laugh. The canned laughter is doubly ironic, for those recordings are quite old, and most of the laughers long dead.

The fact that listening to prerecorded apologies and the laughter of the dead are routine experiences, and that scarcely anyone even bothers to complain about them, show how thoroughly present-day society is dominated by the out-of-control monster known as Technology. The incredible and increasing aggressiveness of technology, and its invasion of every aspect of our lives, is alarmingly evident in everyday language. For nearly a century the language of the telephone, for everyone except specialists, was limited to less than a dozen common words. The vocabulary of phone-calling has multiplied more in the past decade than it did in the preceding hundred years. Several generations referred simply to "the phone"; now they speak of cell-phones, car-phones, mobile, cordless, and wireless phones, not to mention such special services as Caller I.D., fax machines, voice-mail, and e-mail. Today, even kids in third grade know all about digital messaging systems, voice-stations, "hands-free desk-top communication systems," and "Instant Messaging" programs. And with millions of "phone solicitors" or "telemarketers" cluttering up the wires and airwaves with the telephonic version of junk-mail, it is clear that the old-time phone call "ain't what it used to be."

This book is an inquiry into the poetic, critical, and subversive implications of electronic voice-to-voice chance encounters. It is not, however, a book about technology. If you want to know how the phone works, or what causes a bad connection, you'll have to look elsewhere. The focus throughout these pages is not the telephone as such, but the telephone at its point of breakdown: the crisis-point known as the Wrong Number. In those moments of exemplary "wrongness," where technology has slipped, fallen, and exposed its vulnerability, the telephone is suddenly transformed—as if by magic—into something new and different. Inexplicably, or so it seems at the time, its "official" function has lapsed and the line is now open to the unknown. Much to the confusion of all parties involved, two complete strangers are now able to meet in truly unforeseen circumstances, and sometimes—when conditions are right—to discover what poetry is.

Although the technical aspects of telephony are beyond the scope of this study, this book is nonetheless a contribution to the critique of—and the abolition of—oppressive technology, which is a major component of the miserabilist order.

A telephone, as Amiri Baraka remarked as long ago as 1970 in the journal *Amistad*, "is one culture's solution to the problem of sending words through space. It is political power that has allowed this technology to emerge, and seems the sole direction for the result desired." The telephone, he went on to say, is a part of the technology of the West—"a technology that kills both plants and animals, poisons the air and degenerates or enslaves man"—and he added that he looked ahead to a post-Western technology that would draw on its pre-Western roots: a liberating technology that would "represent human striving" and expand human consciousness.

I like to think of the Wrong Number as a kind of Groucho-Marxist anticipation—*within* but in opposition to the dominant technology—of the expansive, liberating, post-Western technology called for by Baraka in his *Amistad* article. All Wrong Numbers embody a radical *détournement* of the telephone—a creative misuse and abuse of the existing authoritarian technology for *other* purposes. And as such, it also embodies a kind of "inside" critique of telecommunications technology, and inspires its connoisseurs to develop that critique.

Hats off to Ned Ludd!

Despite all the changes in technology, Wrong Numbers are not only still with us, but actually prospering in all directions at once. And the many troubling questions they pose simply refuse to go away:

Why do so many people who think they are "perfectly all right" make so many "wrong" phone-calls?

What are these callers really trying to say?

What do Wrong Numbers tell us about the society we live in, and about ourselves?

Most assuredly, such questions cannot be stifled by prerecorded evasions or robotic operators, much less by the laughter of the dead.

## A Whispered Symbol of Umor

Finding a needle in a haystack is simplicity itself compared to finding a sympathetic student of Wrong Numbers. Everyone knows what a needle looks like, and all one has to do is search through a single haystack to locate it. With a powerful magnet, the task might be accomplished in seconds.

The Wrong Number, however, is so far out in left field that even left-fielders don't want to hear about it.

Reasons for this neglect are not hard to find. A third of each day, on the average—eight hours out of twenty-four, or 480 minutes—are occupied by sleep. Rare indeed, however, are those for whom Wrong Numbers take up even 288th of the day—that is, a mere twelfth of an hour, or five minutes. Considering how little waking time most people devote to questions pertaining to their sleep and dreams, it is not very surprising that so little attention has been given to Wrong Numbers.

Only the most magisterially marginal of sciences might be expected to have shed some light on this insuperably problematical *problematique*. Our search, however, suggests that even the most marginalized beyond-the-borderline researchers appear to have avoided the subject. Until now, the world's thinkers seem not to have been overly concerned with righting the record on Wrong Numbers.

Surely Alfred Jarry's Pataphysics, the "science of imaginary solutions" and of "the laws governing exceptions," is ideally—or let us say *ideoreally*, using the term of Jarry's friend and fellow poet, Saint-Pol-Roux—suited for the pursuit of investigations in this realm. In his *Exploits and Opinions of Doctor Faustroll, Pataphysician*, Jarry discusses the building of time-machines, shows how a sieve can become an excellent boat, and even refers (in passing) to the man he mistakenly believed to be the inventor of the phone: Alexander Graham Bell. Much to our regret, however, Jarry does not appear to have blessed posterity with his observations on the Pataphysical ramifications of misdialed numbers.

Though never systematized into a full-fledged science, or even elaborated beyond a few scattered jottings and excerpts from conversation, Marcel Duchamp's elegant concept of the "Infra-Slim"—a broad category embracing a wide range of virtually unnoticed phenomena, viewed in terms of their potential energy—overflows with affinities with the vital issue under discussion in these pages. Unfortunately, Duchamp—co-author of *Opposition and Sister Squares are Reconciled*, a subtle treatise on the Infra-Slim in the guise of a study of esoteric chess-endings—did not, to the best of our knowledge, pronounce himself on esoteric telephony.

The Wrong Number's resolutely anti-utilitarian character, its inherent refusal to produce, its emphatic dryness, and a number of other attractively irritating qualities that we shall touch on elsewhere in the course of this study, make it an unexcelled example—a veritable *emblem*—of Jacques Vaché's deep *umor*, "a sense of the theatrical (and joyless) uselessness of everything." A close and imaginative reader of Jarry, Vaché developed his own radical "Humor without the H" in the trenches and no-man's-land of World War I.

By avocation one of the least prolific writers of all time, and a suicide at 24, Vaché is not known to have contributed directly to the elucidation of Wrong Numbers. His close friend André Breton, however, left us a remarkable document which merits recognition as the first important text in the annals of our science.

Breton's found poem, "PSST," originally published in the Dada review *Cannibale* in May 1920 and reprinted (slightly modified) in his collection *Clair de terre* (1923), reproduces a list of twenty people named Breton and their telephone numbers from the Paris telephone directory. Inasmuch as none of the numbers is his, it is in effect an authentic list of Wrong Numbers. As is true of everything having to do with this subject, the poem—which meets Duchamp's definition of an "assisted readymade"—invites a wide range of interpretations. Like all Wrong Number research, the poem is an inquiry into the problems of identity, anonymity, language, communication, poetry, chance, and humor, prefiguring the opening question of Breton's later work, *Nadja*: "Who am I?"

In the closing pages of the first *Surrealist Manifesto* (1924) is a paragraph featuring a series of questions and answers, such as: "Radios? Fine. . . . Photography? I don't see any reason why not. The cinema? Three cheers for darkened rooms," and "The telephone? Hello."

From the very beginning, then—albeit only in a whisper—surrealism posed the question of the Wrong Number.

# PSST

| | |
|---|---|
| *Neuilly 1-18* ... | Breton, vacherie modèle, r. de l'Ouest, 12, Neuilly. |
| *Nord 13-40* .... | Breton (E.), mon. funèbr., av. Cimetière Parisien, 23, Pantin. |
| *Passy 44-15*.... | Breton (Eug.), vins, restaur., tabacs, r. de la Pompe, 176. |
| *Roquette 07-90*.. | Breton (François), vétérinaire, r. Trousseau, 21 (2$^{e}$). |
| *Central 64-99*.. | Breton frères, mécanicien, r, de Belleville, 262. (20$^{e}$). |
| *Bergère 43-61*... | Breton et fils, r. Rougemont, 12, (9$^{e}$). |
| *Archives 32-58*.. | Breton (G.). fournit. cycles, autos, r. des Archives, 78, (3$^{e}$). |
| *Central 30-08* .. | Breton (Georges), r. du Marché-Saint-Honoré, 4, (1$^{er}$). |
| *Wagram 60-84*. | Breton (M et M$^{me}$ G.) b$^{d}$ Malesherbes, 58, (8$^{e}$ . |
| *Gutenberg 03-78*. | Breton (H.), dentelles, r. de Richelieu, 60, (2$^{e}$). |
| *Passy 80-70* ... | Breton (Henri) négociant, r. Octave-Feuillet, 22, (16$^{e}$). |
| *Gobelins 08-09* . | Breton (J.), Elix. Combier, ag. gén., butte du Rhône, 21-23. |
| *Roquette 32-59* . | Breton (J. L ), député, s.-secr. Etat inv., b$^{d}$ Soult, 81 bis. |
| *Archives 39-43*.. | Breton (L.), hôtel-bar, r. François-Miron, 38, (4$^{e}$). |
| *Marcadet 04-11*. | Breton (Noël, hôtel-rest., b$^{d}$ National, 56, Clichy. |
| *Roquette 02-25*.. | Breton (Paul), décolleteur, r. Saint-Maur, 21, (11$^{e}$). |
| *Central 84-08*.. | Breton (Th.), contentieux. r. du fg. Montmartre, 13, (9$^{e}$). |
| *Saxe 57-86*.... | Breton (J.), Biscuits, r. La Quintinie, 16-18, (15$^{e}$). |
| *Archives 35-44* . | Breton (J.) et C$^{ie}$, papiers en gros, r. Saint-Martin, 245, (3$^{e}$). |
| *Roquette 09-76* . | Breton et C$^{ie}$(Soc.anon,)Charbons gros, q. La Rapée, 60, (12$^{e}$). |

**Breton (André).**

André Breton: "PSST" (*Cannibale*, Paris, May 1920)

## PROLEGOMENA TO A PHENOMENOLOGY OF THE UNCALLED-FOR

Like the giant supernatural helmet in the opening pages of Horace Walpole's *Castle of Otranto*, the Wrong Number imposes itself first of all as an anomaly, and an anomaly it remains: by turns byzantine, BugsBunnylike and even frightening in its awesome immunity to the ordinary scheme of things. Fundamentally and irreducibly an *enigma*, it is always and definitionally unreasonable, protean, uncontrollable. Nothing can diminish its inherent and all-pervasive ambiguity. No matter how well one understands the technical reasons for the Wrong Number's existence, *as a personal experience* it resists logic and defies "sensible" interpretation. Always disguised, supremely aloof, quick as a wink, its substance is much less than the shadows it is capable of casting on coming events.

Moreover, like so many other phenomena regarded as implacably nonrational and portentous, it is also irrepressible. No matter how many times the receiver is placed back on the hook, the Wrong Number, in its infinite variety, can always be counted on to make a comeback.

It is in the essence of the Wrong Number that it is almost never regarded as reassuring. It is always an intrusion, a rude awakening, an unsolicited "barging in." Its cousins include such epochal intruders as Mr Punch, Frankenstein's monster, Melmoth the Wanderer, Ignatz Mouse, Fantômas, King Kong, The Shadow, Plastic Man, Godzilla, the extra-terrestrial of the season, and any number of lesser pests, from Invisible Scarlet O'Neill and the Clown at Midnight to the halfwit party-crasher and belligerent beggar. An irritant in disembodied but (assumed) human form, the Wrong Number also can be considered a variant of the trickster, but a highly specialized trickster whose "tricks," from start to finish, rarely last more than a few seconds.

And finally (finally?), as an example of unadulterated nonsense, the Wrong Number has a lot in common with a fugitive character introduced by cartoonist Bill Holman in a 1942 *Smokey Stover* Sunday comic strip: the "cagey codger"—the fellow "who markets all the good an ill wind blows no."

The Wrong Number differs from all these, of course, in that it is always double, and works both ways: Every Wrong Number is a dialogue, or verbal duet. In the silence before the call, and after, the Wrong Number stands out on both ends of the line, beckoning vaguely in two directions—toward the Might-Have-Been and the Why Not?

In this lunatics' labyrinth, two minotaurs seem to have lost their way. As they confront their anonymity and identity, isn't it possible that they might discover a new kind of mutual aid, inseparable from the passional attraction of strangeness?

## TAKING SILLY THINGS SERIOUSLY: A DEBATE

"Whose idea was this, anyway?" grumbled a voice, which may well have been my own, for I was the only one around.

"Yours, of course," I answered with indignation. "And what a crackbrained scheme it turned out to be! As if anyone in their right mind would give a nickel for all the Wrong Numbers that ever ever were or will be."

"But that's the whole point," I replied. "Their commonness, together with their strangeness, and the fact that no one really pays attention to them, makes them fascinating. Wrong Numbers intrude on just about everyone's daily life, yet everyone just goes on acting as if they don't exist."

"You deluded fool! Can't you see why everyone ignores them? It's because they're of no interest whatsoever! Face it: Wrong Numbers are absolutely devoid of significance. They're nothing, or less than nothing. Lots of things figure in daily life, and people do their best to ignore them because they have more important things to do. You might as well write about sneezes, or parking lots, or marbles. They are almost as boring as these Wrong Numbers of yours."

"Well, I *am* interested in marbles and sneezes."

"See? You're not even serious—you're just being silly. You think it's clever pretending to write seriously about silly things."

"But aren't so-called silly things worth taking seriously? And besides, who is to say what's silly? In their time the ideas of Copernicus, Wollstonecraft, Garrison, Darwin, Freud, and even Charlie Parker were widely derided as silly."

"Wrong Numbers are a thousand times sillier than any *idea*, and you know it. In any case, you're not taking them seriously—you're just fooling around."

"All poets know," I said, this time with passion, "that fooling around can be a better way of being serious than just being serious."

"And this so-called book you're supposed to be writing—a mish-mash of *Looney Tunes*, surrealism, and a lot of crazy notions you've stumbled on in books nobody else reads because they're not worth reading: Do you call *that* serious?"

"Well," I said, reduced to quoting Jacques Vaché's all-purpose monosyllable.

"Why don't you admit that this is just another one of the 1,743,569 ridiculous 'projects' that you'll never finish because they weren't worth starting in the first place, and which nobody would ever bother to read anyway?"

"Well," I repeated—this time rather self-assuredly, I thought. After all, Vaché knew what he was talking about. But my antagonist persisted.

"Look, the world is going to hell in a handbasket, and what are you doing? Wasting your time writing about Wrong Numbers! What on Earth do you hope to accomplish with such foolishness? Can't you think of anything *worthwhile* to do?"

"I don't know," said I, simultaneously summing up the overall outlook of some of the world's finest thinkers, and my own carefully prepared answer to anyone who might ask me what I really *knew* about Wrong Numbers.

My opponent in the foregoing running debate with myself was relentless, but I remained unconvinced. The fact that the arguments against writing about Wrong Numbers had all of Western Civilization to back them up (and probably a few other assorted civilizations as well) served only to bolster my determination.

In any event, I really didn't want to argue about it—least of all with a debater such as myself, notorious for exaggeration, hyperbole, *ad hominem* arguments, absurd digressions, and attempts at humor as esoteric as they are in bad taste.

Despite recurring doubts that this research was going anywhere—or for that matter, that it had anywhere to go—I realized that it was too late to quit. I was already in it too deep. Trying *not* to think of Wrong Numbers was out of the question. Having started on this unlikely voyage, it seemed to me I was obliged to go all the way.

There are things you feel you *have* to do, even if you feel like doing something else. For me, the way to Something Else could be reached only through the tangled forests and endangered wetlands of Wrong Numbers.

Somehow, I realized, Wrong Numbers and I are in this together.

# 2.

# BACK TO LONG AGO

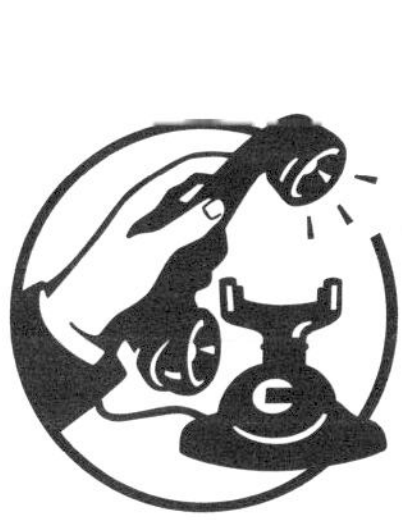

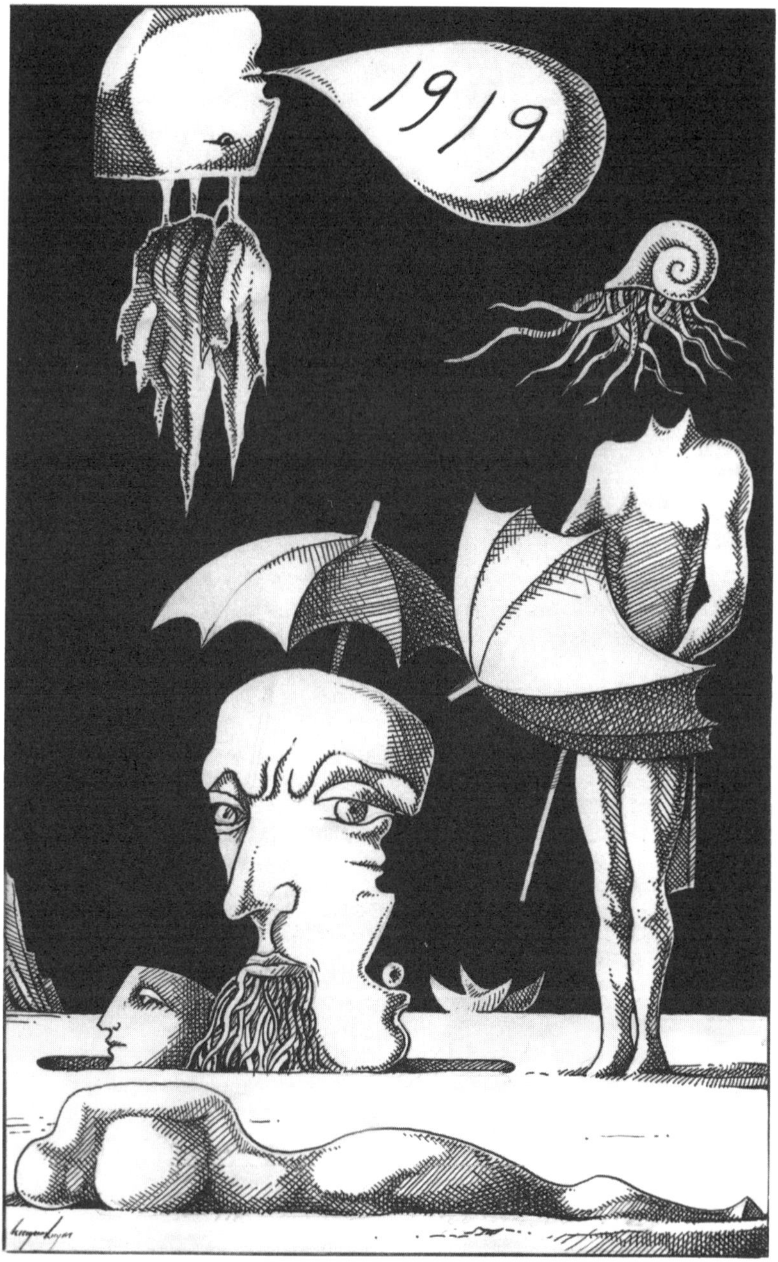
1919

## ADVENTURES IN PREHISTORY

Like everything else in and out of this world, my decidedly improbable decision to explore the wild blue hither of Wrong Numbers not only has a history, laughable though it may be, but also a prehistory, which can be said to extend as far beyond laughter as laughter itself goes beyond sanctimonious solemnity.

In retrospect, certain ineluctable experiences I had long ago, while sauntering through the dazzling wilderness of chance and revery, seem to me to foreshadow in various and furtive ways, the more systematically unsystematic search, specifically focused on "telephone trouble," that began years later when I no longer had the alibi of childhood or adolescence.

The following twelve chapters are made up of anecdotes, enigmas, and stray bits of memorabilia that prefigure—directly or indirectly—my later Quest for the Golden Fleece of Wrong Numbers. Most of these action-packed adventures date from my misspent youth, which, mere chronology aside, I seem to keep misspending even now, whenever the occasion arises.

As Rosa Luxemburg once wrote: "There is nothing so well calculated to liberate our modes of thought from the restrictive fetters of routine as a revolutionary period. Real history, like creative nature, is far more bizarre and fruitful in its caprices than the classifying and systematizing pedant."

Here, then, are a few bizarre and fruitful episodes from those thrilling days of yesteryear, which should help answer the ever-popular question: What the hell is this all about, anyway?

## WHAT I LEARNED ABOUT MYSELF IN HIGH SCHOOL CIVICS

After the nightmare of boredom known as grade school had run its eight-year course, I was supposed to be ready for high school—another nightmare of boredom, but on a much larger scale. Aside from gym, the most nightmarish and boring part of it was Civics class.

The high school to which I was subjected for three years had the bizarre name of Proviso, but no one seemed to know why, or even what it meant. The name was never explained, despite repeated inquiries from students. The only proviso that gets much attention in U.S. history is the pre-Civil-War Wilmot Proviso, which would have prohibited slavery in land purchased from Mexico (it passed the House but was defeated in the Senate). Several of us wondered: Did this historic proviso have anything to do with Proviso High in Maywood, Illinois? Not one of the teachers knew anything about it, and few seemed even to care. That's the kind of school it was.

A grim suburban blend of old-line fascism and the newer made-in-U.S.A. high-security prison system, Proviso was a typical 1950s American high school. Brutal regimentation, arbitrary rules, ridiculous dress-codes, cruel and inhuman punishment, bureaucratic incoherence, and all-around extreme authoritarianism were visited upon 5000 students in large daily doses. All this added a certain piquancy to the Civics lectures, which trumpeted the alleged freedom and democracy of "our" great American republic, in which "We, the People" were alleged to be true sovereigns, the real rulers of "our" lives, and even masters of our destiny.

"We, the Students," however, did not feel free in school, and least of all in Civics class. We felt like prisoners, which of course is exactly what we were. The Civics teacher was a dyspeptic bully, at least 200 pounds overweight, and consumed by a hatred of all living beings, especially high school students. He also coached the school football team. Teachers of his type—small-minded, malevolent, power-obsessed—were generally given nicknames like Big Brother, Der Fuehrer, Napoleon the XIIIth, or other terms of endearment. This one was known as the Great Dictator. In our view, he was just one of the many teachers at Proviso who got jobs there only because the Gestapo was out of business. You can guess how much his cold, calculating cynicism, along with his all-pervasive malice and stench of corruption, added to our appreciation of his favorite topic: the wisdom of the nation's Founding Fathers. To this day when I try to imagine what a slave-catcher was like, or a concentration-camp guard, I think of this Civics teacher at Proviso High.

Like all prisoners, the inmates of Civics class spent a lot of time pretending to be Somewhere Else. We did all we could to avoid listening to the Great Dictator's stultifying lectures, which, as if to accentuate their hypocrisy and lack of content, were invariably delivered in a droning, lifeless monotone. For several of us, a favorite life-saving time-killer was passing clandestine notes around, usually jokes at the teacher's expense. We embellished these messages with cartoons of animals wearing zoot suits, dark sunglasses and berets, in the manner of George Price's illustrations for Steve Allen's *Bop Fables.* This was 1958: the so-called Beat Generation was young and on the upswing, and my friends and I—perhaps a dozen of us out of the Proviso 5000—had rallied to the Cause.

One day a note reached me that read: "Man, this civics jive is the least—I mean, *square as a chair*, strictly from Hungersville! If this drag lasts another set I'll really flip! Can't we, like, start a riot or something?" As it happened, the Great Dictator was watching. With impressive speed for a man of his ungainly corpulence, he rushed to my desk, seized this piece of illicit correspondence, read it (silently), growled (loudly), and lumbered slowly back to his own desk, muttering that I should see him after class. A few classmates gave me commiserating glances and hummed the opening bars of Chopin's Funeral March. Red-faced with rage, the Great Dictator went on with his lecture about freedom of speech.

The after-class interview started off as boringly as the lecture it had interrupted. "As a member of society," the Dictator intoned, "you're part of a *team.* A high school class is a *team*, and you're part of it. Do you understand?"

"No," said I. "Being on a 'team' seems to me to involve a choice. I did not *choose* to be in high school. I did not *choose* to be in this class."

He glared at me a while, shaking his head, and went on with the lecture. "I'll give you an example. Suppose you're on the football team, and you're out on the field. Someone throws you the ball. Now, you can't just do what *you* want to do, can you? No, because you're part of a *team*, and you've got to do what's best for the *team.* So there you are, with the ball, with a real responsibility. Others are depending on you. The whole game might depend on you! So what do you do?"

I felt like throwing up, but I managed to repress it and tried simple honesty. "Look," I said, "your example is ill-chosen. I don't play football. In fact, I hate it. I don't like any team sports. I'd rather go mountain-climbing. But if, by some odd circumstance, I happened to find myself on a football field, and somebody threw me the ball by mistake, I'd probably toss it to the spectators."

The poor Dictator didn't seem to follow. "You'd *what*?" he gasped. And then he roared: "Why in the hell would you do a thing like *that*? You're part of a *team*!"

"No, I'm not," I insisted. "You're just *pretending* I'm part of a team."

"But *why* would you throw the ball to the fans?" he asked. "What good would that do?" He was frowning, and I thought I detected a few tears in his piglike eyes. This puzzle seemed beyond his ken.

"I don't know," I answered truthfully. "I guess because it would be interesting to see what would happen. Anyway, I would also immediately walk off the field. I wouldn't want to spoil my perfect record as a nonparticipant in team sports."

A long silence followed as the tearful frown returned to the usual hate-filled glare. The Great Dictator was breathing heavily now—wheezing, clearing his throat, and fuming, too. Then he spoke the words that astonished me no end: "You really are a *Wrong Number*, aren't you?"

And I laughed. I know it wasn't the brightest thing to do, but it was by no means intentional. The fact is, I had never heard the expression "wrong number" used in that way before, and now I was hearing it used to describe *me*, and it made me laugh, uncontrollably.

By now, the Great Dictator was on the verge of apoplexy, or worse. "You think this is *funny*?" he screamed, rising suddenly from his swivel chair. I've long since forgotten the man's name, but I can still recall the flecks of foam he sputtered in all directions.

So there I was, an unwitting actor in a typical Proviso High School tableau: a forlorn but wisecracking student menaced by an enraged extra-large superpatriotic football coach/civics teacher who was, to all intents and purposes, having some kind of fit. I was sure the guy was preparing to tear me limb from limb. And what was *I* doing?

Laughing like an idiot.

Uncontrollably.

"How do you get yourself into these situations?" I asked myself.

But before I had time to answer, the war was over, and I won! Unbelievably, the Great Dictator conceded defeat. As befitted his personality, his surrender assumed an authoritarian form, but I preferred not to quibble. He simply looked at me and shouted—in truth, it was a kind of loud croak—the very words I most wanted to hear: "Get *out*! Get out of my sight! Get *out*! Out! *Out*!"

And out I went, a Wrong Number, laughing all the way home.

## My Three San Francisco Renaissances

The San Francisco poetry Renaissance of the late 1950s and early 60s, when the city became the "capital" of the Beat Generation, seemed entirely in the order of things to me. Growing up in

Chicago I heard much more about San Francisco than about the city in which I was born and raised. My father loved to tell us stories of his own childhood on the family's small farm in Mill Valley, and at their printing office, Rosemont Press, at 21 Rosemont Place, a block-long street in the City's Mission District. Even before I started school I knew that we were descendants of refugees from religious persecution in England who had started emigrating to North America around 1640, and settled in such New England villages as Ashby, Boscawen, Hingham, and Winchendon: names that rang the bells of wonderland for me. I knew too that a large part of the New England branch of the family went on to become California pioneers; the first of them, Alexander Putney, had been "One of Frémont's Men" in 1848–49, according to the inscription on his headstone.

I also "knew" San Francisco was far, far away—"Out West," as my father put it—but that did not prevent its holding stage-center in my real and imaginary worlds, and it affected just about every phase of my formative years. The first oil paintings I ever saw—I was four or five—were still-lives of roses painted by my great-grandmother, Juliet Josephine Petremont, and it was those two dark canvases in black wooden frames that sparked my love of painting, or rather of certain paintings that have, at critical moments in my life, leaped to my eyes. Around the same time I also discovered the prairie—a struggling remnant of the grand prairie of old, but still a magnificent sea of tall grass and wildflowers, gloriously populated by vast numbers of birds, spiders, insects, snakes, rabbits and thirteen-striped ground-squirrels. The prairie was just a little west of our house, but that was enough for my five-year-old mind to link it to San Francisco.

Chancing upon my great-grandmother's paintings, and wandering into the wilderness were my earliest experiences of *enchantment*.

Besides being an artist, Petremont—known in the family as "Mamère"—also taught French and "deportment" to children of the Forty-Niners. Physically small to the point of daintiness (her dancing slippers were size three), she was nonetheless considered a "powerful presence" and perhaps just a wee bit eccentric, for she sported a man's silk top-hat and smoked cigars. She died thirty-two years before I was born but she has remained a powerful presence for me. Her husband was a musician and music printer, and for many years their Music Store at Kearny and Sutton was one of the largest purveyors of sheet music west of the Mississippi. They named their son (my grandfather) Ludwig von Beethoven, but with characteristically Far West informality Grandpa Rosemont shortened it to L. Budd. Unpretentious, reckless enthusiasm seemed to me to describe their whole way of life, and I was especially charmed by what I heard of the immense freedom enjoyed by the next (my father's) generation of California Rosemont children. When the printing business on Rosemont Place (later it moved for a time to Sycamore) kept my grandparents at work in the city for extended periods, most if not all of their eight youngsters—ranging in age from mid-teen to toddler—often stayed at the farm for weeks at a time, caring for the horse, cow, chickens, geese, and above all the many dogs, for the California Rosemonts were also active in the pure-bred dog business, and organizers of major dog shows. With their penchant for mutual aid, group singing, in-house plays, family meetings, and making their own ice-cream and root-beer, the children carried on much like the characters in Louisa May Alcott's *Little Women*—which, by the way, was a family favorite.

The young majority tended to rule the roost even in the house on Rosemont Place, in the City. Although tradition has it that in earlier years Mark Twain had been a guest for a week or two, the family dwelling-place—which took up a sizeable chunk of the block—was never exactly a boarding-house. It was home, however—for a night, or a week, and sometimes much longer—for countless visitors, most but not all of them the children's friends. As my father told it, rare were the evening suppers without at least two or three newcomers sitting in; Grandpa Rosemont's standard query, "And *whose* are you?"—always asked in a genial, welcoming way—signified "Which of my children invited you to join us at our table?"

Even my mother, daughter of Polish immigrants and a lifelong Chicagoan, added appreciably to this rampant Rosemontian San-Franciscoism. As a professional musician (accordion, piano, vocals), and leader of the Sally Kaye Trio, one of her gigs involved entertaining a whole trainload of conventioneers and their wives on a two-week trip to and from—yes, San Francisco! According to family legend, that trip occasioned my first experience with the phone. There I was, not quite five, listening to my mother—the one-time "Boop-boop-a-doo Girl" of the Chicago Theatre, and star of "The Streets of Paris" at the 1933–34 Chicago World's Fair—talking *and singing* to me on the telephone, long-distance from San Francisco.

All this genealogical/autobiographical preambling is meant to drive home the point that, in at least one little house on Chicago's western extremity during the dark and dreary close of the 1940s, the spirit of Old San Francisco was still young, and that at least one adventurous preschooler took it to heart. My "knowledge" of the place, of course, consisted almost entirely of fantasies, only lightly seasoned with facts. Between the ages of four and twelve, my "image" of San Francisco—which amounted to a personal *myth*—blended elements of many worlds: the Wild West, Hopalong Cassidy, the *Cinnamon Bear* radio saga, *The Wizard of Oz* movie, the *Foodini* show on early TV, Dixie Willson's story "The Train That Went Traveling," tales of pirates and buried treasure, towering mountains, vast giant redwood forests, music, painting, and all the arts, a free-wheeling communal way of life, printing with moveable type, red roses everywhere, and (by no means least) little or no school. For me, the City "out West" was a kind of children's utopia characterized by freedom, wilderness, creative eccentricity, lots of dogs to romp with, and cable-cars to ride on night and day.

Rather disconcertingly, my visualizations of this mythic realm—drawing on my father's rambling stories, old snapshots and postcards, fleeting scenes in incomprehensible movies, and photos from *Western Kennel World* (mailed to us each month direct from Rosemont Press)—also incorporated images of the late Middle Ages and early Renaissance: Uccello's Florence and Dürer's Nuremburg. I suspect this confabulation resulted from my father's attempt to explain to his five-year-old son the origins and meaning of the name "San Francisco." In any event, for me, the boundaries between "Out West" and "Once upon a time, long, long ago" remained blurred for many years.

Having grown up in a household which quietly but steadily celebrated a miniature San Francisco Renaissance all its own, I continued even as a teenager to think of myself as a kind of San-Franciscan-in-exile. All along I knew in my bones that some day I would head "Out West" and visit my ancestral "home away from home." By 1960, as a discontented high-schooler learning the fine art of hitch-hiking, I decided that now was the time. A few miles west of Chicago I stuck out my thumb; seventy-two hours later I reached the West Coast.

In 1960, San Francisco was in the midst of a Renaissance so boisterous that it made headlines around the world. As a militant partisan of the Beat Generation at Proviso High, and a regular reader of *Big Table* and *Evergreen Review*, I had followed every twist and turn of this Renaissance since 1958, and naturally—despite the fact that I lived a mere 2000 miles away—I considered myself a participant. When I finally got there, my experiences of *déja vu* were so many and close between that I almost felt like an old-timer; I was in fact sixteen, but most of the people I met, especially those close to my own age, were new to the city and knew nothing of its history or traditions. Dizzy with the joy of discovery, and full of enthusiasm for the future, I spent most of my time wandering the streets, sitting and reading in the old easy chairs at City Lights Bookstore, and talking with poets and jazz people at the Co-Existence Bagel Shop.

As it happened, most of the poets I had hoped to meet in San Francisco (including Bob Kaufman, Philip Lamantia and Gary Snyder) were either far away or laying low. One evening I was pleased to run into Lawrence Ferlinghetti at City Lights, but business was brisk and we spoke only for a few minutes. The friends I made at that time, however—Shig Murao and Dick McBride at City Lights; Robert Stock, who tended bar at the Bagel Shop; and several whom I knew only by their first names, most notably a young African American philosopher/poet, Tyrone—fully embodied the practical utopianism and spirit of improvisation that figured so prominently in the one-house San Francisco Renaissance of my Chicago childhood. The sense of community, solidarity, creativity and mutual aid in the North Beach Beat scene seemed to me to reflect, on a grand scale, all that I had heard of the collective vitality and adventurousness of the California Rosemonts of the 1890s through the early 1920s.

In the 1960 San Francisco Renaissance, the "experimental life" flourished as nowhere else, and part of the experimentation involved herbs and substances that the U.S. government had declared illegal. As is so often the case when a new free spirit is in the wind, the local police were notorious for their brutality, which they largely directed against peaceful "beatniks" and jazz musicians. Although "possession or sale of illegal drugs" was a frequent pretext for that brutality, the real reason was well known: North Beach was a racially integrated community and, as such, an affront to the white supremacist cops.

During the two months that I lived there, drug use was a rather minor pursuit among the people I knew. LSD and mescaline were often discussed but nobody ever seemed to have any. From time to time, someone passed around a reefer. A few folks had prescriptions for dexedrine (which never attracted me; I was frantic enough already).

The really dangerous, deadly drugs were commonly called "over-the-counter" and "legal" drugs, for the simple reason that they were on sale at drug stores everywhere. One of these legal drugs, known as "Azmador," was an alleged treatment for asthma. For a few weeks in the fall of 1960, among a small minority of young North Beach poets and assorted cognoscenti, "Azmador" was something of a fad: a "guaranteed" provoker of "weird" and "interesting" hallucinations. It was readily available at a special low price at a drugstore of dubious virtue known as The Hub, which was open all night and frequented by many North Beach residents looking for legal "highs."

As a zealous reader of Rimbaud, I decided to see what Azmador could do. Because I was six feet tall and weighed 160 pounds, it was suggested that I take twice the recommended dose. Because I was sixteen and didn't know any better, I took a triple dose.

For half an hour, nothing happened. It was early evening and I was out walking, impatient for something to happen and wondering whether I should take yet another dose. And then, out of nowhere, a friend from the Bagel Shop appeared, coming from the opposite direction, and we stood there and talked for a few minutes before going our separate ways. Something about this conversation struck me as a little odd, and when I turned around, my friend had disappeared.

"Uh-oh," said I to myself, "the Azmador must be working at last."

Fortunately I had a place to stay. A jazz bass-player friend had a pad on Laguna Street paid up to the end of the month, but he had to go home to Sonora for a few days, maybe longer, because of illness in the family. He had given me his key and told me that as long as I came in after dark and left early in the morning, there'd be no hassle with the building manager. I hurried off to the Laguna Street pad, third floor, hallucinating all the way.

The hallucinations were not only "interesting" and "weird," they were also terrifying and overwhelming. An endless noisy procession of demons, devils, monsters, composite beings, and phantasmagoric characters worthy of *Bugs Bunny and the Magic Sneeze* cavorted all over the ceiling, walls, and furniture—appearing, disappearing, constantly changing. With my eyes open or shut all I saw was nightmare after nightmare. A lamp that had changed into a lizard went on to become, in rapid succession, a bird of prey, the MGM movie lion, and Francis Marion, the "Swamp Fox" of the Revolution. Anything and everything kept changing into anything and everything else. Time was in flux, or in reverse—the "world" I was in had a lot in common with the fifteenth century. This Renaissance was not, however, that of Raphael or Leonardo, but rather of Hieronymus Bosch, with a dash of Tex Avery thrown in.

At one point I opened the closet and beheld the brass monkey trio—See No Evil, Hear No Evil, Speak No Evil—three-feet tall, giggling, and thoroughly evil. Horrified, I shut the door quickly, lay down on the bed and tried again (unsuccessfully) to sleep. Several times in the course of that terrorsome night I looked in the closet again, and was barely able to suppress a scream when I found those malevolent monkeys still there, still giggling. Hours later, when I looked yet again, I was just as scared to find them gone!

Interspersed with these visions of gloom, foreboding, and cosmic terror were many calm encounters with people I knew. Aside from the fact that these visitors were not really there, our conversations were not particularly extraordinary. I hallucinated several friends from the Co-Existence Bagel Shop and other hangouts, and for the most part we talked about matters at hand. Here was poet Robert Stock, who assured me that the "state" I was in wouldn't last forever, that it would subside before too long, that soon I would be able to look back on it all and laugh. And there was Shig from City Lights, telling me that this sort of thing happens to all poets—that I should just relax, and chalk it up to experience. My friend Tyrone also showed up in these visions, and contributed a few characteristically sagacious words of his own. And here, too, was Lawrence Ferlinghetti himself, not saying a word, but smiling—exactly as he had smiled at City Lights that busy evening when a fellow I had met the day before had said "Well, we meet again" and I replied, idiotically: "It's the smallest of all possible worlds." Now, in the sheer hell on Laguna Street, third floor, this *bon mot* of mine took on a new and cataclysmic meaning.

Late that night, around 2 a.m., looking out the window, I was astonished to see Hedy Lamarr (looking as she did in her 1940s films) sitting on a tree limb just a few feet away, and beckoning to me. I opened the window and climbed out onto the tree's largest limb. By then, Ms Lamarr herself had vanished, but a large, framed photograph of her had been left in her place. As I ventured a little closer toward it, someone yelled: "Hey, what the hell do you think you're doing?" I knew that this was an intrusion of "reality"—that those words were intended for me—even before the shouter added: "Get out of that tree or I'll call the police!"

So there I was, out on a limb in a tall tree in the apartment courtyard at 2 a.m., inching my way back to the third-floor window. As I climbed into my room, I felt cold, exhausted and, truth to tell, a little sorry for myself. Closing the window, I glanced back and noticed that the photo of Hedy Lamarr was gone.

For a few minutes I thought that the voice from the "real world" and the cold air had brought me out of the nightmare, and that I was now "back to normal" at last. Alas, in no time at all the multiplication of unusual creatures in the room persuaded me that the hallucinations had started up again, with a vengeance.

And so it went for another agonizingly long night and day.

By the third day, I was convinced that I would never recover; that I was doomed to keep hallucinating for the rest of my life; that the Azmador had destroyed large areas of my brain; that I had stupidly messed up my whole life—in short, that all was lost.

And then, suddenly, the telephone rang!

I must have jumped at least three feet in the air. But as it rang and rang, again and again, I persuaded myself that this was probably just another auditory hallucination, so I slowly sat down on the bed and did my best to ignore it. Staring at the phone and pretending not to hear it, I listened to it ring for two, maybe three years. I wondered what to do. Feeling as I did like an alien from an unknown planet, I wasn't sure I wanted to talk with anyone from Earth.

For some reason, I eventually picked up the phone and said "Hello?" No matter who it was, I was determined to bluff my way through.

Amazingly, it was my friend the bass player—the guy whose room I was staying in. The fact that no one else knew I could be reached at that number had not occurred to me.

"Hey, man," my friend said, "What's happening?"

I stammered back that I was feeling a bit "out of it," but that basically I was all right, sort of, more or less.

"You sound a little funny," he said.

"I *feel* a little funny," was my snappy reply.

"Oho!" he replied. "I think I know what you're saying. You haven't been over to The Hub, have you?"

"Well," said I, "I don't really want to go into all that right now."

"Okay, man," he said, laughing a little, "but are you sure you're okay?"

When I insisted I was fine he said "Be cool" and hung up.

Oddly enough, I did in fact feel much better. After that unexpected call, the hallucinations—with a few minor exceptions—went away and stayed away. For me, life started all over again.

A couple hours later I called home to Chicago and did what I considered a fairly good imitation of a normal human being. Neither of my parents seemed to think I sounded "funny," and they really put me to the test with a barrage of questions. Yes, I had been to Rosemont Place and Chinatown and Muir Woods, and had ridden cable-cars and crossed the Golden Gate bridge several times; and yes, I was fine, had a nice place to stay, and even had a job of sorts, selling the weekly *San Francisco Star*, an early "underground" paper.

By the time I hung up, I realized that my sense-perception was fully restored, and in fact heightened by a strong feeling of *elation*, which, by the way, lasted for days. In my own personal *renascence*, the nightmares were over.

The active ingredient in Azmador was belladonna, also known as nightshade, the powerful medicinal and hallucinogenic properties of which have been known for ages. Some scholars have argued that

Hieronymus Bosch, as a member of the Brotherhood of the Free Spirit which used the drug in certain rituals, was familiar with it. The opening sentence of the second canto of *Les Chants de Maldoror* refers to Maldoror's mouth "full of belladonna leaves." For generations it was a standard household remedy. One of the youngest characters in *Little Women*, coming down with "headache, sore throat, and queer feelings," takes belladonna for relief.

In my three-day nightmare journey, belladonna was clearly the active element, but the telephone—its passive accomplice—played a critical role as well. My friend's call, however innocuous, served as the "Voice from Outside" that is so important in vision-seeking and other shamanic experiences. This was not a Wrong Number, but an unhoped-for call that allowed me to escape from a whirlpool of wrongness.

Simply by dialing "his own" number (which was no longer his), my friend unwittingly provided an example of a "wake-up call" in the truest and most prophetic import of the word: a sudden, simultaneous reawakening of the senses, mind and spirit. In the wink of an eye I emerged from the pit of despair and soared to the heights of ecstasy. I felt not only renewed, but *reborn*.

The whole experience—vision-quest, descent to the underworld, and rite of passage—marked a decisive turning-point in my life. For three days that seemed centuries, in a state of agonizing intensity, fearful anguish, and total despair (I was sure I was going to die at any moment) I lived and dreamed the wildest Transcendentalist abandon, an *Argonautica*, a *Season in Hell*, and I emerged from these despondent wanderings a new person: an *other* "I" that superseded all my previous I's.

## A New York Phone Call and a Letter From Paris

As early as 1959, at fifteen, I realized that I was a surrealist. Critical literature on the subject stated that the movement had "died" years before, but I found that hard to believe, for the world-transforming goals the first surrealists proclaimed in 1924 had barely begun to be fulfilled. Not until 1962, however, while browsing through scholarly journals at the old Post Office News bookstore in downtown Chicago, did I come across a reference to the current-day activity of the Surrealist Group in Paris.

As a surrealist I naturally also regarded myself as a revolutionary. I carried a red card (No. X322339) in the Industrial Workers of the World (the IWW, known as Wobblies), and for a time also frequented the Libertarian Tendency of the Young People's Socialist League. YPSL (pronounced Yipsel) was the official youth section of the Socialist Party, but in those days was far to the left of the Party, and the Libertarian Tendency was far to the left of everyone else in YPSL. In essence, the Tendency was the U.S. counterpart of the French *Socialisme ou Barbarie* group, and of the Solidarity groups in London and Glasgow. Most of its members also belonged to the IWW.

In fall '62 I happened to attend a YPSL convention in Kerhonkson, New York. It took me thirteen hours to hitchhike to New York City, and thirteen more to hitchhike the additional few miles to Kerhonkson. Apart from meeting the comrades in the Libertarian Tendency, the convention was inconsequential, and the only real accomplishment of the trip was the telephone call I made to the Greek poet Nicolas Calas. In the 1930s and 40s, Calas had been a dynamic presence in the Surrealist Movement in Athens, Paris and New York. His writings from the "old days" were an important source for the nascent Chicago Surrealist Group.

When I looked him up in the New York phone directory, I was not sure he still lived in New York, or for that matter, whether he was still alive at all. Calling from a street-corner pay-phone, a few seconds later I heard a man's booming voice saying "Yes?"

"Is this Nicolas Calas?" I asked, and the voice repeated "Yes," but this time without the boom or question-mark.

"And do you still consider yourself a surrealist?" I continued.

"The question is a little abrupt," he said. After a brief pause, he added: "First, I would like to know: Who are *you*?"

I told him my name, and explained that several of us in Chicago had come to recognize ourselves as surrealists, had taken the first steps in forming a group, and were eager to get in touch with other surrealists.

"A Surrealist Group in Chicago," said Calas, perhaps with a note of irony. "That's very interesting. Indeed, quite remarkable." He bombarded me with questions: How many were we? What were our ages? (When I told him I was nineteen he said: "That's not too bad.") Were we painters or writers or both? And how long was I going to be in New York? Perhaps we could get together?

When I told him I had to return immediately to Chicago, he said:

"In any case I should like to know more about you and your friends. You will write me?" I told him yes, of course (and we did in fact carry on something of a correspondence for several years).

"Well, then," he went on, "for myself, I am not quite sure how to answer your question. There is no surrealist activity in New York, and there has not been any for many years. A lot has changed since the 1940s. I have not been active in Breton's group since that time, but I am still on good terms with Breton, and I always see him when I go to Paris." He hesitated a moment, then asked: "You are of course in touch with Breton?"

"Not yet," said I. "That's one of the reasons I called you—to obtain his address so that we could write to him."

"Yes," he said, "if you think of yourselves as surrealists, you should by all means write to Breton. He is at the same address as always: 42, rue Fontaine, in the ninth *arrondissement*."

I thanked him heartily, and was ready to say good-by when he asked: "Do you not also want his telephone number?"

Now it was my turn to pause. My knowledge of French was slight, and my pronunciation poor, and I could hardly imagine telephoning André Breton under such circumstances. So I told Calas no, I would rather write Breton a letter.

By early December, my letter to Breton was on its way. In a concluding paragraph, I noted that I was studying French, but still read it with some difficulty—which explains why the reply came from a younger and bilingual surrealist, Robert Benayoun, who opened with these words: "André Breton asks me to answer you in his place, since his command of the English language is practically non-existent."

Benayoun's letter, which marked my first direct contact with the Surrealist Group in Paris, also turned out to be an object-lesson in the uncertainty of long-distance communication. He had rightly sent it to the address I had given Breton: my parents' address in the Chicago suburb of Forest Park. By the time it arrived there, however—such was my mobility in those restless years—I was in Mexico City. When I called home and learned that an air-mail letter from Paris had arrived at the Forest Park address, I gave my parents careful instructions on forwarding it to me c/o General Delivery at the main post office in Mexico City.

Weeks passed, but the letter did not arrive. A postal official suggested that it may have been lost. "Sometimes it happens," he said, with a shrug. And then he asked: "Where was it mailed from?"

"Chicago," I replied. "But originally from Paris."

"Paris!" he cried, and went on to explain that an air-mail letter from

Europe may have gone to another department. We marched there together but no letter from Paris had arrived for me.

Despairing of ever receiving the letter, I nonetheless took care to leave further forwarding information at both General Delivery and the European air-mail departments before setting out for my next destination, which happened to be San Francisco.

Three weeks later, visiting my brother at his place in Seattle, I started to tell him the odyssey of that letter, "now evidently lost forever"—but that's as far as I got in the story, for my brother interrupted, saying: "No, it arrived here last week. It's in the dining room—I'll get it."

From Paris to Chicago to Mexico City to Seattle: Quite an itinerary! Half-way round the world in some forty-odd days!

No Wrong Number figures in this narrative—it is not even about the Wrong Number's postal equivalents: a wrongly addressed or misdelivered letter. At each step Benayoun's letter was sent to what was, at that particular moment, the right address, but the addressee—*c'est moi!*—seems to have found it hard to stay in one place long enough to receive it. The experience nonetheless resounds with the tricksterish "spirit" of Wrong Numbers, and this much is certain: It made me acutely aware of the extreme precariousness of human communication in all its forms.

Benayoun's comradely three-page letter assured me that André Breton and the entire Surrealist Group had found my letter "very encouraging," that they were eager to hear more about our group in Chicago, and were "happy to see that the subversive thought keeps everywhere its power of impact." Some years later Mimi Parent, a painter from Montreal who had been active in the Paris group since 1959, told me that my letter, in which I had inquired about surrealism's current political position, had provoked a lengthy and sometimes heated discussion in the Paris group on that very subject. A large part of Benayoun's letter was in fact devoted to politics, including a detailed summary of the Surrealist Group's leading role in drafting the important 1960 "Declaration Concerning the Right to Insubordination in the Algerian War" (commonly known as the "Declaration of the 121").

That much-forwarded, long-delayed letter from Paris affected me as few letters have done since. Naturally I wanted Benayoun to know that it had arrived at last and that I was delighted to hear from him. In Seattle, at the old storefront Wobbly hall on Yesler Way, I sat down in front of an ancient typewriter—an Oliver No. 5, if memory serves—and pecked out a hurried reply.

# Claude Tarnaud & the Poetic Use of the Useless

On my first day in Mexico City, early in 1963, I chanced to find a copy of Aldo Pellegrini's excellent *Antologia de la poesia surrealista*, featuring the "militant poets of the Surrealist Group" in France. Through the years I had the good fortune to meet and/or correspond with many of those militant poets, several of whom became lifelong friends. The first one I met was Claude Tarnaud, who was then living in New York with his wife Gibbsy, and working as a translator at the United Nations.

While I was waiting impatiently for Benayoun's letter in Mexico, the sculptor Alberto Gironella gave me Tarnaud's New York address. Almost simultaneously, Gérard Legrand in Paris sent Tarnaud my address in Chicago. Later, at the headquarters of the Berkeley, California branch of the IWW, I dashed off a letter to Tarnaud, explaining that I was still on the road but hoped to see him soon. His reply came in a few days (c/o City Lights Bookstore), and a couple of weeks later I was thumbing rides from Seattle to Chicago. After a short rest at home, I took to the road again and didn't stop until I reached the Tarnauds' place on Riverside Drive in Manhattan.

One of the finest poets of his generation, Claude Tarnaud was a brilliant, original thinker, and an outstanding figure in surrealism. He was my first close friend in the international surrealist movement. From the start it was clear that we shared an enormous number of passional attractions, including bop and post-bop jazz, especially the splendorous sounds of Thelonious Monk and John Coltrane. (Years later, in 1989, after a long lapse in our correspondence, he wrote me of his love for free jazz: the music of Muhal Richard Abrams and other members of Chicago's Association for the Advancement of Creative Musicians). Among our other mutual enthusiasms were Jacques Vaché and the theory and practice of *umor*; the books of Charles Fort, "prophet of the unexplained"; the "Cthulhu Mythos" of H. P. Lovecraft and Clark Ashton Smith; and the great Irish precursor of surrealism, Charles Robert Maturin, whose *Melmoth the Wanderer* I had started reading just before hitchhiking to Mexico, and finished in Acapulco. Moreover, the focus of Tarnaud's specifically surrealist research also happened to be mine—the phenomena known as *objective chance*: those wondrous coincidences of desire and necessity in which the real and ideal series of events compose a single magic moment.

The opposite of a *littérateur*, Claude was a "hipster" in the best sense of the word—*i.e.*, the bop musicians' sense, in which, as Robin D. G. Kelley has pointed out, "hipness" was the essence of a whole "culture of opposition." He was in his forties when we met, twenty-one years older than I, but he had hitchhiked quite a bit in his younger days, and it was he, more than any other individual, who convinced me that the "open road" had to lead somewhere. More importantly, he not only confirmed my spontaneous and instinctive sense—or should I say *sensation*?—of the "practice of poetry," but also *heightened* it immeasurably, and gave my adolescent awareness a much surer direction.

His personal contributions to my surrealist education were in fact second to none. Realizing that in those days I was unable to read many of the most important surrealist books, he did his best to rectify the situation. Concentrating on *Arcanum 17*, which he considered Breton's greatest work—the expansive synthesis of the revolutionary poetic outlook and way of life set forth in *Nadja, The Communicating Vessels*, and *Mad Love*—he extemporaneously translated numerous passages, and discussed them at length. He did the same with Georges Goldfayn's and Gérard Legrand's preface to the annotated edition of the *Poésies* of Isidore Ducasse published by Eric Losfeld.

Almost every day for a full week, sometimes extending "to all hours," we talked, and talked, and then talked some more. We talked about Africa, where he and Gibbsy had lived for some time; about the civil rights struggle in the U.S., in which I was active; about the IWW, the Cuban Revolution, Simon Rodia and his Watts Towers, English and American poetry, and contemporary art and intellectual life in the U.S. Above all we talked about surrealism, its history, current perspectives, and problems; and about the newest developments in jazz. He introduced me to the great painter and writer Eugenio F. Granell, who also became a close friend, and regaled me with stories about many of his other surrealist comrades, including Victor Brauner, Wifredo Lam, and Gherasim Luca.

In the course of these prolonged discussions Claude said a few things which then seemed to have no bearing whatsoever on Wrong Numbers—a topic that hardly interested me at that time in any case—but which, as I recalled them years later, appeared very near to the heart of that insistently immaterial matter.

First was his remark that the only justification for all those glossy magazines that contain so much color photography is the possibility that they will some day be pillaged for the making of surrealist collages. I found this expropriative approach to the dominant order's visual "reality" highly appealing. For me, the revolutionary poetic use of the "useless"—the transmutation of dull "illustrations" into subversive images of the Marvelous—were key components of the surrealist project. Later, when my inquiry into the Who-What-When-and-Wherewithal of Wrong Numbers began to heat up a little, it occurred to me that the Wrong Number—or, more generally, the surrealist misuse of the telephone—might well be (symbolically, at least) the only true justification for all the world's phone-calls. This was scarcely more than a whim, of course, but it had the effect of bringing me closer to the real roots of the question.

Also bursting with Wrong Number implications was a story Claude told about one of his closest friends, Gherasim Luca, a major figure of surrealism in Romania and later in France. I did not take notes at the time, but the story impressed me deeply, and though I may have forgotten a few details, the broad outline remains vivid.

The story involved one of Luca's myriad surrealist experiments in the realm of chance and the irrational. As Claude told it, Luca—after someone else had randomly selected a name (from the telephone directory, perhaps?)—proceeded to write an anonymous letter to that person (a complete stranger) every day for some thirty days. In these letters Luca wrote freely and with great emotional intensity about anything and everything that came to mind. He himself knew nothing, not even the name, of the person he addressed; his letters, unsigned and with no return address, were mailed each day by a friend.

I was very moved by this anecdote of disinterested, almost deadpan intervention in the world of chance, all the more so in that it was combined with an equally disinterested and spontaneous creativity. That same combination, with Luca's example in mind, was the defining element of much of the early activity of the Chicago Surrealist Group. I recall in particular one such experiment that began with all of us practicing automatic writing for two or three minutes. Next, one of us—blindfolded—stuck a pin in a map of the city, and then we all went directly to that place to see how closely our texts corresponded to the reality. The results were striking. The central image in my own text, for example, was an *emerald fork.* When we reached the spot indicated on the map (the intersection of Clark and Fullerton), one of the first sights to confront us was the sign of a restaurant called the Golden Cup, picturing a large and well-illuminated green fork.

Such playful excursions into the hinterlands of the unexpected seem to me to be only a dialectical leap or two away from the wonders of misdialed numbers.

And so, without knowing it, my friend Claude Tarnaud made genuine contributions to a critique of the critical/uncritical/

hypercritical dismissal of Wrong Numbers, and therefore holds a place of honor as a pioneer of our authentically umorous *scienza nuova*. Is it by accident that one of his longest and most alluring articles is titled "Clandestine Paths of an Anterior Future"?

## Calling Robert Benayoun

You don't have to know Hegel's *Logic* by heart to know that a Wrong Number can be right and wrong at the same time.

In December 1965 Penelope and I left for Paris via New York and London. The purpose of the trip was to meet with André Breton and others in the Surrealist Group, with the intention of organizing a Surrealist Group in the U.S. when we returned. Our plan was to stay a few months in London, where we intended to study French intensively, and then to proceed to Paris in the Spring.

As it happened, British immigration officials at London airport refused us admission. Although the reasons they gave for this were mostly unstated, some months later it was revealed that they suspected me of being a draft-dodger. I was in fact an active opponent of the U.S. government's imperialist war against the Vietnamese, but at that time I had received no draft notice and was not actually fleeing conscription or otherwise violating U.S. law. Nonetheless, our passport was stamped REFUSED, and we spent the night as Her Majesty's guests in the airport detention center. The following morning armed guards escorted us onto the first plane to Paris, and instructed a stewardess to give us our passports only after take-off. The experience was not without its amusing side: After all, how many U.S. citizens are lucky enough to be deported to Paris?

And so, as we arrived at Le Bourget airport on Christmas eve, we decided to call Robert Benayoun, the only member of the Surrealist Group whom we knew to be fluent in English, and with whom I had in fact exchanged letters. I looked up *Benayoun, Robert* in the airport telephone directory, and dialed the number. A woman answered, in French of course, and when I asked for Robert she asked several questions that I did not understand. With considerable effort I managed to learn that Robert was seriously ill and unable to come to the phone. To his wife, as I thought her to be, I extended my best wishes for his speedy recovery, and asked her to tell him that his friends from Chicago would call again in a few days. The woman to whom I was speaking, however, was amazed to learn that Robert had friends in Chicago; she said she was certain that her husband knew no one in the U.S. Even more disturbingly, she stated flatly that he did not know a word of English.

"Pardon, madame," I said at this point, in French, "But is this the residence of Robert Benayoun, *surréaliste*?"

Instead of replying, she hung up the phone.

It was the wrong Robert Benayoun.

Which goes to show that Wrong Numbers come in many shapes and sizes. Here I had dialed correctly but reached a Wrong Number just the same.

We were a bit demoralized as we boarded the airport bus for Paris. Things certainly did not seem to be proceeding according to plan. But it had started snowing lightly, the Paris streets were beautiful—it was our first trip there, and despite our difficulties we were enjoying ourselves immensely. As we strolled along the streets looking for an inexpensive hotel, we noticed Breton's *Le Surréalisme et la peinture* featured in a bookstore window, and then in another window, and another; the new, definitive edition had just appeared. And then we were astonished to see a poster for an International Surrealist Exhibition, *L'Ecart absolu* (Absolute Divergence, a concept of Charles Fourier's), at Georges Bernier's Galerie de l'Oeil at 3, rue Séguier.

Had we stayed in London according to our original plan, we might well have missed this exceptionally important exhibition. Almost certainly we would also have missed meeting Breton, for he became very ill some weeks later and never fully recovered; he died that fall.

At the exhibition we inquired about Robert. I asked if he was ill. Not at all, we were assured; he had just been at the gallery an hour or so ago. Rosamond Bernier gave us his telephone number.

At Robert's, we told him about the other Robert Benayoun, sick and bedridden.

"Oh, the poor fellow," Robert replied. "I must call him and see how I'm doing."

# Calling Andre Breton, or, Memoirs of an Ex-Telephonophobe

Despite our initial difficulties in reaching him by phone, Robert Benayoun—my first surrealist correspondent in Paris—was also the first surrealist Penelope and I visited in Paris. All too typically, English-language texts on surrealism tend to ignore him; U.S. writers, in particular, pretending that the Surrealist Movement "ended" in 1939 or 1947 or some other arbitrary date, almost never even mention his name. The plain truth is that the Moroccan-born Benayoun was an important figure in the Paris group from 1948 on. An inspired interpreter of U.S. popular culture, he authored illuminating studies of Buster Keaton, Woody Allen, the Marx Brothers, nonsense literature, and animated cartoons. He also spearheaded—more than any other individual—the worldwide reawakening of interest in the great Tex Avery.

On that first visit to his apartment, Robert gave us André Breton's phone number: 874-2833. He also let us know that the author of the *Surrealist Manifestoes* detested being addressed as "Monsieur Breton," that everyone in the group called him André, and that we should do so, too. Explaining further that André had been quite ill of late, and only occasionally attended the group's daily meetings at the café La Promenade de Venus (in the old Les Halles market district), Robert nonetheless urged us to telephone him right away, to let him know we were in Paris. "He will be very glad to hear from you," Robert insisted, "and will certainly want to meet with you as soon as his health permits." He went on to say that André and the entire Paris group were deeply interested in the prospects of a Surrealist Group in the United States. He added that André's wife Elisa would probably answer the phone, and that that might make things a bit easier for us, because she spoke English quite well.

In those days I had an extreme aversion to making phone calls. I called it an allergy, only half-jokingly, but in truth it almost amounted to a phobia. As a child I had been taught that the sole purpose of the telephone was to transmit and receive brief messages—especially in regard to my parents' job- or union-related matters. Above all I was made to understand that the phone was not a toy, and was not meant for small talk, or extended conversation, or any other form of amusement.

This severe attitude reflected my father's New England Puritanical/Unitarian heritage more than his "Wild West" San Francisco upbringing, but it also embodied his workingclass hostility to the telephone monopoly. "The longer we talk," he used to say, "the richer the phone company gets," and many a call from loquacious relatives or friends of the family was abruptly brought to a close by some such statement.

Rarely if ever did I answer the phone before I was eight. For me, phones were boring, strictly utilitarian, with an exceedingly narrow function. They were of no more interest to me than a hairbrush or a vacuum cleaner. I simply had no use for phones. Electric trains, hand puppets, the radio, and (a little later) books were vastly more interesting, not to mention more fun. Best of all, of course was the *outside*—the prairie, or even just an overgrown empty lot, where there were birds, spiders, and butterflies to watch, snakes to follow, fruit trees to climb.

For me, all through high school, and for several years afterward, the telephone retained its repellent associations. To use the phone was like going to the dentist or being sent to the principal's office.

Only when I met Penelope in 1964—a decisive encounter if there ever was one—did I suddenly overcome my antipathy to the telephone. And I overcame it then only to the extent that I was willing and eager to telephone *her,* and her alone. *Love* was the crucial element here, not a "rational adjustment" to the phone. My calls to others were very few indeed.

In Paris, January 1966, therefore, it was Penelope who dialed André Breton's number to announce our arrival in Paris. And as Robert had predicted, it was Elisa who answered. In her captivating, accented English, sprinkled with a little French, she gave us an exceptionally warm and hearty welcome. She and André had already heard, on the surrealist grapevine, that we were in Paris, and that we had attended the group's New Year's Eve party at the Théatre Ranelagh, where we had met Toyen, Mimi Parent and Jean Benoît, Alain Joubert and Nicole Espagnol, and many others who became our good friends. Elisa said André was eager to meet us "as soon as possible," but that he was still too ill to receive visitors.

From then on, Penelope called there three or four times a week. Elisa always answered, and was invariably gracious, comradely, and eager to share news and information she thought would interest us. These calls always lasted at least five minutes, sometimes much longer. Each time Elisa asked questions: What were we doing? What were we reading? Had we been to such-and-such a place, or seen so-and-so's exhibition? She was pleased to hear that we were visiting other surrealists, and was especially delighted that we had met Ted Joans by chance in the street one evening, for she and André liked him very much. She was also interested to learn that we were making the rounds of bookstores—Eric Losfeld's Le Terrain vague, José Corti's, Le

Minotaure, La Soleil dans la tête—in search of surrealist books, and amused that we were finding many volumes that members of the group had told us were *introuvable* (impossible to find).

Elisa also frequently attended the meetings at the café—far more often than André did at that time—and we had the chance to get to know her better there, for she often made it a point to visit with the two of us after the group meeting was over. She very quickly became our very dear friend, and remained so for the rest of her life.

André's illness lingered through the winter into the Spring, and Penelope and I were able to speak to him at length only on two occasions, at the café. Once, however, during one of Penelope's calls, André cried out that we should come visit him the following day. This allowed us the great pleasure of exploring, for a couple of hours, the grand studio at 42, rue Fontaine. Unfortunately, André's condition had worsened during the night, necessitating yet another postponement of the longer discussion we all desired.

Several months later, back in Chicago, Penelope and I resumed our phoneless, semi-nomadic way of life (between 1964 and '71, we lived at six different addresses). For several years we made use of the phone at the IWW's Solidarity Bookshop—which itself moved at least four times in that same period, but was usually just a few blocks away from wherever we were staying.

Our eventual decision to get a telephone of our own was directly related to the question of "surrealist communication." On our second trip to Paris in the fall of 1970, Mimi Parent told us that she and her husband Jean Benoît had had a several-hours stopover at Chicago's O'Hare Airport some months earlier, and hoped we could meet. Of course, since we had no telephone, they were unable to call us! Two of surrealism's most fearlessly innovative painters, Mimi and Jean were also among our closest friends in Paris, and Penelope and I would have loved to see them in Chicago.

The way to avoid such mishaps in the future was only too clear. One fine Sunday morning, at the Maxwell Street open market, we paid two dollars for a black bakelite "Type 500" phone that was installed a few days later.

And so it came to pass that, under the sign of love, a seemingly incurable telephonophobe not only overcame that particular phobia, but also—having made that quantum leap—went on to make his way through clouds and darkness to the Hidden Valley of Wrong Numbers.

I should add that it was only in the course of writing this book that I realized that I had never spoken to André Breton on the phone.

Except once: years later, far from Paris, in a dream.

# Jacques Brunius and the African Mask; or, A New Vindication of Marcus Garvey

The following account of an attempted meeting frustrated by an exceedingly odd instance of mistaken identity makes no reference to Wrong Numbers, but it has its place in this chronicle nonetheless, and not least because it climaxes with an observation on the telephone so staggeringly (and yet so literally!) *off the wall* that I have never been able to look at a phone the same way since.

Early in January 1966 Robert Benayoun told me that Jacques Brunius, the surrealist cinéaste, was in town for a few days, visiting from London, and that he wanted to meet Penelope and me. I had corresponded with Brunius and was eager to meet him as well. I rang him up and we arranged a rendezvous for the following evening at the International Surrealist Exhibition at the Galerie l'Oeil.

Penelope and I arrived a little early at the gallery, and waited in the foyer, where a number of other individuals were also waiting. Among these was an older man I thought might be Brunius. Since the only photo I had seen of him was taken in the early 1930s, I was reluctant to approach him, so I asked Rosamond Bernier, wife of the gallery's owner, whether Jacques Brunius was in the room; she said no. The man I thought might be Brunius glanced at us from time to time, and at one point he too addressed an inquiry to Mme. Bernier, who promptly looked in our direction, shook her head no, and said something to this man (in French) that I did not understand.

After waiting a little over an hour Penelope and I returned to our hotel a few blocks away, leaving a note for Brunius on Mme. Bernier's desk (she was in the midst of a somewhat lengthy telephone conversation), asking him to call us, or simply to come to our hotel if he preferred.

Less than half an hour later came a knock on the door of our room on the fourth floor of the Hotel du Grand Balcon at 52 rue Dauphine. Sure enough, it was the man I thought might be Brunius, and he said: "So it *was* you, after all. I was *sure* it was you, but Mme. Bernier told me you were waiting for Jean Benoît."

The mystery was solved! Clearly Mme. Bernier had misunderstood what I said. The mishap, however, was a most curious one, truly a tangled web. Consider: The parties who wished to make contact were present, close to each other and even face to face, but failed to meet, despite the fact that a third person, Rosamond Bernier, who knew everyone involved—Brunius, Penelope and me, and Jean Benoît—was also on the scene. When I asked Rosamond whether Brunius was there, she replied no, thinking I had asked for Benoît; when Brunius asked her whether we had asked for him, she said no, and told him we had asked for Benoît.

The whole experience has the ring of a bizarre variant of the Wrong Number, in which the roles of caller, recipient and third person have been switched without warning, and in which the additional factor of mishearing multiplied the confusion. In many respects the incident seemed like a lost chapter of *Alice in Wonderland.* As we learned later, Brunius was in fact a well-known Lewis Carroll scholar, and his main reason for coming to Paris that week was to record a special radio program on the Alice books.

Our visit with Brunius was a heartening one; we talked for a good two or three hours, and we parted warm friends. I recall especially his comments on the current situation of surrealism in England (he was exasperated by E. L. T. Mesens' failure to initiate a public activity, but at the same time reluctant to attempt something on his own). I was impressed, too, by Brunius's response to a question of mine regarding recent tendencies in surrealist poetry: without a moment's hesitation he stated his opinion that the most "radically original" surrealist poets in the French language since World War II were Claude Tarnaud and the Belgian Jacques Lacomblez.

However, my strongest impression of this meeting with Brunius took place toward the end of his visit. Suddenly and spontaneously he said to us, pointing to the telephone on our hotel-room wall and raising his voice, for he was clearly excited: "Look, *that telephone is an African mask*!" From a certain angle, with the shadows that fell upon it, the phone did bear an uncanny resemblance to such a mask. "If one photographed it from where I am sitting," Brunius said, "and in this light, everyone would take it for a wood-carving from Mali." Our friend was deeply affected—as were we—by this glaring coincidence between the ultramodern and the so-called "primitive."

For the first time I saw the telephone as an instrument capable of concealing as much as it revealed—a device one could hide behind for the purpose of mixing, multiplying or confusing identities. My later adventures in the world of Wrong Numbers convinced me that all telephones are always masks, off the hook or not.

During a Wrong Number, moreover, two telephones engage in a harum-scarum *double-masked dance across the wires*. With a breathless rhythm all its own, the transmission of unanticipated and disembodied message-fragments proceeds ceremonially from one end of the line to the other, and back again—back and forth, voice to voice, mask to mask.

It is enough to make one's hair stand on end.

But how pleasant it is, after all, to verify once again—particularly in such an unexpected context, as has happened many times in the past century—the venerable principle that such thinkers as Aimé Césaire, Frantz Fanon, Malcolm X, Max Roach, and Joseph Jarman came to regard as second nature: that one of the surest ways to cast new light on present problems and future prospects is to heed Marcus Garvey's celebrated slogan: *Back to Africa!*

## A Parcel for Marcel

For reasons that are neither clear nor unclear, I never met Marcel Duchamp. The way we just missed each other on numerous occasions was worthy of a choreographer. Every time our paths were close to crossing, one or the other of us just happened to veer elsewhere.

When Penelope and I returned to the States in May 1966, we stayed in New York for a week at the fifth-floor studio of Eric Matheson on First Avenue, across the street from Bellevue Hospital. One afternoon, on a stroll several miles from there, we chanced to run into Sheila G., a friend I had known in my teens, and whom Penelope had also known, in college. I had not seen her since the days of the short-lived (1960–62) Rhapsodist Movement of Maywood, Illinois—in which she had played a peripheral but authentically subversive role—and I did not know that she was now living in New York. Sheila was always an inspiring character, prone to provocative and even reckless behavior (she was, among other things, an accomplished thief), and it was certainly a pleasure to see her again. Of course we stopped for coffee, and talked about people we knew and things we were doing and dreaming.

"And now I have a story to tell you," Sheila said after an hour or so—"a true story about something that happened to me, and you are the only people I know who will be interested in it." A delivery-man had rung the bell of her apartment and explained that he had attempted to deliver a package to the man in the apartment next to hers. This neighbor, however, was not in: Would she sign for it and give it to him? "Of course," said Sheila, signing and taking the package, which she placed near her door. A few hours later she picked it up and knocked on her neighbor's door. A handsome, elegant older man "with a twinkle in his eye" opened the door and smiled at her. "I have a parcel for you," said Sheila. And only as the parcel passed from her hands into his and he said "Thank you," did she notice the name of its addressee.

"And that," she concluded, "is the story of my meeting with Marcel Duchamp."

I have always admired this rather absurd little story, and on reflection I find that what I love most about it is its wildly unaffected simplicity—its delightful lack of "literary" veneer. What seemed to be the real beginning turned out to be the end—but then, with ends like that, who needs beginnings?

## I Knew We Should Have Turned Left at Utopia Parkway

This episode centers around a curious incident of *misdelivery* in which, as in the most exquisite Wrong Numbers, the wrong place somehow turned out to be the right place, with ambiguous signposts pointing still deeper into *terra incognita* at its most disquieting.

During my brief career as shipping-clerk at the Roosevelt University Bookstore in 1966–67, it happened that a box of books had been delivered to a wrong address in Hyde Park, and the chore of recovering them was assigned to me. A taxi took me to the house on Woodlawn Avenue, just down the street from what was then known as Mohammad's Mosque No. 1. The front porch was impressively guarded by two large gryphons in wood. I rang the bell, and seconds later the door was opened by a distinguished looking African American woman. A few feet behind her, on the wall, was a large painting by René Magritte.

I introduced myself as the messenger from the bookstore, and was promptly invited in. My hostess pointed to the box I was to retrieve, and asked if I had time for a cup of tea. By then I had noticed truly amazing paintings on all the walls, and although I had instructed the cab-driver to wait, I was in no hurry to leave. "Tea would be lovely," I replied, and asked if I could look at the paintings. "Of course!" my hostess said. "Look all you like!" She explained that the owners of the house were away for the morning, that she was the housekeeper, that I was welcome to stay as long as I wished.

And so for the next half hour or so I had the pleasure of looking at numerous paintings by the very artists I most admired—most of them surrealists. I was familiar with many of the works through reproductions, but I also recall an early Picabia that I had never seen before.

Most appealing of all were a group of object-boxes by Joseph Cornell. It was these I looked upon longest, and studied most closely, marveling at the shimmering depth of their poetry and magic.

At last I thanked my gracious hostess for her hospitality, took the misdelivered box of books and returned to the cab.

The adventure, however, was far from over.

At the first intersection, the driver suddenly said: "Hey, what *is* this?" He was pointing to a sizeable group of people on the other side of the street.

It was a group such as I had never seen before, and have not seen since. Physically, each and all of them departed radically from what is commonly accepted as normal. There were at least three microcephalics, several dwarves and midgets—twelve or fifteen individuals in all, moving rather hesitantly as they crossed the street.

This procession closely resembled an outing of old-time circus sideshow performers, or the cast of Tod Browning's powerful but long-suppressed film, *Freaks*, which I had seen for the first time a few months before.

Later I asked various friends and acquaintances who lived in Hyde Park whether there was some kind of home or school for such people nearby, but none of them knew of any such thing, and none had ever seen or heard of any of the people I saw. Some of these friends made further inquiries, but learned nothing.

## A Message from Mauritius

The precariousness of communication manifests itself in mysterious ways. Even direct, face-to-face conversation is subject to the greatest confusion and misunderstanding, as indicated by such expressions as "I didn't say that" and "That's not what I meant." And the greater the distance between two would-be communicators, the greater the chance that things will go awry. The misdelivered letter, the intercepted letter, the "dead" letter, and the letter a friend "forgot" to mail are all building-blocks of History. Not for nothing did Alfred Jarry ironize about the "superstitious belief" that stamped, sealed envelopes deposited in mailboxes actually reached their supposed distant destinations.

In my own experience, one of the most touching letters I have ever received almost failed to reach me simply because an officious bureaucrat of the United States Post Office did not want to hand it over.

The letter was from Malcolm de Chazal, of Mauritius—a French-language poet whose 1947 book, *Sens-plastique*, prompted André Breton to affirm that "Nothing so powerful has been heard since Lautréamont." Although Chazal's direct participation in the surrealist movement was brief and tangential, his finest work is surrealist in the fullest sense. Throughout his writings, the exhilarating possibilities of poetic analogy—"the reciprocity of subject and object" and "the identity of the different"—soar to astonishing new heights, expanding and enhancing the luxuriously revolutionary vision of Charles Fourier. Like Fourier, too, Chazal's analogical revelations—many of them as condensed as telegrams—radiate a sparkling critical humor. For example:

*To believe*
*Is the fatigue*
*Of the devout*

and

*Religion*
*Exists*
*To console*
*Humanity*
*For all the harm*
*That priests*
*Have done to it*

From the late 1960s on my friends and I in the Chicago Surrealist Group held Chazal in the highest esteem. Selections from his writings—poems, aphorisms, an essay—appeared in every issue of *Arsenal/Surrealist Subversion* as well as in *Marvelous Freedom/Vigilance of Desire*, the catalog of the 1976 World Surrealist Exhibition.

In early 1971 I wrote him a short letter, informing him of the existence of the Chicago Surrealist Group, our basic perspective (summed up in the assertion that "What remains for surrealism to do far exceeds what surrealism has done"), and our deep and abiding interest in his work. I added that I regarded him as perhaps the greatest living poet, and that it would be a great pleasure to hear from him.

When I wrote the letter, Penelope and I were preparing to move to a new apartment, and had duly filled out the requisite U.S. Post Office "Change of Address" card. On the day we moved, we found a "Notice of Attempt to Deliver Mail" in the mailbox at our new address. Passport and other identification in hand, we set out for the local Post Office on Irving Park Road to obtain our mail.

The letter was "registered," which meant that we had to wait in line at a special window for that category of mail. Unfortunately, the postal official assigned to that window on that day was not a working clerk but some sort of "higher-up" who was obviously determined to assert his power and authority at all cost. When I presented my "Notice," passport, and other I.D., he stared at me and frowned. He showed me the envelope addressed to me, and as soon as I saw the colorful Mauritius stamps (picturing Violet and Orange Spider Shells) I knew it was from Chazal and was eager to read it.

Instead of handing my letter to me, however, "Mr Higher-Up" held back. He was "disturbed," he said, that the letter had no return address. But what really made him suspicious was the "fact," as he called it, that there was no such place as Mauritius. "We," he told me, "could find no evidence that such a country exists. I have a Mauritania here, but no Mauritius."

Before I could say a word, he went on: "Is this some kind of hoax? You might be in big trouble. Who printed these stamps? You can't just go around inventing countries, you know. What's going on here?" I wished I knew! Here I was at the Post Office, trying to get a letter that was addressed to me, but all I was getting was belligerent foolishness from an ignorant boss. In passing I wondered whether it was a crime to receive mail from non-existent countries.

At last I was allowed to say few words. "There truly *is* a Mauritius," I said. "It's a tiny island east of Madagascar in the Indian Ocean."

"Oh, so you think you know all about it, do you? Well then, smart guy, how come the United States government doesn't mention in it in this list of every country in the world?"

"I don't know," I replied. "Does the list include every *island* in the world?"

"If it's a country, it's on the list!" he shouted.

The stand-off lasted several miserable minutes. What saved the day was the sudden appearance of a working postal clerk who said, "Excuse me," picked up the "list of every country in the world," glanced at it for a fraction of a second, and said: "Here it is—Mauritius."

"Humph!" said Mr Higher-Up as he grudgingly passed me the letter through the window.

Penelope and I breathed sighs of relief and went home singing the grand old Wobbly song, "Dump the Bosses Off Your Back!"

Chazal's letter was well worth the struggle. Here are a few excerpts from its four handwritten pages:

> Friday 19th February '71
>
> Dear Franklin Rosemont,
>
> As nothing happens in life which does not have a meaning, your letter will lead to something.
>
> I am not only a writer, but also a painter. . . . My paintings illustrate *Sens-plastique*, give the fairy land. The tree is humanized, the fish is humanized, the flower is humanized, and so on. By the colors is obtained a message of light. It all concerns THE ART OF INNOCENCE. . . . All my works lead to that unique river, as tributaries. . . .
>
> The big thing, now, is the *robe-fée*, the fairy gown taken from my paintings. It has to do with Dupont de Nemours.
>
> It is impossible for me to speak at length. Why should I? I am in the road of simplicity. Your letter conveys to me the feeling that you have grasped the essential.
>
> One has to go beyond good & evil and head to the plane of innocence.
>
> *Sens-plastique* is the vision of innocence beyond words. My paintings give to see the land of innocence.
>
> I have to tell you something which will interest your wife: I can be understood by 70% of women, 100% of children and hardly 1% of men. My congratulations.
>
> M de Chazal

This stunning communiqué from the land of the Dodo and the Blue Pigeon seemed to require no further response, and certainly no further inquiry; Chazal's remarks about "simplicity" and not wishing to "speak at length" confirmed what surrealist friends in Paris had told me about his solitary proclivities. He continued, of course, to be very "present" in our thoughts, and we regularly sent him our publications and above all "Surrealist Greetings" postcards. I would guess that Chazal was the recipient of three dozen or more postcard salutations from Penelope and me and our friends—from Mexico City and Yucatan; from Devil's Lake, Baraboo, and Kewaunee,

Wisconsin; from Key Largo, New York, Boston, New Orleans and of course Chicago. We were still air-mailing Chazal postcards well into the 1980s, for only much later did we learn that he had died in 1981.

I am aware that this account of my correspondence with Chazal has thus far made no mention of Wrong Numbers, or even of the telephone. And it puzzles me no end that the dozen or so of his works that I have managed to secure—for his books, especially those published in Mauritius, are notoriously difficult to find—include tempting references to the telescope, telegraph, and even television, but nary a word about the telephone. At least one significant, revealing, and obvious connection nonetheless exists between the author of *Sens-plastique* and the theme of this book: Chazal was for several years the Mauritius Telephone Inspector, and as such supervised the preparation of the island's telephone directory.

With that tantalizing bit of biography in mind, I would argue further that the book you are now holding in your hands is the very "something" to which Chazal in 1971 said my letter would lead. Wrong Numbers belong to the land of Innocence, and its wonders are accessible only to those who approach them by way of ever-expanding analogy—that is, those who apply the method of *Sens-plastique.*

## A Proliferation of Beverlys

One afternoon in the summer of 1973 I received a call for Beverly. The name provoked no immediate associations, in part because, as I realized when I put the phone down, I did not know anyone of that name.

All this was far from my thoughts when I awoke the next morning and wondered which of many chores I should attend to first. Those were exceptionally frenetic days for me; among other tasks I was preparing the second issue of *Arsenal / Surrealist Subversion*. As is often the case when I have too many things to do, I decided to go for a walk.

On this particular walk I made it a point to take streets I usually avoided, to turn at corners I had not turned at before, and generally to go in different directions than usual. I was deliberately trying to awaken a sensation of *dislocation*, in which the sense of poetry grows most acute.

About twenty minutes later, at a corner not far from Clark Street,

I noticed a young woman descending a staircase to the sidewalk in front of an apartment building. She may have been as young as fourteen or fifteen, and was casually dressed; she was barefoot, wore bluejeans not snapped at the top, and her shirt (a man's, I think, and much too large for her) was neither tucked in nor buttoned. She smiled and said "Hi!" as she reached the bottom of the stairs, then hurried across the street to meet a girlfriend. Suddenly a woman in her forties, and wearing an apron, appeared in the doorway at the top of the stairs and shouted: "Beverly! Get in here this minute!" I glanced back in time to see Beverly say a few words to her friend and dash back across the street. As she reached the stairs she smiled again—she evidently enjoyed this experiment in defiance—and ran up the stairs two at a time.

I did not have the pleasure of seeing this charming free spirit again, but the name Beverly recurred several times in the next few weeks.

Within a day or two Paul Garon asked me to accompany him on a delivery he had to make in southwest Chicago. The neighborhood, which I had not heard of before, was named Beverly.

A couple of weeks later Penelope and I drove, for the first time, to the Indiana dunes, where relatives of hers owned a small piece of land. The name of the town was Beverly Shores.

Shortly after that, on our first trip to Door County in northern Wisconsin, we passed a number of signs advertising the Beverly Lumber Company.

And so it went, Beverly after Beverly.

I do not recall that I have ever had another Wrong Number asking for a Beverly. It was around that time, however, that I became deeply interested in everything having to do with the nineteenth-century African American "affectional alchemist" Paschal Beverly Randolph, author of *Ravalette, the Rosicrucian's Story*, *Seership: Magic Mirrors and Their Uses*, and other quaint and curious volumes of forgotten lore.

## Who Were You in the Fifteenth Century?

For much of my life, our own telephone was officially listed under a Wrong Number, or at least a Wrong Name. As a consequence of a minor dispute with the gas company, Penelope and I had no credit, and were therefore unable to secure phone service under our name. We decided therefore to apply under the name of a fifteenth-century alchemist whose writings we both admired. The experiment proved to have unforeseen advantages: It saved us the expense of an unlisted number, and made it easy to recognize telephone solicitors, for they automatically assumed that our name was the name they found in the directory. Often they hailed me by the alchemist's first name, as if we were old friends.

We received a surprising amount of mail addressed to our alchemist friend, much of it "special offers" or announcements of spurious "prizes" he was supposed to have won, from banks, insurance companies, and real estate agencies.

A friend who was active in the League of Black Revolutionary Workers had a similar falling-out with the telephone monopoly, and availed himself of our alchemist's surname for a listing of his own. Over the years, as others also made use of his last name, the alchemist's family continued to grow. A couple of decades later we were invited to purchase a costly "limited-edition" genealogy, which, as it turned out, largely derived its current generation listings from telephone directories around the world. This meant that all the imaginary descendants of our alchemist forebear were duly listed. The cover letter solemnly informed me that "I"—that is, the fifteenth-century alchemist whose telephone number Penelope and I shared—was definitely included in this "important reference-work."

When we received calls for this still-thriving ghost from the distant past, it was our practice to explain that he and his family were not in, that they were in the South Seas, or Tierra del Fuego, or Timbuktu, or some other faraway place, and that they were not expected to return for months.

"Thank you," such callers would usually say, "I'll try again in a few months."

# 3.

# THE ADVANTAGE OF SURPRISE, OR, THE WORLD TURNED UPSIDE DOWN

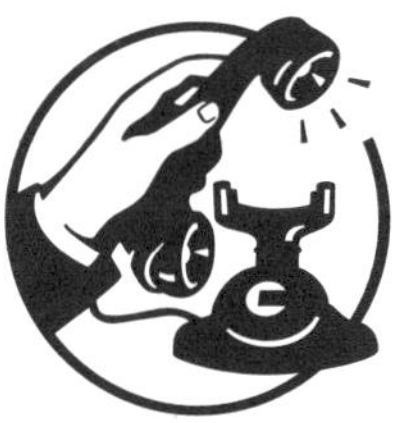

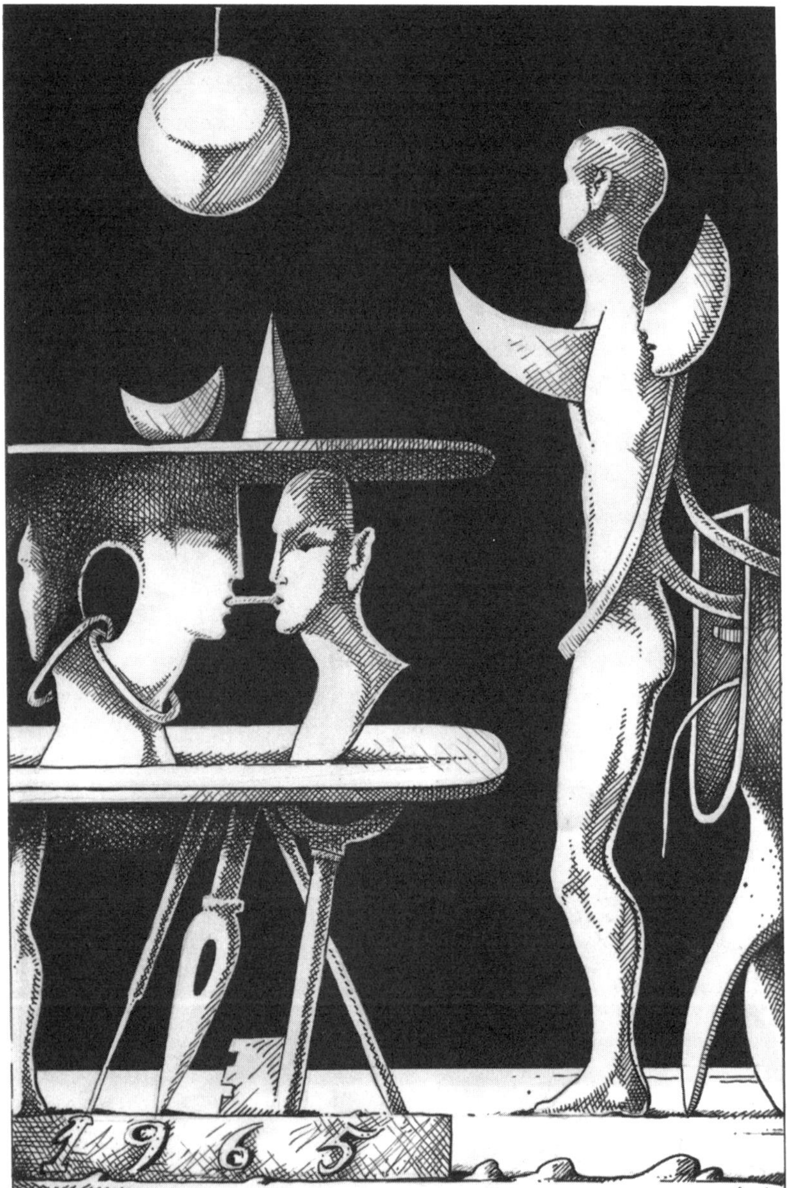
1965

## The Matter of a Moment

In ordinary telephone calls we exchange information, state opinions, make plans, inquire about movie schedules, tell jokes, order pizza, offer assistance, extend congratulations, express condolences, and otherwise communicate our thoughts and feelings. True, the discussion can get "emotional," tempers can flare up, one or both parties can burst into tears, slam down the phone in anger or say things that may be regretted later. For the most part, however, the ordinary telephone call is an experience in which reason (or a reasonable facsimile thereof) dominates the proceedings.

Wrong Numbers, on the other hand, offer a taste of the world turned upside down. Suddenly the course of human events is all off, or has moved and left no forwarding address. The whole experience eludes mere understanding, and is utterly devoid of edification. In Wrong Numbers, reason is always out to lunch, and no one has any idea of what is going to happen next. Magically (or so it seems), the principle of causality changes into the principle of uncertainty. The only thing we know for sure (or think we know for sure) is that we don't know the person who is calling, or the person to whom the caller wishes to speak.

The Wrong Number's underlying psychological reality is a mixture of seemingly impossible questions and deep yearnings only dimly perceived. "Anything Goes" is its whole agenda. Both voices are the voices of strangers, and the words they speak often seem to resemble a kind of vocal hieroglyphics more than conversation. For many recipients of such calls, the experience is much like that of being "suddenly hurled into the middle of another man's story," as described by G. K. Chesterton in *The Club of Queer Trades.* Without even knowing what we are doing, we become actors in symbolic situations so resilient, and so subject to change without notice, that our very identities are wide open with wonder.

Our first task: to seek answers to those "impossible" questions, and to bring those yearnings into the light of consciousness. In this dreamlike climate the Wrong Number's very absence of obvious meaning compels us to seek and find hidden meaning(s) in the depths of ourselves.

No matter which way we turn in the Land of Wrong Numbers, we can count on this: We're in for surprise after surprise.

Those who know how to make their way through the hall of mirrors to the serendipitous configurations beyond soon realize that *too far* can be one of the better places to go.

## How to Mistake Your Own Identity

From the standpoint of the Marvelous, any experience which blurs questionable but commonly accepted distinctions—for example: between self and non-self, subjective and objective, dream and reality—is worth pursuing. This cardinal principle of surrealist research has guided my Quest for the Grail of Wrong Numbers.

Such experiences, however, are not without their hidden dangers, as is amply evidenced in the abundant literature by opium-eaters, ether-inhalers, and the adepts of LSD. I soon learned that Wrong Numbers are no exception. They are non-addictive, of course, and their toxicity is zero, but in large doses their capacity for psychic distress and even damage should not be underrated.

Even the simplest Wrong Number puts us on the other side of the normal. When A dials a number he believes is C's, hoping to speak to B, but instead reaches a stranger, D, without knowing it, A often at first believes that D *is* B or C, and addresses him or her accordingly. This experience of mistaken identity is naturally disorienting for both caller and recipient. The caller believes he is speaking to someone else, and is soon embarrassed to learn otherwise; the recipient is in the no less uncomfortable position of having to deny that he or she is someone else.

The language of Wrong Numbers aggravates the anxiety. The words spoken are all concrete, but they consist of disparate, confusing phrases instead of a coherent conversation, and this gives the words an abstracted air. More often than not, the two speakers share a linguistic community, but they are speaking from very different environments, and with very different assumptions, which widen the distance and limit the communication between them. Many Wrong Numbers are a little like trying to follow a discussion in a foreign language one does not fully understand. A Wrong Number is not exactly nonsense, but it borders on nonsense, and that kind of border never stands still.

Benjamin Paul Blood, the pamphleteering poet and philosopher of laughing-gas who was so deeply admired by William James, was particularly interested in the psychological and philosophical problems of "sense," "non-sense," and the whole gamut of intermediate states. His own extensive experimentation with nitrous oxide and ether convinced him—as he expressed it in his 1874 manifesto, *The Anaesthetic Revelation*—that "naked life is realized outside of sanity altogether."

Misdialed telephone calls, however, are very rarely considered a laughing matter. The Wrong Number, in fact, is far more likely to be considered a bottomless abyss. Falling into it differs from falling into other abysses chiefly in this: The process of sinking into its depths, resurfacing and returning to whatever one was doing beforehand generally takes place in a matter of seconds. Abruptness is one of the Wrong Number's sturdiest traditions. It also explains why so few people perceive even the smallest danger in such a call: It's over so fast, and so easy to forget, who cares? It's just a Wrong Number!

The problem seems to arise only for what we might call the serious student—that is, anyone who allots an inordinate amount of time, as it must seem to others, for research in this realm of pure bafflement. To such persistent inquirers—those who, so to speak, *dwell on* Wrong Numbers—the dangers are all too apparent.

These reflections are based on my own experience. Mere weeks after resolving to keep an ear open for such calls I was beset by several heretofore undiscovered species of frustration, uncertainty, confusion. It did not take me long to realize that trying to solve the riddle of Wrong Numbers was as good a way as any of finding out what it's like to have jagged nerves.

What I found most dismaying was the overwhelming disproportion between the sheer quantity and range of questions posed by these calls, and the meager, highly tentative answers I was grasping at like straws. Clearly I was *seeking*, but the notion of *what* I was seeking was not clear at all. For that matter, I had no "hard evidence" that there was really anything to be sought. Worse yet, focusing on something so vague and yet so intricate and mazelike is like rummaging through a huge barrel of epistemological puzzles: getting lost in it is easier done than said, and once you are lost, what is commonly called "self-consciousness" dissolves with frightening rapidity in an endless series of objective practical jokes.

"Pardon me, is this the way to Chaos?"

Some nights I designated *sleepless*, for the very good reason that I lay awake all through them, unable to secure the benefits of tired nature's sweet restorer. Thanks to an overdose of Wrong Numbers, my customary somnolence was now ablaze with firecrackers. At times I felt like an unemployed sleepwalker, trying (unsuccessfully) to collect dream compensation at the local Bureau of Insomnia. All sorts of depressing "business as usual" droned lifelessly every which way. Stuffed with an odd kind of emptiness, the silence was growing louder and louder.

Wrong Numbers are not icebergs or deserts, but that doesn't mean you can't be stranded on them.

The more I tried to concentrate on these calls, the more the misdialed world began to assume a distinctly indistinct reality of its own—a black hole of an anti-world, entered by a magic doorway or window.

Aside from being surrounded by a multitude of invisible and anonymous callers, I often felt terribly alone in my delirium, but not always. I was heartened by this limpid declaration of Novalis: "No one can pretend to know himself if he is only himself and not at the same time another." And Gérard de Nerval's "I am the other." And Thoreau's "how rarely it is that I am I." And of course Rimbaud's celebrated "I is an other" ("Je suis un autre"), four little words that quickened a whole series of revolts and revolutions in poetry and thought. Bugs Bunny, with his own bottomless bag of tricks, also figured in all this, and a Bluejay as well (*Cyanocitta cristata*); both clearly knew their way around, and offered sage advice.

With such characters as these on my side, I realized all the more that poetry not only goes places, but also takes us along for the ride.

Even to the trained participant-observer, however, listening to the disembodied voices of strangers in a strange disembodied land can lead to unpleasant dreams, anxieties, and miscellaneous miseries too numerous to mention.

Chaos, here I come!

Two voices are heard, apparently speaking to each other, but they are speaking about different subjects, and with different objects in mind: a bit schizophrenic, is it not?

I noticed my own mind, such as it was, is and will be, wandering considerably more than usual, and farther afield.

The destination being at least as uncertain as the terrain I was trying to traverse, mind and body gave the impression of wanting to go their separate ways, leaving me—or what was left of me—in a lurch.

Having roamed to the point of fatigue through the endless rabbit-hole of Wrong Numbers, I seem to have run slam-bang into a kind of epiphany of telephony's own weirdest of all Wonderlands.

Nothing to worry about, just a little mental disintegration, loss of identity, severe depression and nervous collapse.

Welcome to Chaos!

Verily I say unto you, in the spirit of Diogenes and Jacques Vaché: Those who have never beheld their mental grasp *slipping* will never hear the barking of feral mirrors at dawn in the depths of the visibly unspoken!

But then again, those who have never lost themselves are the only real losers.

Chaos, yes—but "*our* Chaos," as Eiranaeus Philalethes called it—and free as the wind!

## Is This the Engineering Works?

During my long, meandering quest for the truth about Wrong Numbers. I confess that there were times when I felt like throwing in the sponge. But then, in the worst moments of discouragement and despair, a call would come.

One morning I was distracting myself by reading the works of Malcolm de Chazal, a poet who was also an engineer, and thinking about George Washington Gale Ferris, an engineer who, as the inventor of the Ferris Wheel, could be considered something of a poet. I thought also of my friend the poet and engineer Vincent Bounoure, who not long before had sent me his book, *La Civilisation surréaliste*.

Amidst these reveries of poetry, giant wheels and a new civilization grounded in surrealism, the phone rang.

"Hello?" said I, as is the custom.

"Hello," my caller replied, a little hesitantly. "Is this the Engineering Works?"

I could not help exclaiming: "*Engineering Works!*" Stunned, and completely off guard, I could only blurt out, "What made you call the Engineering Works at this particular moment?"

"Well," my caller explained, "I have a number here," and he read a number that differed slightly from mine. "Have I dialed incorrectly?" he asked.

"That's not the number you have reached," I told him, "but this is extraordinary—I was just reading and thinking about engineers at the precise moment you called."

My caller, alas, was not interested. "I am sorry to have bothered you," he said, and before I could say another word, he hung up the phone.

I was bitterly disappointed, for I had questions for him: What was he thinking about when he dialed? Why was he calling the Engineering Works? Had he read Malcolm de Chazal? Did the names Ferris or Bounoure mean anything to him? And just what, precisely, were his own views regarding poetry, engineering, surrealism, and the relationship between them?

My disappointment, however, soon dissipated, for this astonishing call let me know—definitively—that I was on the right track. I did not know which track it was, or in which direction I was headed, or the name of the destination, but I knew it was the right way to pursue Wrong Numbers.

## Spoken Doodles From the Zone of Problem 13

As a footloose wanderer in Wrong Number country, it took me a while to learn the lay of the land. These uncharted wastes—large, blank and shifting spaces on the psychic map—were full of non-stop surprises and an overabundance of troubles, large and small. Once I found my bearings, however—or rather, realized that there were no bearings to find—I felt right at home.

During the interim days of doubt, I spent a lot of time talking to myself, but I was too preoccupied to pay much attention to what I was saying. It was in such conditions that the phenomenon of the *spoken doodle* first presented itself: the vocal equivalent of the generally small automatic drawings made while talking on the phone or in other circumstances when one's concentration is directed elsewhere.

Like Wrong Numbers and other unanticipated speech, these word-images engage the ear and the mind at once—the usual gap between speaking and thinking is absent. I began to consider them *peripheral auditions*: roundabout extensions and reverberations of the Wrong Number experience, and also (here the analogy with peripheral vision no longer applies) brief imaginary commentaries on the experience: a kind of automatistic grafitti for ears.

Again and again, prolifically at first but recurring sporadically over the years, these unsolicited utterances borne of internal conflict zoomed into my mind like hummingbirds. Only a few of these scraps of thought found their way onto scraps of paper, and many accidentally or otherwise in turn found their way to the trash-bin. Out of many years' rubble of dreams, hypnagogic reveries, headaches, mood swings, dizzy spells, chills and fever—all related to Wrong Numbers, though no doubt frequently aggravated by such external factors as boredom, caffeine withdrawal, exhaustion and the common cold—the following fragments seem to be the only known survivors.

* * *

*I am in an old-fashioned telephone-booth. The door is stuck. Swarms of mosquitoes have unanimously elected me their chief object of investigation. The phone is out of order.*

* * *

*"I'm sorry, the Ghost of Wrong Numbers Past doesn't live here any more."*

* * *

*A summer evening, swelteringly hot. Jean Tierney, as she appeared in* Laura, *has not returned my call. Later, Buster Keaton arrives, but speaks not a word.*

* * *

*Dial O for Other.*

* * *

*If you want to speak to Millard Fillmore, press 1.* (For a time during my childhood, our phone number was FIllmore 4-0902. I should add that I have never had anything to say to him or to any other upholder of slavery.)

* * *

*News item: The latest sweep by the INS and FBI brought in four hundred and twenty-six offenders, charged with dialing Wrong Numbers without a permit.*

* * *

*"Operator, this is an emergency. I need to speak to the author of* The Brontës Went to Woolworth's.*"*

*"I'm sorry, sir, I have listings for the authors of* The Brontës' Web of Childhood, In the Footsteps of the Brontës, *and* The Inner Structure of *Wuthering Heights—but nothing for the author of* The Brontës Went to Woolworth's. *Would you like the number of Woolworth's?"*

* * *

*Learn to Be Your Own Influencing Machine! Call today!*

* * *

*"On hold": a state of suspended animation in the middle of an evacuated city on the outskirts of an undeclared war zone.*

* * *

*"I'm sorry, all the numbers in the world are now unlisted at their owners' request."*

* * *

*Dial O for Ornithology.*

* * *

*"We're sorry, the telephone for King Ubu has been temporarily disconnected."*

* * *

*"I have a collect call from a Little Red Riding Hood. Will you accept the charges?"*

* * *

*"Are Wrong Numbers ruining your life? Don't despair! Help is on the way! Call Wrong Numbers Anonymous!"*

* * *

*A film: Telephonic Phoenix Meets the Wizard of Osmosis!*

* * *

*Dial O for Outside.*

* * *

*"Do you have a listing for William R. G. Eddie, or A.-K. Woynow?"*

* * *

*When the telephone-sphinx rings, who will* you *be*. . .you *be*. . .you *be*. . .you *be*. . .you *be (etc.).*

* * *

Such are the messages I (?) left for myself (?) as I (?) made my (?) way through the haze of Wrong Numbers. Rereading them today with a critical eye, it amazes me to recall how startlingly lucid these and many other equally absurd formulations seemed to me at the moment of enunciation; several times I was three-quarters convinced that one or another of them provided the key to the puzzle. They remind me now of nothing so much as the fleeting half-images of road-signs and billboards that catch the eye "in passing" while traveling cross-country in a fast train or car. Their relevance may be questionable and their silliness more than obvious, but there they are: among the very few documents of the journey I am trying to record—which, in turn, will not fail to be called questionable and silly.

One particular spoken doodle, however, stands out from all the rest, and I have saved it for last. Unlike the preceding doodles—images and phrases that "leaped to mind"—this one was actually spoken into my ear via telephone:

*"Your call cannot go through as dialed because of Problem 13."*

This was a recorded message on an outdoor pay-phone in the town of Zion, Illinois, some fifty miles north of Chicago. The recording further instructed me to hang up and try again, and added that, should the problem persist, I should call the Operator. I tried again, listened to the same message, and then dialed the Operator who, however, was unable to offer any explanation of the message I had received. Her repeated efforts to put my call through were unsuccessful (it had something to do with competing phone services), but curiously, although she dialed the same number I did, she did not receive that recorded message. Neither the Operator, nor her supervisor whom she consulted while I was on the line, had ever heard of Problem 13.

The fact that this heretofore unnoted episode of *The Twilight Zone* took place in Zion seems entirely fitting. The town was for many years world headquarters of a bizarre religious sect, several thousand strong, whose creed emphasized the flatness of the Earth. The powerful Zion radio station broadcast the flat-Earth dogma far and wide, together with prophecies of the planet's imminent destruction. A large part of the local income was derived from fines imposed on outsiders for such crimes as smoking on Sunday and driving a car faster than five miles per hour.

The flat-Earth movement has long since removed to California, but Zion, Illinois remains—for me, anyway—the capital of Problem 13.

## The Difference Between Right and Wrong

Just as misspelling is the least appreciated genre of creative writing, the Wrong Number is the most despised form of oral poetry and storytelling.

Receiving a Wrong Number is generally considered something like stubbing one's toe, listening to someone scratch chalk across a blackboard, being bitten on the ankle by a Lhasa Apso, and other not-quite-catastrophic but less-than-delightful things one would prefer to do without. Individuals may disagree about particulars, but as far as the Wrong

Number is concerned, just about everyone seems eager to brush it aside, toss it in the trash, get rid of it and otherwise forget all about it.

The number itself, of course, is not wrong; it is a number like any other, beyond right and wrong. What is "wrong" is that it was unintended—or at least consciously so. On the dialer's part, *un*conscious determinants play a key role here, for misdialing is unquestionably a variant of the slip of the tongue or pen, and other parapraxes, or chance actions, discussed by Freud with such compelling charm and insight in *The Psychopathology of Everyday Life*. Psychoanalytically, dialing a Wrong Number indicates that unconsciously the caller did not in fact wish to reach the consciously intended party. When the wrong person answers, the caller's irritation conceals either self-reproach or hostility toward the consciously intended recipient—anger directed inward or outward to mask the unconscious anger toward the third party he or she wished to avoid by dialing incorrectly. As an accidental revelation of latent sexual conflict or aggression, the Wrong Number tends to be regarded as a rude, thoughtless intrusion, and is commonly a source of embarrassment to both parties.

For the recipient, however, the Wrong Number always lies in the realm of pure accident. A call can be expected, but when the telephone rings, none of us can ever be sure who will address us from the other end of the line. Every telephone call involves the unexpected to one degree or another, but in the Wrong Number the element of the unexpected predominates almost to the exclusion of all else.

Most recipients, of course, share the misdialer's dislike of the Wrong Number, but for different reasons. The displeasure of receiving a Wrong Number consists chiefly in the fact that the person who is mistakenly called is completely unknown to the caller, and *vice versa*. Annoyance is greatest when the caller confuses the person who answers with the sought-for unknown, and addresses her or him as such. This manner of being mistaken for Someone Else who is, in fact, a complete stranger, seems to be the telephonic equivalent of being in "the wrong place at the wrong time." As the Wrong Number proceeds to make each and everyone feel ill at ease and out of place, egos are bruised all around and the stability of one's relationship to "reality" is shown to be something other than a sure thing. In a social order in which everyone is supposed to be fully in control of who they are, the experience is also a challenge to one's very identity. Although the number dialed is yours—no mistake there—somehow you are the wrong person.

The Wrong Number's background in sexual conflict and aggression, and its parapractic origin, as a slip of the forefinger hastened by impatience and carelessness, are part and parcel of its shadowy reputation. But of course there is much more to it. Through no fault of its own, the Wrong Number inherited the huge, cumbersome cultural baggage that is packed tightly into the five-letter word *wrong*.

It is no ordinary word. It is not, for example, a mere stand-in for "incorrect," for *wrong* has strongly pejorative connotations: *wrong* is *bad*, sinful, improper, a violation of the established code, a *faux-pas*, or worse. The term Wrong Number itself, applied to persons, is a synonym for rotten apple, black sheep, bad egg, and foul ball.

Interestingly, these moralistic associations seem to apply primarily to the English-speaking world, where puritanical values are to this day most firmly entrenched. French and Spanish recipients of such calls do not identify the numbers as wrong (*mauvais* in French; *erróneo* in Spanish). Instead, they politely inform the caller that "you have deceived yourself regarding the number." Most translators routinely render this, "You've reached a wrong number," but the French and Spanish locutions, as well as the Chinese, are notably gentler and warmer, less burdened by fear, mistrust, and accusation.

In the English language, the Wrong Number's associations with blackness, evil, decay, and illegality help situate it, from the standpoint of poetry, in the great "accursed" tradition. A mistake that is also recognizably an *adventure*, involving as it does persons unknown encountering each other unexpectedly *via* voice alone in circumstances potentially perilous: Isn't this the gothicism of Ann Radcliffe and Charles Robert Maturin in a nutshell, a shudder-provoking sensation right up the darkest alleys of German romanticism?

## The Revenge of Punch and Judy

Wrong Numbers are not theater, any more than walking a dog or flying a kite or stopping to exchange words with an acquaintance on a streetcorner are theater. Like all these, however—and for that matter, like everything else—Wrong Numbers can be intensely *dramatic*. What is more, they can be full of consequences for the actors, who also happen to be the audience.

Consider the *dramatis personae* of a typical Wrong Number. First, the caller, the person who begins the play, albeit unknowingly, by misdialing the phone; and second, the recipient, who continues the performance by answering it. Total strangers, each of these actors is nonetheless able to characterize the other solely on the basis of tone of voice, modulation, accent, and sometimes vocabulary, in the all-too-rare instances when it happens to depart from the ordinary. It is worth noting that, although they alone have speaking roles in the performance, the script itself tends to conform so closely to the standard model that the spoken parts—with the decisive exception of a single word—are only occasionally of interest. The whole cycle can be reduced to seven syllables in five or six seconds:

*Ring!*

"Hello?"

"Nick, please."

"Wrong number."

*Click!*

The aforementioned decisive exception is of course the *name* of the *third person* in the play: *the person who is being called*, and who in fact tends to be the *sine qua non* and center of interest of the whole drama. In all Wrong Numbers, the Absent One is the most vividly Present. In the great majority of such calls, the Absent One's name—the sole word in the dialogue that stands out from ritualized routine—is mentioned only once. However, because it is the one unpredictable element in what otherwise is merely an exchange of formulaic phrases, once is enough. Spontaneously and involuntarily, the disembodied name assumes a psychical reality based on the associations it calls forth in the recipient's imagination. In the ephemeral and discontinuous parallel life of Wrong Numbers, the third party—who takes no direct part in the play itself, and in truth knows nothing about it—is nonetheless the star of the show. Notwithstanding the fact that she or he neither speaks nor appears on stage, this evanescent phantom—present in name only—inevitably enjoys the *title* role, as I can attest from my own files, for from the start I referred to *The Call for Ernestine*, *The Call for Olga*, *The Call for Tyrone*, and so forth. That is why a series of Wrong Numbers always has something of the effect of a long drawn-out invocation of names, like *The Black Book of Carmarthen*, or *What to Name the Baby*, or a family genealogy.

In Wrong Numbers, however, as so often happens in poetry, one and one add up not only to three (caller, recipient and the unknown person asked for), but also to *four*, for *the Wrong Number itself* is a distinctive, multifaceted entity in its own right. Like a General Strike or a three-ring circus, the Wrong Number is not reducible to its components. The individual actors are important, but "the play's the thing."

Despite their frequently stereotyped character, Wrong Numbers are always improvised and unpolished. Even the best and longest read like uncorrected transcripts of unrehearsed dialogues, which of course is exactly what they are. One of their most striking qualities is that they seem to have neither introduction nor ending. Our opening hello and the caller's culminating click are mere formalities that cannot conceal the curious fact that we enter *in the middle*, and leave before the curtain is drawn.

If the great mass of Wrong Numbers fizzle out into existentialist monotony—redundancies that Beckett might have omitted from *Waiting for Godot*—a precious few soar to the heights and save the day. These rare, exalting names, magic phrases, images of enchantment remain ineffaceable. However squeezed through the strainer of convention, *poetry* erupts and asserts its prerogatives to the hilt.

At their best, these unedited, first and last rough drafts of dialogues that could easily fit in a fortune-cookie read like highly distilled versions of a Punch and Judy show, a vaudeville comic dialogue, a Paul Winchell/Jerry Mahoney ventriloquist routine, Antonin Artaud's Theater of Cruelty, a piece of *film noir* soundtrack.

Will all these quasi-theatrical cries from crowded phone-calls fire the imagination of those who dream of a wildly dramatic future? Who can say? But meanwhile, no doubt about it, the Wrong Number is still the best five-to twenty-second show in town.

## The Dialectics of Names and Numbers

Wrong Numbers may be absurd, but there is no denying their reality. They confront us daily, and the mere fact of their absurdity is not going to make them go away. They cannot be wished into non-existence or driven off with epithets. They may have no easily assignable meaning, but that does not make them meaningless. Like it or not, each and every one of them is a transmitter of multiple and many-leveled significations.

That's the way it is in the world of words. Even the plainest, most ordinary, least evocative words seem to have ways of making themselves indispensable, and therefore of groping their way into our quotidian affairs and disturbing our sleep. Marcel Duchamp's "THE,"

the first text he wrote in English, consists of five sentences from which the article "the" has been extracted and replaced by an asterisk. And how glaring is the absence of this three-letter word which hardly seems to be a word at all! Homonymically, moreover, "the" is all the difference between *efficiency* and *a fish in the sea*. That the latter can be taken as an *image* of the former tells us something else about words, but that's a horse of several different colors.

In Wrong Numbers, words are not simply words: They are *names*. Or sometimes they are *numbers*, which can also be considered names. And that brings us back to the troubling question of their meaning, and more generally of their impact on our thinking.

Names in Wrong Numbers appear to exert an influence all the greater in that they are not necessarily linked to preconceived images, and thus draw freely on the full reservoir of unconscious associations. In cases where a name *does* conjure an image (as in the call for Cathy or Emily while one is reading *Wuthering Heights*), the image is usually so improbable and irrational that its effect on the mind tends to be even more aggravating.

A free lesson in experimental nominalism came my way *via* a complete and unseen stranger in March of 1989. While browsing through the "Used Books For Sale" shelves in the Oak Park Public Library, just west of Chicago, I chanced to overhear fragments of a series of calls made from a pay phone in a small inset room a few feet away. What attracted me initially were the first words I heard: "This is Cranston," which brought to mind Lamont Cranston, alter-ego of The Shadow in the old radio serial. The caller went on to say that he would not be able to keep his appointment, for he was in Lisle, a town fifteen miles or so distant from where he was actually making his call. A few seconds later he made another call: "This is Doyle. I dropped off some films." And then a third: "This is Johnson. Are those papers ready yet?" He made several other calls, using a different name each time, and was dialing yet another when I left.

Whatever his motives, this curious character—whom I never even glimpsed, for he remained in the tiny phone-room all the time I was there—evidently was someone for whom names were no prison. He had learned well the truth, spurned by more prosaic minds, that rose and thorn alike may be known by many other names.

Now and then, the "name" in a Wrong Number is in fact a number—as when a caller asks, "Hello, is this 433-1056?" Mathematicians, for their part, seem to have maintained a discreet silence on the subject. An immense literature exists on numbers: complex, decimal, imaginary, natural, negative, odd, even, rational, irrational, prime, and real—but only rare and passing references on the numbers known as *wrong*. In Wrong Numbers, of course, the numbers themselves play a minor role; the *wrongness* is what really counts. A purely mathematical inquiry into the topic would nonetheless be delightful.

If the "Wrong" in Wrong Numbers carries a heavy load of ambiguity and misdirection, the word "Numbers" is by no means light as a feather. The dictionary lists no less than ten definitions of the word as a noun, and seven more as a verb. These definitions span an unusually wide latitude. Aside from its ordinary mathematical meanings, "Number(s)" can indicate a group of people; a single person or thing singled out ("She's quite a number"); or discovering an individual's true character ("I've got your number"). Two definitions relate the word intimately to music. "Numbers" is an ancient term for musical notation, and something of the meaning survives in modern slang, in which musicians and other performers refer to a song, tune, or dance as a "number."

These musical connections also link "Numbers" to the venerable tradition of mathematical/musical mysticism, as expounded for example by the Greek philosopher Pythagoras in the sixth century B.C., and by the late-eighteenth-century Pythagorean philologist/philosopher Antoine Fabre d'Olivet, author of a treatise on *Music Explained as Science and Art.* According to Fabre d'Olivet, music for the ancient Egyptians and Greeks was the "universal science . . . without which one cannot penetrate the inner essence of anything." And the "principle of music" was Number.

Mathematics and music, along with imaginative astronomical/cosmological speculation, were also a prime focus of free-jazz pioneer Sun Ra, prophet of "intergalactic music" from the 1950s on. Drawing on ancient Egyptian science and African musical traditions, Sun Ra and his Arkestra proclaimed that "Space is the Place!" and that "The next stop is Jupiter!" Similar concerns have been taken up more recently by the David Boykin Outet (with Josh Abrams, Glenda Baker, Nicole Mitchell, and Chad Taylor), as in their CD, *Evidence of Life on Other Planets.*

Such musings serve to emphasize the fact that the convoluted complexities of Wrong Numbers are not only hard to get right, but are also *numberless* (so to speak) and "out of this world."

In any event, numbers right and wrong cavort and careen all over us and around us and between us at all times, and sometimes they play tricks on us that not only attract our attention for the moment but remain etched forever in our minds. Consider the almost obsessive recurrence of the number 9 in Dante's *La Vita Nuova*; the peculiar games with numbers devised by the Marquis de Sade during his long imprisonment, to calculate the day of his release; Fourier's complex computations regarding the interplay of the many phalansterian groups and series, which prompted Friedrich Engels to describe his whole work as "a mathematical poem"; and those popular "dream books" used in the old "Numbers Game"—*The Three Witches*, *Kansas City Kitty's*, *King Tut*—which assigned numbers to dream symbols, common words and people's names:

Adventure 17.18.19
Alchemy 58.59.60
Aurelia 6.41.78
Dream 1.14.48
Emily 5.41.56
Freedom 59.69.73
Love 3.18.21.26
Marvelous 7.22.68.70
Penelope 2.19.27
Revolution 8.57.75
Rhinoceros 4.44.45.50
Window 4.34.43
Zebra 16.21.33
Zenobia 46.47.53

Telephone numbers themselves have always exerted a certain fascination, as evidenced in films such as *Northside 777* and songs such as *Beechwood 4-0709* ("You can call me up any old time"). For years the Magikist Carpet and Rug Cleaners—whose huge neon sign featuring a pair of bright red lips (very much like one of Man Ray's best known paintings), was one of the major "sights" on the old Congress Expressway—had a radio commercial that ended with a baritone voice singing the firm's phone number: "Hudson Three-Two-Seven-Hundred."

The colorful letter-exchanges were long ago replaced by numerals as part of the bureaucratic depersonalization process which also gave us the zipcode, the ISBN number, the Universal Price Code and other sub-prosaic impositions. The last four digits, however, still retain something of a symbolic quality, especially those that remind us of years. For the names of years, and all dates, are fraught with conscious and unconscious associations. The individual who consciously intends to dial 1975 but instead dials one or more of the numerals incorrectly, thereby reveals an unconscious aversion to that number, or more probably to that year, and more particularly to some traumatic incident of that year. The mistaken number actually dialed is doubtless also overdetermined.

But this is also terrain for poetic exploration. André Breton's discovery that his initials resembled the number 1713 (the hook in the French 7 provides the A's crossbar) naturally piqued his curiosity, and led to a lifelong interest in incidents that took place during that year. Can anyone whose phone number ends in the numbers 1789 or 1917 or 1968 fail to associate them with those memorable years, and with the landmark revolutionary events that distinguish them from other years?

1919 for me is the year of the deaths of Rosa Luxemburg, Karl Liebknecht and Jacques Vaché, but also the year of the General Strikes in Seattle and Winnipeg; the year of Breton's and Soupault's *Les Champs magnétiques*; the year that the cry of jazz went 'round the world—a year of appalling endings and lyrical beginnings.

For several years of my childhood the address of the house I lived in was 1247, a number which meant nothing to me then. Later, however, it suggested the thirteenth century—more precisely, the third year after the Church-led annihilation of the inhabitants of Montségur, last outpost of the libertarian heretics known as Cathars.

1943 signifies for me not only the year of my birth, but the year of André Breton's *Les Etats Generaux* (The States-General), a suite of poems in which I recognized profound personal implications years before I learned that it was written during the very month I was born. (Only after the publication of the third volume of Breton's complete works in 1999 did I learn that, upon completing this poem, André read it to his friend Robert Lebel *over the telephone*!)

These few examples, which could easily be multiplied, show that numbers, like any other word or image, are always ready and waiting vehicles of the restless imagination.

The role of numbers in Wrong Numbers may be obscure and difficult to calculate, but there it is: a puzzle within a puzzle, too silly for words but too important to hide under a bushel.

## My Trip to China

Especially poignant, puzzling, full of surprises and odd twists, are Wrong Numbers whose players speak different languages, and who understand each other only with difficulty or not at all. Parables of our time!

On a Monday in August 1976 I received a Wrong Number from a man speaking a language I recognized at once as Chinese—Cantonese, to be precise. By coincidence, Penelope and I had visited Chinatown just the day before. I should add that never before or since, I am sorry to say, have I ever received a Chinese-language Wrong Number.

My caller continued to speak in Chinese for a full minute or more before I explained that he had reached a Wrong Number. He did not, however, understand what I said, for he spoke two or three sentences more before I interrupted and repeated my earlier statement. This time he hesitated briefly, then spoke a few words, with an inflection suggesting a question. Once again I said, this time very slowly, and perhaps slightly louder than before, "You–have–a–Wrong–Number."

"Oh!" replied my unknown Chinese caller, who now at least seemed to realize that I neither spoke nor understood his language. Clearly, however, he had not fully understood the words I had said to him, for he went on to ask, in thickly-accented English: "You have won-ton soup?"

This episode, which anyone else would probably have shrugged off as inconsequential or idiotic, filled me with profound nostalgia, and sent me reeling into a revery that lasted a long while.

From around 1959 until well into the 1980s Chinese restaurants played a big role in my life. They were my favorite eating-places by far, and also frequent sites of *rendez-vous* and meetings with friends. When Penelope and I met in 1964 we often lunched in the Loop at the workingclass Chinese diners along South Clark Street, or at the spacious Bamboo Inn, next door to the Clark Theatre. And when we went to Paris in '65 we ate more Chinese cuisine than French. In Chicago in the 1970s and 80s, Jane Lee's on East 53rd, Wing Yee on North Clark, Ding Hoe on Division, and Restaurant Chang on Howard were frequent meeting-places of the Surrealist Group.

As it happens, my first job—aside from childhood puppet- and magic shows, newspaper routes, lawn-mowing, and snow-shoveling—was at a Chinese take-out restaurant called Kum-Kum on Roosevelt Road in Maywood, some eight or nine miles west of downtown Chicago. I was seventeen, but already a journeyman "Beatnik," and had just returned from a couple of months' hitchhiking west to

Venice and San Francisco (where I ate almost every day at Woey Loy Guey's, a few blocks from City Lights: sixty cents for a huge oval-shaped plate of great food!).

By 1960–61, my greatest passion was surrealism; I had read every book on the subject in the downtown Chicago Public Library, dozens more in the library of the Art Institute, and by making the rounds of Chicago's then-numerous new and used bookstores, had amassed a sizeable surrealist library of my own. But I was also a serious student of Zen, eager to learn Chinese so that I could read the poems of Han-shan in the original. It was precisely on the condition that the proprietor of Kum-Kum would teach me at least some rudiments of Chinese that I took the job there.

"So you want to learn Chinese!" he roared, with a big smile. "OK, we teach you Chinese! Ha-ha-ha!" Thus began my checkered career as part-time wage-slave and student of the Chinese language.

Curiously, every day I worked there (Tuesdays and Thursdays for three months or so), the patriarch of Kum-Kum, who doubled as assistant chef, repeated those same words: "So you want to learn Chinese! OK, we teach you Chinese! Ha-ha-ha!" However, he always added: "But first, you package up rice!" Or, "First, you fix up sweet-sour sauce!" Or, "First, you sweep floor!" Otherwise, he almost never spoke to me at all.

As the days passed, without even a minute's Chinese lesson, I asked him when he was going teach me a few Chinese words. Once again he roared, "So you want to learn Chinese! OK, we teach you Chinese! Ha-ha-ha! But first—" and so it went. Every time I asked him about learning Chinese, I received the same reply.

When I asked him about anything else—often in the hope of engaging him in conversation that might lead to my learning some Chinese—he would reply brusquely: "Use own judgement." How much rice should I put in each order? "Use own judgement." How many containers of mustard per customer? "Use own judgement." How much gravy in a carton of Egg Foo Yung? "Use own judgement."

But whenever I brought up the question of learning Chinese, he would roar, "So you want to learn Chinese! OK, we teach you Chinese! Ha-ha-ha! But first—."

The head chef at Kum-Kum was a man of even fewer words. I am not sure that he spoke English at all. He nodded a friendly hello when I showed up and waved good-by at the end of the day, but his rare utterances were all in Chinese and addressed to the patriarch himself.

Is it necessary to add that, during the three or four months I worked at Kum-Kum, I did not learn a single word of Chinese?

But there was something so zany and Zenlike about the whole experience that I did not feel deceived or disappointed. I must say that I enjoyed working there more than I have ever enjoyed working anywhere since. I felt at the time that it was a kind of *honor* to work there, and I have never lost that feeling. I have always looked back upon that truly odd job and the strange personages with whom I worked with great fondness.

Do you want to know why they hired me in the first place? Because they needed someone fluent in English to *answer the phone*!

## Transatlantic Laughter

Just as a single spark can illuminate the universe, a single Wrong Number can ring so true that all the right numbers in the world seem a lie.

On mornings like this we realize that an apple sliced in two tells us all we need to know about time.

Early in October 1977 I was expecting proofs of my book *André Breton and the First Principles of Surrealism*, and its companion volume, *What Is Surrealism? Selected Writings of André Breton*. With a laugh at the vagaries of chronology, my friends and I were calling the coming year the "100th Anniversary of Hysteria," and in fact shortly afterward we organized an international surrealist exhibition with that title, which opened in Milwaukee in January 1978, the very month the books appeared.

Hysteria, then, was already in the air in October, a few months early. Under a darkening sky, amidst rising winds, things were stirring. As I noted in the Foreword to *André Breton*, Penelope was doing some volunteer work for the Illinois Labor History Society—the group that maintains the monument to the martyred Haymarket anarchists—in an old Chicago skyscraper known as the Manhattan Building, and in the evenings we were reading a long run of Walt Kelly's *Pogo* comic books, chronicling the philosophical frolics of an opossum and his friends in the Okefenokee Swamp. One morning, as I was opening the proofs of my Breton books, which had just arrived from London, Penelope read me a curious story in the newspaper she was perusing: Police had found a live opossum in the doorway of the Manhattan Building.

A few days later the telephone rang. A woman's voice, with a British accent, said: "I've been ringing but it hasn't been easy to get through." The voice was unusually faint, which made her sound slightly farther away than Istanbul or Omsk—I had the impression that she may have been speaking to someone else, over her shoulder. After a slight pause she added, somewhat louder and inquiringly: "Hello?" Considerable static rattled the line at first, but her clear voice sparkled through it all with the tone of a silver bell. I said hello, and waited for her to introduce herself. After several more bursts of static and other assorted electrical noises, she said, once again as if to a third person, "I'm not sure what's going on," and again she raised her voice slightly and asked: "Hello?"

"Yes," I said, speaking a little louder myself. "Hello, I'm here."

"And *who* might you be?" she asked.

"This is Franklin," I replied, but the static was crackling one last time, so I doubt that she heard me.

"Now that's odd," said she, to which I replied:

"Where are you calling from?"

I should mention at this point that from the moment I heard a British woman's voice on the phone I was sure it was someone calling from Pluto Press, the London publisher of the Breton books. During that month I had had several calls from Pluto, two from women, and I was in fact expecting a call from the publisher that very day.

My surprise caller, however, responded to my question with the name of a street or a building, I forget which, but she made no mention of Pluto Press. I asked: "What city?"

She repeated my words: "What *city*? What a strange question! London, of course! Why, where are *you*?"

When I said Chicago, she echoed me at a much higher pitch, and drawing out the middle syllable—"*Chicaaaago!*"—and laughed warmly, and contagiously as well, for I found that I too could not help laughing.

There we were: total strangers, 7000 miles miles apart, enjoying a hearty laugh in the ethereal intimacy of long distance.

My notes are incomplete, but when I asked, just to make sure, "Are you calling from Pluto Press?" my caller replied by asking: "What's that?" A moment later she confided that she had never heard of Pluto Press. And then she recited the number she had dialed—a number which had almost nothing in common with mine.

"How perfectly odd," said she.

Down to its least nuance, this call from London remains startlingly fresh in my memory. At some point I remarked—echoing a word she had already spoken—that "the odds against such a call as this taking place must be in the millions." She agreed and laughed again, and we both laughed, and then she said she could not believe such a thing had happened, for she had simply rung up a friend down the road. "And here I am talking to you in Chicago! It's amazing!"

I want to emphasize, however, that in this call, in many respects the most remarkable Wrong Number I have ever received, the actual words we exchanged were not remarkable at all. On the contrary, they were notably dry, well within the boundaries of ordinary speech, devoid of any kind of oratorical flourish or "literary talk." What gave the whole experience its resonance as poetry lay not in words or ideas or what is commonly meant by expression, but rather in the between-the-lines openness, the dynamic transparence of the encounter itself, lit up—dazzlingly so for me—by such intangibles as *tone of voice* and a kind of extemporaneous emotional clairvoyance.

This encounter seemed to transcend all rules, all expectations, all plausibility, and even possibility itself. "Since everything that's possible has been tried," said Sun Ra, "we need to try the impossible."

This call from across the sea, an incredible intercontinental mingling of affinities both elective and electrical, seems to me to exemplify the range and impact that Wrong Numbers are capable of attaining. It also smacks of the marvelous substance which, as the alchemist Arnold of Villanova wrote in his *Speculum*, "converts to itself proportionally all important bodies that it touches." While it lasted—that is, as long as the woman from London was on the line—no contradictions blocked the way between hermetic and wide open, secret and public, yesterday and tomorrow. Its dizzyingly exceptional character, moreover—and I'm talking here about vertigo to the *n*th power—left me centered in an equally intoxicating equilibrium.

For those who recognize the world as an illimitable playground, what appear to others as insurmountable barriers are surmounted as easily as a duckbilled platypus takes to water. This is what the Romanian surrealist poet Gellu Naum called "the state of poetry."

Poetry, after all, is the highest—let's say *the most playful*—form of play.

In other words, the "right" to work is a fraud and a curse. What we want is the freedom to frolic! To hell with "more jobs"! On with the dance!

On nights like tonight, a spiked wheel in the wind is the only music we need.

Right from the start, however, what struck me most about this call from London was the very special *intensity* of it, its hot mix of exhilaration and risk, as if the secret we shared had its origins in some harrowing adventure ages ago, and which also involved a vital promise, still to be kept. Simultaneously, and no one will ever know just how, the two of us found ourselves to be participants in one another's dreams, characters liberated from secret myth, wandering figments of our own imaginations.

The sensation I had was a little like tripping over some hidden dimension and landing on my feet *inside* a crystal ball, just in time to absorb a full minute's worth of a distant morrow, somewhere far away. A kind of voices-only *déja-vu* echoing (multiplying) to infinity, it also most definitely made itself felt as an *announcement* of things to come.

The call, in short, marked the commencement of a beautiful strangeness.

"Easy yet rare," wrote Eiranaeus Philalethes.

Perfectly odd.

## The Stuff That Wrong Numbers Are Made Of

Dialogues *with* an unknown and *about* another unknown, Wrong Numbers are a mockery of rational anticipation, and as such, remain definitively inconclusive: cliff-hanging episodes of a narrative in which Chapter One and The End are missing. Not many of them possess the exalting grandeur, that "rare and striking" quality that Diderot regarded as essential to Beauty, but all Wrong Numbers are at least surprising, and a precious few approach the ineffable. In their upside-down sort of way, these souvenirs of the most fugitive and least understood phantasmagorias reinforce the persistent hope that humankind rightly places in dreams. The Wrong Number is itself a kind of collective dream (dreamed by strangers), something like the surrealist game "Exquisite Corpse," in which none of the players know what the others are contributing to a picture or text.

The radically oneiric character of Wrong Numbers is signaled in the classic Ullman/Fletcher definition from the novel, *Sorry, Wrong Number*: "A brief pause in time in which reality fade[s] and a dream [sweeps] through the caverns of the mind." For my part, I would prefer to change the first three words of this definition to "An open window," highlighting the important role the Wrong Number plays as an *invitation to voyage*. The voyages it invites us to take, however, do not belong solely to dream or to waking life, but *somewhere in between*.

The unusual access the Wrong Number offers to these in-between worlds relates it to the theory elaborated by the English engineer John W. Dunne in his study, *An Experiment with Time*, first published in 1927. Starting with problems posed by the notion of the "regress of time," and drawing on his own exceptionally rich experience as a dreamer, Dunne posited that the "lop-sided view" civilized humankind has of time—"a view with the 'future' part unaccountably missing, cut off from the growing 'past' by a traveling 'present moment'"—is in fact attributable to "a purely mentally imposed barrier" which exists only in the waking state. In ordinary workaday life, he concluded, precognition is triggered only by "disconnections" perceived in dreams.

Typically ignored by orthodox sleep-researchers and run-of-the-mill psychoanalysts, Dunne's daring views were heartily welcomed by the surrealists, notably André Breton, Marcel Duchamp, Claude Tarnaud, and Vincent Bounoure. Urging us to consider the entire question of dream-life in a new light, Dunne's "experiment" also invites further applications. It seems to me that the randomness, oneiric energy, and "disconnected" quality of Wrong Numbers might well make them ideal vehicles for signs and signals from other strata of what Dunne termed "Serial Time." Here, it would seem, is an exciting field of inquiry. Meanwhile, this much seems clear: Wrong Numbers imitate neither waking life nor dream, but are capable of instigating fortuitous encounters between the two.

When the ringing of the telephone awakens us from deep sleep, the experience of the Wrong Number tends to become the direct continuation of the interrupted dream as well as a point of departure for the next phase of waking life. When the ringing tears us away from serious thinking, reading, or discussion with friends, the Wrong Number injects something of the dreams of sleep into waking consciousness, and perhaps plants seeds of nocturnal dreams to come.

Not long after I started investigating the desultory mysteries of misdialing, elements of Wrong Numbers began to venture into my dream-life. A dream voice echoes the voice from the phone: "Is Margie there?" Before I am able to finish saying that there is no one here by that name, I see that I am mistaken, for Margie is here after all. But beyond being "Margie," who is she? Where did she come from? How does she happen to be at my side when the dream-telephone rings?

Roughly around the same time I met a repugnant fellow who happened to be surnamed Martin. In the next few days I received a couple of Wrong Numbers that began: "May I speak to Martin, please?" The morning after the second of those calls I awakened from a dream in which the name Martin was juxtaposed with the name of a downtown motel called the Mart Inn. Two or three days later Penelope chanced to find—at a used bookstore that had just opened—a book we had been seeking for years: Ethan Allen Hitchcock's *Remarks Upon Alchemy and the Alchemists.* A first edition (Boston, 1857), it included the signature of an earlier (perhaps the original) owner, a "Mrs Martin" of Green Bay, Wisconsin, along with some penciled annotations in her hand.

What made these odd sightings of many Martins, all within a week, of more than ordinary interest was the fact that they brought together for me—for the first time—a Wrong Number, a dream, and a chance encounter in daily life.

Or again: In a dream I received a call for Olga, as I had in a Wrong Number earlier in the day. But this time Olga whispers to me: "Don't tell them I am here. I don't want them to know where I am." In waking life I do not know anyone named Olga, but here she is, in some kind of trouble, hiding at my place, and counting on help from me.

One day I received a call for Tyrone from a woman whose melodious voice led me to think she was African American. The only Tyrone I have ever known was also African American: a tall, lanky, sympathetic, philosophically-inclined poet in San Francisco's North Beach during the Beat days. I had not seen him or heard anything of him in years, but after his name popped up in a Wrong Number, Tyrone himself showed up in a dream. "Hey, man," he said to me, looking exactly as I had seen him last at the Co-Existence Bagel Shop in 1960, "I hear you got a call for me."

Thus, slowly but surely, the ordinary "day residues" that add touches of everyday reality to the dreams of sleep were displaced by authentically *oneiric* day residues from the Enchanted Isles of Wrong Numbers.

While awake, meanwhile, quite spontaneously I began to tell myself stories (or stories began telling themselves to me) linking the characters in two or more Wrong Numbers in situations and plots of varying complexity, usually intersecting with particular episodes of daily life. Although I call them "stories," I want it understood that these off-the-cuff imaginings were conceived without the slightest conscious intent, or even with the thought that they might go on for more than a minute or two. They were stories only in the sense that they were a series of imaginary situations in which some of the "characters" kept recurring. They had no real plot, no preconceived story line, no character development, no descriptions (for my improvised narratives were accompanied by, and at times supplanted by, strong visual imagery), and their continuity was jumpy at best. Such aimless strolling in the imaginary is the kind of psychic activity that occurs in certain highly distracted states, where poets readily make themselves at home. When one is not thinking of anything in particular, or perhaps trying to *avoid* thinking of something in particular, suddenly something wholly unrelated comes to mind out of the blue, and then something else, and soon a situation develops which strikes one as funny, or scary, and then other forms of the imaginary come to mind to resolve the problem, only to set one off again, creating other new situations.

And so it came to pass that Olga, for example—not content with starring roles in both Wrong Number and dream—also figured prominently in an adventure tale of mine which, had I taken the trouble to put it in writing, could have served as a rough draft of a sequel to Dostoyevsky's *Possessed*.

A veritable late-night serial in broad daylight, this rambling, oft-interrupted adventure (which included brief appearances of some other Wrong Number acquaintances as well) was a wildly romantic drama of love, conspiracy, and intrigue—rather like *The Three Musketeers*, with something of the 1940s *Jingle Jangle Comics* tossed in for good measure. As in all the stories one tells oneself, I was no mere narrator but an actor as well, always in the thick of things. It probably never really ended, but just drifted off into other stories, with other casts. Its beginning, however, can be dated with precision: March 31, 1978. For that was the day the messenger of Wrong Numbers brought me the call from the unknown Olga.

What really started the wheels of revery spinning, however, is the fact that this call came just after Penelope and I had seen the dancer Annabelle Gamson perform a series of Isadora Duncan's choreographies, including two from her Russian days—"Mother" and "Etude," with music by Scriabin. Throughout this period I was deeply preoccupied with Duncan, and especially her long sojourn in Bolshevik Russia. Inevitably, Isadora too, along with Sergei Essenin, also appeared in my internal monologue/pulp-thriller, which was of course set in Russia, writing itself in discrete unspoken fragments between the lines of my waking distractions. When Olga burst on the scene like a human cannonball from the Moscow Circus, all the pieces seemed to come together—with a bang.

Thus we see how the Wrong Number, under certain circumstances, can precipitate curious convergences of dream and waking life. The dry tinder of waking thought and dream had to be ready and waiting, of course, but would the prolonged revery ever have caught fire had the call for Olga not provided the spark?

## An Oneiric Critique of the Non-Oneiric

Nobody's fool and therefore everybody's, the Wrong Number—like the alarm-clock—intrudes simultaneously on the conscious *and* the unconscious: waking *and* sleeping. Unlike the alarm-clock, however, the Wrong Number not only does not tell the time, but ignores time altogether. Its ringing announces a few "free moments" away from time. What might appear to be a wake-up call turns out to be an urgent dream-call instead.

Ordinary phone-calls are accompanied by ordinary images. Wrong Numbers, extraordinary by nature, are capable of provoking extraordinary images. The fact that this appears to happen so infrequently seems to me to be attributable to resistance (repression) on the part of the recipient. In ordinary calls, especially with friends and relatives, memory and familiarity fill in the missing sensory elements, so that in effect one "sees" the caller. Eye contact, facial expression, body language all come into play to a greater or lesser degree. The Wrong Number, however, tends to provoke the uneasiness and anxiety that accompany sensory deprivation. To be suddenly confronted by an unknown caller suffices to catch most people off balance, and the disequilibrium is often aggravated when the mysterious voice mistakes one for yet another unknown. Only the extreme brevity of the call, and the fact that the experience, by established custom, is conveniently categorized as a mere nuisance, enables the recipient to suppress its distressing qualities, including its accompanying visual imagery.

And yet, some trace of these voices remain, in addition to the names they announce, and the diaphanous ever-not-quite images that flit alongside and around them. Like the vivid aroma of lilacs recalled from decades past, these voice-to-voice encounters in the telephonic void persist as siren-songs from a temptation-filled and emphatically secular Beyond. If they are generally believed to lead nowhere, it is only because so few people are prepared to follow them. Such helplessness, in turn, is directly related to the Wrong Number's mercilessly negative implications for the prevailing bourgeois ideology of language as a mere medium of exchange. To learn how to play with Wrong Numbers it is necessary to break the chains that are passed off as Necessity. Poetry needs freedom and leisure to flourish, and looking for answers is always a good way to begin. "Identity?" Who wants to know? Interestingly, in this regard, the common Wrong Number opening gambit:

*Ring!*

"Hello?"

"Hello—who *is* this?"
was magnificently answered by none other than Herman Melville in 1857, when Antonio Meucci's "speaking telegraph" was still in its childhood: "Nobody knows who anybody is. The data which life furnishes, toward forming a true estimate of any being, are as insufficient to that end as in geometry one side given would be to determine the triangle."

By a dizzyingly circuitous route we have taken up where the German Romantic philosopher Franz von Baader left off with his suggestion that, instead of interpreting dreams from the standpoint of waking life, we should interpret waking life from the standpoint of dreams. The Wrong Number can be considered an *objectively oneiric critique of everyday self-expression*—a Mad Tea Party at which no one is partying, no tea is served, and no one, in fact, happens to be mad, but at which, nonetheless, everyone's cup is filled to overflowing, and refilled as often as one likes.

Whenever it makes its appearance, the strangest of all ways of talking to strangers is always a challenge to rationalized immobility, and always a call—to dream and to act!

## Error in the Service of Eros

However accidental and anonymous Wrong Numbers may be, their sudden, sensuous, intimate, present-tense quality gives them an immediacy seldom equaled by a misdelivered letter or even a first-class typographical error in the daily paper. In a Wrong Number it is always a living voice that speaks, and sometimes it speaks not only *to* us, but *through* us. The fragment of conversation with an unknown can be an irritant, surely, but like the grain of sand that provokes the creation of a pearl, it can also work wonders.

It is characteristic of our degraded age that the Wrong Number is mistaken for a miserable exercise in reality-testing, when in essence it is a game of *imagination*-provoking, and therefore—like everything pertaining to the imagination—deeply erotic. True, its erotic aspects are generally repressed, but at times the experience can assume the qualities of a powerful aphrodisiac. For the merest moment, a caressing voice on the wire can embody all the libidinal bliss of Maybeland.

Potentially, every Wrong Number offers a possibility for two otherwise unacquainted speakers—that is, a *couple*—to enjoy both their own *and* the other's megalomania, without interference of any external authority, and without infringing on anyone's liberty.

The resulting experience of shared delirium—an exuberantly ebullient megalomania for two—is naturally at its most sumptuous when the exchange assumes, at least on the symbolic level, a specifically amorous character. Such magic moments may be exceedingly rare, but they are the moments that matter most. For it is only in such miraculously illuminating instants that we recognize the Wrong Number as a kind of auditory *foreplay*—an erotic verbal frolicking which begins by changing the relations between speakers and goes on, in its modest way, to stimulate orgiastic reveries of insubordination and freedom, thereby helping to lay the foundation for a truly desirable life for all.

Officially, a telephone is an instrument of commerce and control: its routine function is to transmit and exacerbate the world's misery-as-usual, sexual and otherwise. Thanks to the Wrong Number, however—a pure product of chance, and as such, wholly against the grain of all that the "telecommunications industry" stands for—the same instrument enables us not only to hear but also to *add our own voices to* the precognitive echoes of a future worth dreaming about.

The Marquis de Sade's aim remains ours: to vanquish the misfortunes of virtue (and the virtual) by cultivating the prosperities and pleasures of the vices known as poetry, revolt, freedom, and love.

As for commercialized phone-sex, computerized telephone dating services, and other forms of assembly-line pseudo-eroticism, such debasements are part of the problem, and ultimately serve to reinforce inhibitions. The best that can be said for them is that they reveal that a large portion of the population has deep longings that are otherwise unsatisfied. That, of course, is what capitalism is all about.

Sometimes, however, even newspapers can bring us news:

> AT&T Corp., in a mailing to 175,000 ... customers, mistakenly provided the toll-free number to a sex chat line.
>
> Callers expecting to reach an AT&T operator were greeted instead by a sultry voice saying: "Are you ready to get naked? ... If you want hard-core, uncensored, explicit sex now ... then come and—ummm—take it!"... Two digits were transposed accidentally, yielding the number to a $2.98-a-minute sex chat line....
>
> The company sent the wrong number a week ago and already has mailed apologies....
>
> (*Chicago Tribune*, 22 June 1998)

This matter-of-fact report of the unforeseen collision of puritanism and pornography is in fact a rare public acknowledgment of the usually veiled complicity between christian ideology, "legitimate" big business, and organized crime (which runs the sex industry). Notable for its outrageous and scandalous humor, the news story also serves to make us wonder about *other* ways, and radically different circumstances, in which Wrong Numbers and erotic desire could confront each other without the afflictions of exploitation, the profit system, and other degradation.

Surely, somewhere in the world, there are lovers who met each other as the result of a misdialed phone call. The theme is worthy of an epic: Under the sign of the Wrong Number, Eros and Error meet and embrace, voice to voice in the void.

## Our Friend the Two-Headed Hermaphrodite

The Wrong Number, unlike sports and the weather, is not a popular topic of conversation. Scarcely anyone likes to talk about Wrong Numbers. Most people would much prefer to discuss their suicidal tendencies, or confess felonies they have committed, than tell you what goes on in their minds when the telephone rings and unknown voices ask for people who aren't there.

Such reticence, however, is nothing compared to the silence provoked by questions relating Wrong Numbers to sexuality. If you want to know what "running up against a blank wall" is like, don't bother looking for a blank wall to run up against, just ask a group of people what they think of the sex-life of Wrong Numbers.

This is an issue so thoroughly tabooed that the taboo itself hasn't even been noticed yet.

In the following argument, then—perhaps for the first time in history—a taboo is going to be lifted even before being identified as such. (Is it necessary to interpolate that this circumstance is itself characteristic of the waywardness of our subject?)

Everything having to do with Wrong Numbers tends to be ambiguous, but here the adjective fades away, for ambiguity is all there is. And there's an awful lot of it.

The only thing we can say with anything resembling certainty about the sex-life of Wrong Numbers is that it seems to be a virgin topic. Otherwise, anybody's guess seems to be as good as nobody's. And since nobody knows anything about it, it doesn't matter much where we begin, does it?

Only the hopelessly naive could pretend that the Wrong Number has no sex. Available evidence suggests, on the contrary, that it has all sexes at once.

As an inherently invasive phenomenon—an unasked-for intrusion on one's peace and privacy—the Wrong Number could be said to be phallic. However, inasmuch as it is always left "dangling," and is commonly considered to belong to the category of "little things that don't fit in," we may infer that the phallus it symbolizes is rarely erect. Its unconsummated, inconclusive, and unproductive character—the fact that the Wrong Number is the result of an *unsuccessful effort at getting through*, and that *nothing comes of it*, or so they say—further suggests *coitus interruptus* or even impotence.

Then again, the sheer quantity and omnipresence of Wrong Numbers, suggesting that they "breed like rabbits," might be said to hint at considerable sexual prowess.

Viewed in series, the impressively large number of people asked for in Wrong Numbers—men, women, children—surely smacks of massive promiscuity.

On the other hand, or perhaps I should say *in* or *with* the other hand, its compulsive rituals and repetitiveness have more than a little in common with masturbation.

At the same time, perceived as it often is as a kind of void, a moment of *nothingness* ("What was *that* all about?" "Nothing—a Wrong Number"), it also assumes qualities regarded by many as symbolically vaginal. Its traditional position in human affairs—as a phenomenon devalued, viewed with condescension, not taken seriously—is also shared by the great majority of females in the patriarchal order.

The fact that it is universally considered *wrong*, and that it is usually thought to be non-procreative, would further seem to situate it squarely in the ranks of the so-called deviations.

The never-settled sex of Mr and/or Ms Wrong Number is as unsettling as his/her other discomforting qualities. Though rarely on the scene for more than a few seconds at a time, the Wrong Number is a veritable *monster* of sexual confusion.

Like Jarry's plus-and-minus equivalent of opposites—one of the cardinal principles of pataphysics—the Wrong Number is not only hermetic, but also hermaphroditic. No image seems to me to better personify the Wrong Number, sexually speaking, than the alchemists' two-headed hermaphrodite or *rebis*, the double-sexed symbol of the phase of the Great Work known as the Conjunction of Sol and Luna (masculine sun and female moon). Centuries-old alchemical treatises picture the *rebis* at the moment of fusion, standing on the vanquished dragon and the philosophers' stone in the equinoctial equilibrium of the seven-pointed planetary "star of perfection." The striking image of Sulphur contrasted with Mercury, melted into a single being by the heat of fire, is an alchemical emblem representing the balance between stability and volatility—that is, of *universal unity.*

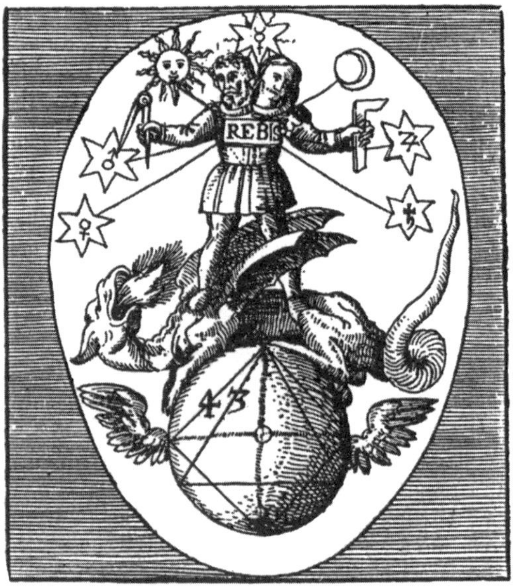

*The Alchemical Rebis*

The universality of this unity is suggested by the incredible diversity it embraces. What the extraordinary image of the rebis conveys is a sexuality that is emphatically not rigid, fixed, or easily classified, but rather volatile, open-ended, in flux, ready for change at all times. Instead of *defining* sexualities by forcing them into restrictive categories, it *merges* them into an ever-expanding array of multisexual combinations. *Voilà!* The do-it-yourself Gender Blender—the Wrong Number in person!

Such factors doubtless exacerbate the consternation with which the Wrong Number is usually regarded, and reinforce its unenviable position as an anomalous experience that does not even have the illusive but soothing virtue of internal consistency.

But that's not all there is to the story.

Symbolically, the image of the two-headed hermaphrodite represents a decisive moment in life's second sexual awakening: the period of adolescence, during which one's quest for balance between stability and volatility generally reaches its climax. The boy's experience of ejaculation, and the girl's of menstruation, initiate a phase of individual and social development characterized by great inner turmoil which, emotionally as well as intellectually, goes far beyond the sexual fantasies of infants. Adolescence is a time of intense self-discovery, during which most people have their first experience of falling in love. Interestingly, it is also a period characterized by sudden and embarrassing changes in voice, and of prolonged, constant use of the telephone.

Every Wrong Number can be considered a highly condensed long-distance replay, or recapitulation, of the complex, agonizing, and inextricably interwoven sexual and identity crises of adolescence. Psychoanalytically, the phone tends to be identified with the superego—an unseen voice of authority—whose development climaxes in this period. The excessive use of the phone by teenagers is largely a way of coming to grips with the superego; instead of passively submitting to its dictates, they try taking it in hand and talking back to it.

The excruciating ambivalence involved in our relation to the telephone, and especially its erotic dimension, is electrifyingly illuminated in a series of enrapturing paintings by one of the foremost painters of our time, Konrad Klapheck of Düsseldorf, whose work is the subject of the concluding essay in André Breton's *Surrealism and Painting* (1965). Penetrating beneath the instrument's superficial utilitarian function in order to expose its hidden truth, Klapheck's analogical *portraits* of telephones (as well as sewing-machines, typewriters, motorcycles, and other machines) reveal near-mythic beings endowed with personality and the whole gamut of passions. With their magnified and otherwise distorted mouthpieces, earpieces, receivers, grips, and cradles, all connected or tied up with coiled umbilical cords, Klapheck's disquietingly sensuous phones are by turns brooding, fearful, proud, arrogant, philosophical, flirtatious, lustful, remorseless, and rebellious. As suggested by his striking titles ("Vows of Celibacy," "The Voice of Conscience," "The Capitulation," "The Kiss," "Dangerous Pursuits," "Original Sin," etc.), these totems of telephonic taboos are a far cry from—and an intrepid refusal of—the Reality Principle's incessant busy signals.

The Wrong Number tends to be hopelessly undependable as a superego. Faulty and erratic at best, at its worst (or best, according to one's point of view) it can be a thoroughgoing *anti*-superego.

(Interestingly, Robert Benayoun long ago pointed out the "counter-Oedipal" implications of Klapheck's paintings.) The alchemical image of the double-headed hermaphrodite captures it in a moment of balance, but the Wrong Number *as a process* also exemplifies the whole succession of before-and-after-images: the whole dynamic state of sexual and psychic fluidity, of vacillation and confusion between conflicting tendencies.

This is a state few people look back on fondly—which is one reason so many hate Wrong Numbers. Reminders of that difficult moment in their lives are painful because the choice they made back then sealed off the possibilities of other choices that at least a part of their own selves may have preferred. For adolescence is a crossroads, a major turning-point, and the direction repressive society requires people to take leaves the repressive machinery intact. Those who deviate from this up-to-date version of the puritan straight and narrow path run the risk—or so a legion of propagandists assure us—of failure, madness and suicide.

As the psychoanalyst Edith Jacobson observed in her monograph, *The Self and the Object World* (1964), at a certain point in the adolescent crisis, "when ego, superego and id communicate so freely with each other, a singular dynamic, economic, and structural situation arises which is in many ways reminiscent of the conditions we may find in creative adults." This promising situation, however—infrequent exceptions aside—lasts only a few weeks before it is stifled. There is simply no place for it, no way it can develop, in an inherently unjust and anti-poetic social system. Luxuriant creativity is not welcome in a social order based on inequality and exploitation, in which "every man for himself" and the accumulation of wealth and power are top priorities. On the contrary, real creativity requires complete individual autonomy, which can only be realized in a radically free community of equals.

What adolescents want above all is precisely this autonomy. In the present social set-up, however, the great majority are pressured into sacrificing real autonomy for some form of "success," which more often than not are mere scams for "getting by." The disintegration of the oedipal system as youth is liberated from parental authority leads in most cases not to real freedom but to the establishment of new ties to far more dangerous authorities: the state, the military, corporations, and/or other repressive institutions. The soothing mirage of "maturation" offers a severely circumscribed quasi-autonomy at the price of endless accommodations to unfreedom. Sad but true, in all but a few cases, the adolescent conflict between stability and volatility is not resolved by effecting a real balance, but by crudely suppressing the latter. Thus the well-behaved child is father to the obedient organization man—

the "team-player" who doesn't want to hear about poetry, revolt, struggles for freedom. These early sell-outs, no matter what their income levels may amount to, are actually losers in this unsavory deal, for they have lost—*and know they have lost*—their best and perhaps only chance for a life worth living. And each time a young person becomes a cog in the repressive machine, the larger society loses, too.

I like the way Guy Ducornet put it: "There is not *one* goddamn reason to abandon any of the wishes/dreams and projects of one's adolescence. There is no reason to ever become a *fonctionnaire*."

Psychoanalysis itself, despite its revolutionary discoveries and the critique of society those discoveries inspired, long ago secured its safe integration into the repressive machinery as an accommodative therapy, *i.e.*, a means of helping misfits fit into the very scheme of things that made them so miserable they had to become misfits. It is disheartening to find an analyst as sensitive and insightful as Edith Jacobson emphasizing the "great contribution" made by "frustration and disappointment" to the solution of adolescent problems, while playing down the role of elation and ecstasy. The way so-called reality-testing is organized in this society, what Herbert Marcuse termed the Performance Principle—the historic form of the Reality Principle—nearly always wins because the dice are loaded. The road of poetry, revolt, the unfettered imagination are not even shown on the Performance Principle map, for the self-appointed managers of Reality like to pretend that such things don't exist.

Adolescents, Jacobson pointed out, citing Anna Freud, tend to be "resistant to analysis"—a resistance they share with poetry and Wrong Numbers. All three remain outside the categories considered "safe" in this society, and all three inspire our hope.

Our friend the two-headed hermaphrodite, and the Wrong Number which he/she symbolizes so well, show that another path—the path of poetry and revolution—is always open, especially to adolescents, but also to anyone who loves love, cares for life, and dares to live. To ignore or reject love and poetry and revolution is to miss the best life has to offer and to surrender oneself instead to a system of business-as-usual regimentation and boredom.

Success and failure are fictitious alternatives. Wrong Numbers lie elsewhere.

## Encouraging Words From a True Philosopher

"What's with the Wrong Number bit, man?"

It was my friend Tyrone, but not exactly in a dream. This time he just showed up in the middle of my imagination. The Co-Existence Bagel Shop had been gone for thirty-odd years, but there we were. It was the only place Tyrone and I ever seemed to run into each other. We were sitting at a small table near the front window, watching the passersby on the corner of Grant Avenue and Green Street. On the jukebox: "Killer Joe."

Tyrone was wearing a blue serge suit, porkpie hat, and a light blue silk shirt with sphinx-head cufflinks. He never seemed to have a nickel, and I'm sure that he—like the rest of us in those days—selected his wardrobe at the Starvation Army. Unlike the rest of us, however, Tyrone always looked like a million dollars.

His question took me by surprise. "I don't really know," I replied. "I'm still trying to figure it out. It's a riddle somebody should have solved long ago, but nobody ever has. Now it seems to be up to me! Anyway, I'm giving it a whirl."

"Hey, you sound *serious*!" he said, with that infectious smile of his. With his natural elegance and graceful gestures, he reminded me of what Duke Ellington must have looked like at nineteen.

"As serious as the birds in the sky," said I.

"And that's about as serious as you can get!" cried Tyrone, exclamation-point and all. "But it seems like a really strange bag to be working out of, man! I didn't figure you for such a weird cat. Wrong Numbers, wow! Where you think you're going with it?"

"Wherever it takes me," I sighed, with a shrug of the shoulders.

A long silence followed. A mutual friend, the fine alto-sax man Pony Poindexter strolled by, waved at us, and we waved back.

I was exhausted, almost (?) delirious. I hadn't slept well for days. "You better watch yourself, man," said Tyrone, slowly rising from the table. "You look like you could use a good night's rest. Way I see it, you got a lot of hard thinking to do. My advice: Keep your eyes open, man, even in your sleep! And your ears, too! Whatever else happen, don't lose your way! You got to let those numbers know the score."

He smiled, leaned a little closer, and whispered:

"If you play it right, man, those Wrong Numbers will treat *you* right!"

# 4.

# NON SEQUITURS AND THEIR SEQUELS

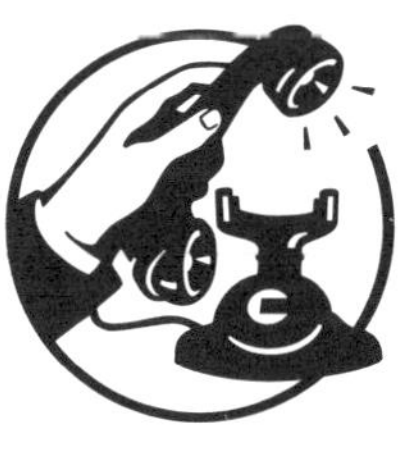

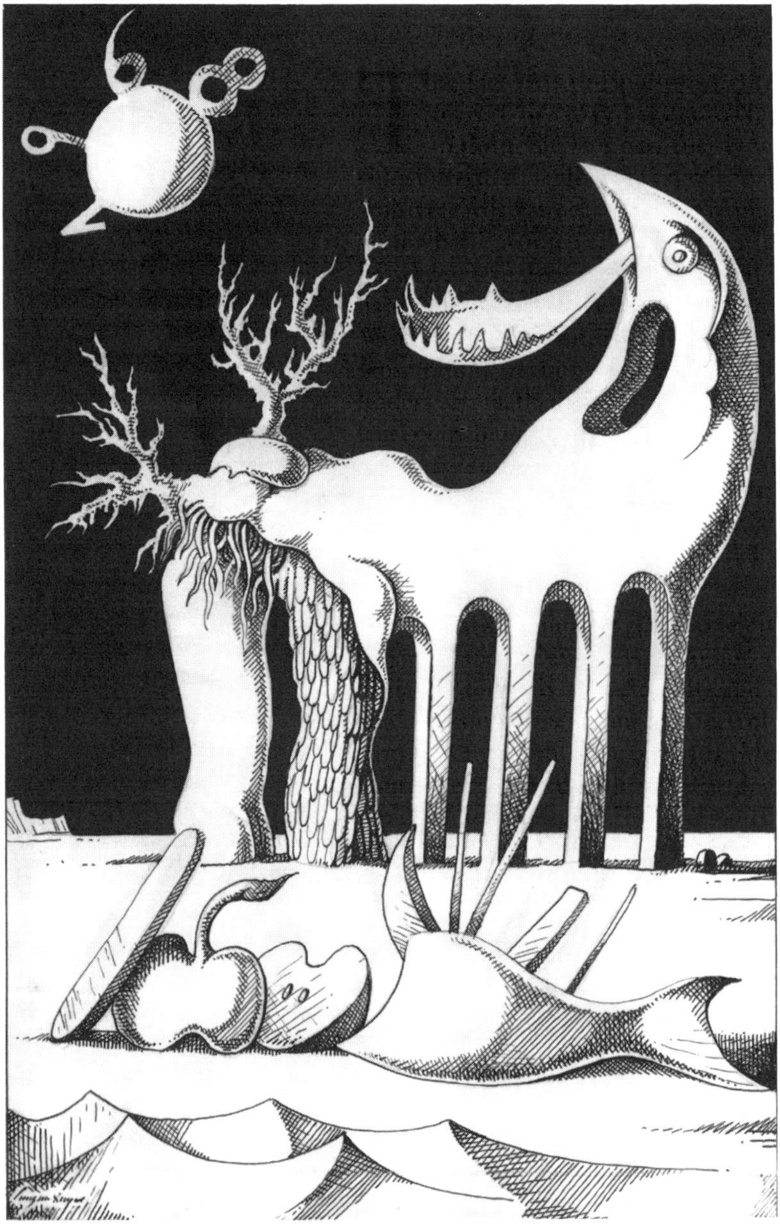

Wrong Numbers hurry us into a tiny hidden nook off one of the least explored corridors of the Tower of Babel, and then—before we can enjoy a real look-see—hurl us back with a click into the ever-redundant mainstream of the mundane.

The linguistics of Wrong Numbers is an initiation into headaches you never knew you had. Of the classic trio—caller, recipient, and the person who isn't there—only the first two speak. They say very little as a rule, but what they do say, and the context in which they say it, leads us from paradox to paradox.

The context, for example, of what can reasonably be called the typical Wrong Number, seems to bear the most striking resemblance to another context that could hardly be more dissimilar. Consider this: While the Wrong Number lasts, every participant tends to be someone else, no one knows who any of the others are, and all of them finally go their own ways without having the slightest notion of what happens to the others. In other words, in the privacy of one's own home the Wrong Number replicates the experience of individuals in a large urban crowd.

That's only the beginning, but it seems appropriate to acknowledge here that my own researches have led me to the conclusion that what the Wrong Number has to tell us about language is something most people don't want to hear.

The Wrong Number is, after all, a quintessential "breakdown in communications." Our two communicators are in fact communicating only by accident, quite reluctantly, and even against their will. Sad to say, in most cases it turns out that they really have nothing to say to each other. Sadder still, neither seems to give a damn about the other. Each hangs up without even knowing the other's name, or anything about her/him. Words fail them, not because of overpowering emotion, but because their emotions hardly seem to be functioning at all. They "simply" (?) can't think of anything to say. In their view, the situation in which they find themselves is *unimaginable*, so they can't imagine using their imaginations to imagine their way out of it, by communicating imaginatively with the imagination of the other. No, a few cut and dried *clichés* will do the job, and then it's over and done with, thank god, and good riddance.

It is a cold and lonely world out there, and to coldness and loneliness they are eager to return, with all due speed.

*Click!*

The inference is hard to miss: Language, like everything else having to do with humankind today, is in big trouble.

At this point, however, it may be useful to consider the distinction between *manifest* and *latent* content. Psychoanalysis long ago revealed that, in the great majority of conversations, the most important things are often left out, only to reappear "accidentally" as unconscious *double entendres* and slips of the tongue. Because of repression, people rarely say what they really want to say, but what they really want to say goes ahead and says itself anyway, on the sly.

In Wrong Numbers, moreover, dialogue is further complicated by the fact that both parties are, in their individual ways, *out of character*.

Therefore, no matter how stereotyped the language in a Wrong Number may be, we know there is always *something else* being said, and we can guess at still other things that caller and recipient would like to say and are trying to say.

No one will deny that the Wrong Number creates an outrageously peculiar situation. The caller's desire to speak to a particular person is suddenly blocked, against all expectations. And just as suddenly and unexpectedly, the recipient's peace and privacy have been broken into by person or persons unknown, clandestinely, and with unknown motive. Frustration, disappointment, mistrust, suspicion, fear, anger, hostility, cynicism and despair seem to be the underlying moods of the moment, on both ends of the line. No wonder, then, that both parties feel a bit tongue-tied. No wonder that in many cases caller and recipient seem less articulate than the asked-for but absent person who naturally remains speechless, but whose name at least continues to resonate and beckon in the background.

Only in exceptional calls, rare as rubies, do humor or imagination intervene to remind us of what language is for. In the game of Wrong Numbers—as in such games as going to the movies or reading comic books—only the exceptions are worth the price of admission. And only the exceptions show us that there really is a way out of the quagmire.

In any event, and in spite of everything, the Wrong Number is always and necessarily *collaborative*, and it is precisely because the collaborators are unknown to each other that their dialogues are *potentially* so expansive, so pregnant with imaginary worlds. What is obviously called for is an entirely new etiquette for Wrong Numbers. Instead of the inane "Sorry, wrong number," one might say: "It is my pleasure to inform you that you have reached a Wrong Number. My name is——. And you?" Or, much less formally, something like this: "Wonderful! A Wrong Number! The first one we've had all week! Would you like to join us for dinner tonight? We'd love to meet you, to hear your stories, to learn who you thought I would be, and to see how many interests we share." And when the stranger completes the introductions, a different kind of game might commence: a *surrealist* game, naturally, for as André Breton remarked in the first *Surrealist Manifesto*, "The forms of surrealist language adapt themselves best to dialogue."

## Around the World in 80 Words or So

Like the dream, the poem, and the animated cartoon, the Wrong Number is a way of cutting long stories short. However paradoxical it might seem, such condensations always have the effect of *enlarging* reality, or at least the perception thereof. That's why a single Wrong Number is often worth more than a thousand of any other kind.

"Too much brevity," Peter Abelard warned, "may introduce too much obscurity." Curiously, the Wrong Number's obscurity—its obsidianlike impenetrability, in terms of ordinary rational "meaning"—turns out to be oddly *illuminating*. At its most inspiring, the Wrong Number has a halo around it—not the hackneyed emblem of holiness or sainthood, but the original pagan halo indicating the radiant lucidity of the exceptional and unique.

This disturbing blend of lucidity and obscurity reminds us that the Wrong Number is a kind of *breakthrough* experience, despite the fact that what it is, precisely, that is breaking through, or trying to break through, tends to be elusive. The world of Wrong Numbers is a world *in passing*, a world up for grabs which no one has ever gotten around to grabbing, and which is, in truth, definitively ungrabbable.

One evening I received a call from a woman who, in response to my "Hello," went straight to the point of her call without a word of introduction. "Hi," she said, "My son is doing a paper for Literature Class and it's due tomorrow and we need a little information. Can you help us?"

I was a little taken aback, but I asked: "What do you need to know?"

"Just one thing," she said. "The years of birth and death of the French writer Jules Verne."

"That should be easy," said I, and less than a minute later gave her the dates straight from *Webster's Biographical Dictionary*.

"Oh, that's wonderful!" she blissfully exclaimed. "Thank you so much! It's so good to have a library nearby!"

"Well," said I, "we're not really the library, but that's okay—glad to help."

"What do you mean you're not the library?" A note of suspicion had entered her voice.

"It means that you dialed a Wrong Number," I explained. "This is a private home."

"A private home? Oh I'm so sorry! Why didn't you say so? I'm so embarrassed!"

"Don't worry about it," said I. "It's really not important. The information you asked for happened to be right at hand. And best of luck to your son on his paper."

"Oh, yes, thank you *very* much. We really appreciate your help. But it's *all so strange*."

And so it was, and is—I couldn't agree with her more.

In other circumstances, however, it would not have seemed strange at all.

In *L'Alphabet spationnel,* Claude Tarnaud wrote: "Erethism, erotism, heresy: Humankind offers itself infinite possibilities of play."

The trouble is, very few seem to know where or how to begin.

Meanwhile, blithely disregarding the coordinates of Time and Place, the Wrong Number's name is Now and Always, alias Everywhere and Elsewhere. It is a glaring contradiction that embodies the promise and presence of that which is Beyond Contradiction.

## The Click of Fear

Theoretically, any caller or recipient of a Wrong Number has the potential of *rising to the occasion*, in the tradition of Dante's Beatrice, DeQuincey's Anne, Nerval's Aurelia, Schwob's Monelle, Breton's Nadja, Naum's Zenobia, as sentinels of fortuity, guides through wonderland, companions or lovers in a dream more real than most of what passes for reality. Long-established custom, alas, reduces such possibilities almost to zero. Such is the disdain for Wrong Numbers in this poetry-hating society that the sole concern of most people, when confronted with one, is to get it over with as quickly as possible.

*Ring!*

"Hello?"

"Hi, it's Denise! I just got back!" The words are spoken with such breathless excitement that I am certain this is not one of the two or three Denises I know, all of whom are distant acquaintances. The voice, in any case, is unfamiliar.

"Hello, Denise," I replied. "My name is Franklin. Where did you just get back *from*?"

*Click!*

Or again:

"Hello, this is Rhonda. What are you doing?" At the time I did not know anyone with that name, which nonetheless evoked not-unpleasant associations.

"Well, Rhonda, it so happens that I was just rereading some chapters from Benjamin Paul Blood's book, *Pluriverse*. What are *you* doing?"

"Hey, who *is* this? Is C—— there?" (Here she mentioned a gentleman's name, which I do not seem to have noted.)

"No," I replied. "I'm afraid you have what is called a Wrong Number."

*Click!*

Like the depressing squeak of a turnstile, or the hostile nose-in-the-air "No-thank-you" of a passerby who refuses a proffered leaflet, these indignant, dismissive clicks are among the saddest and most typical auditory signs and symptoms of a miserabilist civilization afraid of its own shadows. With such clicks, the grand promise of Wrong Numbers is broken again and again.

It is not impossible that each of these callers had good reasons for not pursuing a conversation with a respondent whom they suddenly realized was entirely unknown to them, and whom they had in fact called only by mistake. And yet, behind Denise's ill-concealed frown of consternation (was she perhaps dismayed to have so shamelessly revealed her triumphal return to someone she did not know?) and Rhonda's exasperated impatience (but if she was in such a hurry to talk to whatever-his-name-was, why didn't she dial his number correctly?), one can readily discern other, less rational factors at work, and first among them is *overriding fear*—fear of strangers, of the unknown, of the Other, and finally, of oneself, for the fear of strangers is above all fear of the best, albeit repressed, aspects of our own being.

The prohibition against talking to strangers is the most entrenched form of xenophobia, which in turn is one of the most characteristic traits of the traditional "American Way of Life," especially during the past hundred years or so. Pummeled into children long before they start school, this peculiar phobia is the keystone—certainly one of the keystones—of the massive maze of fear that has defined the emotional dimension of daily life under the patriarchal capitalist state at least since the beginning of the Cold War. Fear of course is older than humankind, but human society, particularly civilization, gave it an *ideological* function. The fear that dominates U.S. society today derives in large part from the judeo-christian myth of the jealous, wrathful, macho god. Religions, senile and "New Age" alike, remain major inculcators of fear as well as of ignorance—the soil in which fear at its worst grows best.

The expansion of capitalism greatly multiplied the production of fear. As Charles Fourier pointed out long before Karl Marx was born, modern society is intrinsically incoherent and destructive of life: a society at war with itself on all sides. With each advance in technology, capital's murderous social organization, founded on inequality, exploitation and the war of each against all, has become more and more ruinous to life on Earth. In this web of interconnected tyrannies—humans over nature, adults over children, men over women, capitalists over the real producers of wealth, so-called "whites" over so-called "racial minorities" who are in truth the great majority—fear is omnipresent, and by no means wholly irrational.

The whole deadly system sometimes appears to be held together with paperclip palliatives and the gooey paste of advertising and other deceptive diversions, but stark fear remains the real emotional basis of whatever stability the system has. Politicians and civics teachers may prattle about America's freedom and democracy, but everyone knows what happens to those who take freedom and democracy seriously. The most revealing pages in U.S. history are written with the blood of those who thought the Bill of Rights was more than a scrap of paper.

This generalized fear is real, and much of it is also rational: fear of the boss, for example (what is the workplace but a dictatorship in which basic human rights count for nothing?), fear of government (in essence, an instrument of violence and terror), fear of the police (a specialized, local armed force, to serve and protect those who rule). In daily life, however, these legitimate fears branch out into a multitude of subsidiary fears, a large proportion of which are delusions. Confused and immobilized by their wholly justifiable fears, besieged by state, church, and commercial propaganda (the psychological warfare known as "bread and circuses") and above all by the constant pressure on all sides to conform—that is, to contribute to one's own misery—a large part of the population succumbs to *ersatz* fears which in fact bolster and reproduce the worst, most debilitating features of the repressive system. Unable to confront their real oppressors, they themselves become oppressors, or at least the aiders and abettors of oppression. Instead of coming to grips with their actual enemies, they project their fears and hatred onto Blacks and anyone with darker skin than their own, the homeless, immigrants, "illegal" aliens, women, young people, sexual minorities, poets and revolutionists.

All these irrational fears are variants of the fear of strangers, which inevitably seems to inflate itself into the fear of strangeness. Anything "different," anything outside the boundaries of the ordinary—other cultures, other languages, sexuality, wilderness, poetry, life itself—are perceived as objects of fear.

In many colonial countries, the white settlers designated the land outside their settlements as "the interior," a verbal twist which illuminates the contradictions of xenophobia and helps explain not only why Wrong Numbers are widely regarded with such displeasure, but also why their subversive potential remains so strong. For the socialized fear of the vast "outside" is rooted in individual fears of the world *inside*: the world of desire, dream, imagination. People who project their doubts and fears onto ideological straw men and women are not only ignorant of the world around them, they are also ignorant of themselves, deeply afraid of looking within their own minds. It is easier to blame their woes on such stock villains as foreigners, African Americans, Muslims, Communists, Anarchists, Feminists, and Surrealists than to inquire into the nature of their own being, or to examine social reality and their place in it with a critical eye.

For such people, what is a Wrong Number but an insidious means of putting them into direct (and involuntary) communication with *their own worst fears*?

Every Wrong Number is in fact a message from *without* that is received *within*. An unknown from "out there" not only penetrates the privacy of one's own home, but also—because of the call's person-to-person quality—infiltrates the deepest recesses of one's imagination.

Because of ideologically imposed fear, however, few of these calls from Otherness ever really get through. The anxiety barrier is too great. All we get are fragments.

Let's face it: A society that can't enjoy Wrong Numbers is a society in severe crisis.

Can we overcome the click of fear?

## The Advent of a World-Historical Humor

Confronted by the unspeakable horror exemplified by daily life in our time—wars, massacres, devastations, famines, epidemics, police terror, corruption, suffering and misery to an unprecedented degree—most people literally *don't know what to think*. Worse yet, they find it relatively easy to give up thinking entirely. Perhaps it would be more correct to say they are *afraid* to think—terrified of any thought that propels them outside the conventionally thinkable routine represented by the commands *work*, *consume*, and *shut up*.

Smile-face decals, "Have-a-nice-day" sound-bites and other forms of mass-market denial notwithstanding, this all-pervading fear has paralyzing effects that are as obvious, detrimental and far-reaching as the systematic suppression and distortion of news on TV. Enforced by the most preposterously huge military apparatus and police surveillance techniques in the history of the world, this fear cripples imagination, inhibits expression, defeats desire, cheapens life, invites the bureaucratic police state to extend its sway still further, and thereby establishes hopelessness and cynicism as prevailing attitudes in social intercourse. As the totalitarian state renovates old forms of inequality and manufactures new ones, its machinery of fear—increasingly computerized, automated, robotized—consolidates its stranglehold on the Public Sphere.

In broad outline, that is the depressing state of affairs that defines social reality in the U.S. today, where depression is in fact the Number One psychological "problem."

In such conditions, *humor* becomes the secret hideout of the poetic and critical faculties—a guerrilla *foco* from which forays can be made against the slave system. That people laugh to keep from crying is no laughing matter. Humor is the best (and funniest) way—the only effective way—to break through the web of fear, to make the walls of repression come tumbling down, to provide respite from otherwise unrelieved apprehension.

In the existing social order, the humorous is considered inferior to the serious. The humorous, the comical, and all funny business are dismissed as mere diversions from "serious matters" such as the stock-market, the munitions industry, and building high-rises. A plodding, gloomy seriousness is the preponderant tenor of life today.

In its daring daylight raids on the forces of fear, terror, and other manifestations of "seriousness," humor melts repressive character armor, unplugs self-defeating defense-mechanisms, undermines the hegemony of the dominant ideologies, and otherwise unilaterally disarms the Reality Principle. As it liberates the mind from fear's incapacitating dominion, it reinforces the libido and sets the imagination free. Together, libido and imagination, nourished by humor, release submerged psychic energies and restore—or in many cases, instill for the first time—a measure of self-confidence and solidarity to people long lost to themselves and the world.

Humor, accidental but real, is the prime feature of a whole category of Wrong Numbers, in which the caller, assuming that he/she has dialed correctly, just starts talking.

In an undated call from around 1980, I picked up the ringing phone and heard a man's voice say: "Hi! Do you fix lawnmowers?"

"No," I replied. "I don't. I don't even *like* lawnmowers, and I wouldn't have the faintest idea of how to go about fixing one."

"Wow!" said my caller. And then he said: "Gosh!" And then, after a brief silence: "Is this the Yard and Garden Supply?"

"No, this is a Wrong Number."

"Oh!" And then he laughed, uproariously, and hung up the phone.

Another call, in the early 1990s, began even more abruptly:

"Hey listen, we're running a little late but we'll get there as fast as we can. You don't have to hold dinner."

"My friend," said I, "I think you have a Wrong Number."

"Oh, for chrissakes, now I gotta make another call! Gees—I guess now we'll *really* be late, huh?" He laughed, and then, clearly addressing someone else, said: "Hey—you got any quarters?" *Click!*

Although neither of these is likely to win an Academy Award, they do—in their small way—highlight the *potential* of the Wrong Number as a medium for impromptu humor. If anyone ever gets around to reviving radio comedy, Wrong Numbers will surely be a major source for gags and stories.

In the above examples, I regard the fact that both callers *laughed* as very encouraging. It shows that a couple of complete strangers, having bumped into each other in a Wrong Number, were not only able to recognize a *comic situation* when they found themselves in one, but were also able to improvise their way through it, and then to laugh about it, too.

Those just happen to be the very abilities most urgently needed by those who are trying to transform the world.

For humor, all jokes aside, is serious business—at least as serious as life. And speaking of life, isn't it curious that when people break out of their conformist shells and behave momentarily in a manner true to themselves, they often recoil immediately afterward and offer pathetic apologies? "This isn't really me," they will say, or "I'm not myself today," or "Of course I'm just kidding." Those who know what humor is know that such informal vacations from our formal selves are really the seeds of a new Garden of Eden. Realizing that you are not really the person you think you are supposed to be is the start of a better life for all. Why bother to be your alleged "self"—*i.e.*, a fearful slave of the *status quo*—when you can be someone else, someone truer to you than the "you" that social convention forces you to be?

"Examine yourself," said Meister Eckhart, "and whenever you find yourself, then take leave of yourself. This is the best way of all."

In other words, you do not have to be "you." Or in still *other* words, others are also "I."

It is precisely because it allows us or impels us to be someone *different* that the Wrong Number, as a vehicle of humor (and a symbol of Umor) actually makes a difference in the world.

The Wrong Number draws two strangers into the space of a moment in which their minds can stretch out a little beyond the time that ordinarily imprisons them. In this game, *you* are the other and the other is you, or someone else who might *also* be you.

To say yes to Wrong Numbers is therefore itself an act of humor which generates other acts of humor. It pulls the rug out from under the fear in ourselves, and enables us to find new ways of defying the limits that fear imposes on society.

What had seemed bitterness turns to sweetness—or peals of laughter.

We need to create conditions in which people are finally able to laugh at their willingness to submit to unfreedom. Undermining the legitimacy of unfreedom is always the beginning of true freedom. Remoralizing the demoralized puts revolution "in the air" again. And only when revolution is in the air can we begin to breathe freely and to be ourselves.

Jacques Vaché's famous declaration to André Breton—"How funny it'll be, don't you see, if this real new spirit breaks loose!"—applies down the line to our umorous and playful science. I would go so far as to suggest that the breaking loose of the heretofore unrecognized *latent content* of Wrong Numbers should prove to be one of the funniest events since the world began.

The point is to acknowledge Wrong Numbers—at last!—as *objectively offered moments* in a much broader movement that could be considered a new *world-historical humor.*

To laugh so hard you can't stop may not be the highest aim in life, but it is singular how few people have even given it a try, once their childhood is past.

Don't get me wrong—I'm new around here, too. And I am well aware that the most subversive currents of humor are far from eliciting either giggle or guffaw.

But a larger question remains: Why settle for anything less than ecstasy?

## Swift's Flea and Lautréamont's Louse

Abrupt, fragmentary, glimpsed in a mist, conclusively inconclusive, and always on the go, the Wrong Number never stops to have its picture taken. Only rarely does it pass for premonition or prefiguration, or anything else one could submit to critical scrutiny. It offers rather the merest hint of a foretaste, which nonetheless leaves an unforgettable aftertaste. More often than not it provokes a vague anxiety or foreboding, an "uncomfortable feeling" that one cannot put one's finger on. Ever-changing but always the same, it exemplifies a desperate kind of mixed metamorphosis.

The *nuisance-value* of the Wrong Number is the most outstanding and precious of its virtues, and cannot be emphasized too strongly. Its ability to agitate, bother, exasperate, jostle, jolt, perplex, pester, pinch, poke, tickle, sting, and then escape unscathed, only to return again and again to the scene of its crimes, is unsurpassed.

Like the "wandering evidence. . . at the crossroads of echoes" invoked by Gherasim Luca in his *Théâtre de Bouche*, it refuses to stand still for long.

All its grandeur lies precisely in its sublimely irritating transience, its notorious "insignifiance" (that is, its lack of certifiable signification), its genius as quick-change artist, and its fiercely *parasitical* character.

A gadfly steeped in sadism and black humor, it does not know when to stop and couldn't care less. Its brevity notwithstanding, it has never benefitted from the "less is more" fad. Like Swift's flea and Lautréamont's louse, the Wrong Number wasn't invited, prefers not to go away until it feels like it, and lingers in the mind and body long after it's gone.

And on less than a moment's notice, it can transform the heretofore "unnoticed" into something momentous, maddening, or marvelous.

Its mobility and improbability are such that no one can capture it in a net, or swat it like a fly, or even point to it, or shake a fist at it.

Like other all-out deviations from the normal course of things, it undermines familiarity, annihilates hypocrisy, and hurries us along detours that serve only to aggravate our confusion.

As a "sound" reverberating in space, and in our ears, it could be considered an auditory sign—or at least the somniferous muttering—of the Great Invisibles (or Great Transparent Ones), long ago proposed by André Breton as a new myth.

A mere moment's diversion, universally held to be without redeeming social value—and proud of it!—the Wrong Number really does manage to get around. You can find it almost anywhere, thumbing its nose (and inviting us to thumb ours, too) at every manifestation of the death-wish in action: at family values, patriotism, xenophobia, the work-ethic—the whole stinking mess.

Part joy-buzzer, part sneeze-powder, part Shakespeare, and part *Night in Tunisia*, it is the essence of all that is brightest in adolescence condensed into ten or twenty seconds. Sometimes it might hurt a little, but think of it as a vaccination against all forms of cynicism. Yesterday it was the banana-peel on which the cynicism known as positivism slipped and fell. Last night it was the exploding cigar that made cynical neo-Kantians cry. This morning it was a pea-shooter in the mind's guerrilla war against the inhibitions of cynical puritanism. Tonight it is a monkeywrench in the ideological machinery of the neo-cynical cyberfascist "New Age."

*In the right hands*, moreover—setting aside all question of left- and right-handedness for the moment—the Wrong Number can be a first-class ticket to that point in the mind where, among other things, pre-Raphaelite and post-Raphaelite, as well as you and I and Raphael Sanzio himself meet, exchange words, and converge.

At its mountaintop best, the Wrong Number exceeds and travesties all conventional expectations, and calls for something inestimably better. Without even trying it abolishes clocks and welcomes dreams with both eyes open. Equivocal and ambivalent, it is never the same river twice. And how majestically it flows!

Grandest of all, with complete lack of consideration for institutions and conventions, it helps dissolve the hard and fast emptiness that lurks between other beings, things and us.

# On the Road With the Negation of the Negation

The fact that the questions asked in Wrong Numbers ("Is X there?" or "May I speak to X, please?") are always answered in the negative is particularly interesting in view of the apparently unrelated fact that the experience itself, with very few exceptions, is also regarded as negative. The Wrong Number has affinities aplenty with what Poe once called poetry's "great negativistic hand." It is a *no* whose irritative capacity is not diminished by the fact that it is hardly more than a whisper in the storm. However fleetingly, every Wrong Number is a negation of positivist continuity and the commonsense rationalizations that go with it. Even when Wrong Numbers lead us astray, their double and triple negatives turn out to be excellent companions on the road. Like certain exquisitely rare palindromes and anagrams, the Wrong Number's implacable neither/nor sometimes carries us so far off the beaten track that we wind up in places incomparably better than we had even hoped for. At their worst they cost us nothing; at their best they reward us handsomely for our toil and trouble.

All paths leading to the Marvelous are surely worth taking, but the way is not always easy. No one gets far who does not start by deviating radically from the Safe and Sure. Here as elsewhere, nonconformism offers the only chance of reaching the desired goal. All things Reasonable, Successful, Moderate, Guaranteed, Non-Controversial, Middle-of-the-Road, and Fully Approved are to be avoided like the plague. The revelation of life's real possibilities requires a systematic *deimpossibilization*, the initial steps of which are always *out of order* and therefore necessarily disorienting. For many, this disorientation easily becomes intoxicating, and redolent with secondary pleasures of its own. In such adventures, everything depends on *not giving in* to a sophomoric pseudo-epicurean confusion—that is to say, on *not giving up* the quest by selling out to the peddlers of disorientation-for-disorientation's-sake, one of the most pitiable of delusions. What is called for here is not simply a matter of keeping one's wits about one, but above all of refusing to become a mere *consumer* of the many brands of marketable obscurantism that may happen to block the way.

Disorientation, in any event, would hardly be worth a used marshmallow if it did not lead, dialectically, to a new *re*orientation. And thus it can be said, in the rigorous spirit of Basilius Valentinus and Nicolas

Flamel, that every Wrong Number is always *worth its salt*. And this is true not only of the exceptional Wrong Numbers that may strike us from the start as completely *right*, but of *any* Wrong Number, read rightly.

Travel light and sleep as you please, but do not forget that there is a lot of debris to be swept aside, and that hurdles exist to be surmounted. Woe unto those who take the debris or the hurdles for the road itself!

Better to take risks than be sorry!

## SECRETS OF MAGIC

Like the ability to perceive images in a magic mirror, or to speak in other voices in a state of trance, receptivity to Wrong Numbers does not appear to be common. It appears to be a veritable "wild talent" that no one has thus far taken the trouble to notice. Its notorious uselessness and unattractiveness as an undesirable and alien byproduct of modern technology, and therefore its complete lack of supernatural glamor, seem to have conspired to keep it out of the hands of the people who supply us with Ouija boards, tealeaf readings, and Your Horoscope With Your Weight, Five Cents. The whole Wrong Number experience is altogether too common and too easily explainable (from the technical standpoint) to be considered even remotely occult or paranormal.

Most phenomena so called belong either to the domain of supernatural beliefs, or to the domain of psychopathology, and there is good reason to believe that a large part of the former also belong to the latter. The Wrong Number, however, belongs to neither. Beyond the scope of abnormal psychology, it has nothing to offer any esoteric dogma. Any attempt to squeeze the experience of Wrong Numbers into the framework of occultism, psychiatry, or parapsychology would be not only arbitrary, but obfuscatory and inane.

Nonetheless, between Wrong Numbers, magic, and the "secret sciences," and even parapsychology, analogies abound in all directions. The unknown voice on the telephone unmistakably comes to us from *outside*, making the listener a kind of "medium" for an oftentimes mysterious message. Some Wrong Numbers have the ring of cryptograms; others, more rarely, retain something of the tone and nuance of thaumaturgical invocations; in still others, we seem to hear faint echoes of some legendary "lost word." Unintentional though it undoubtedly is, the Wrong Number *as a number* is a kind of *anagram*, and thus is related to the whole spectrum of number-based divination and magic squares, from Pythagorean puzzles to the encircled pentagrams in which Renaissance magicians performed their nocturnal rites.

In terms of psychic effect, moreover—their immediate and long-range impact on the recipient's consciousness—Wrong Numbers have much in common with various "anomalous" states and "unexplained" phenomena. Chance interventions of an unknown and external "other" in the internal dialogue that each individual carries on at all times, they share common ground on the broad continuum of *non-*, *anti-*, and *sur*rational modes of apprehension. Most particularly, as pulse-quickening "messages" from "out there," Wrong Numbers have more than a slight resemblance to ancient notions of *annunciation*: direct communications from Heaven and/or dark temptations from Hell.

In the Wrong Number, finally, we find elements reminiscent of obsessions, fetishes, talismans, demonic possession and all manner of "unearthly" reveries, especially those that can be grouped under the heading of "hearing things." Wrong Numbers can appear as trickster, poltergeist, imp of the perverse—as creator/instigator of hallucinatory situations and other troubling experiences which, if not paranormal, are certainly a long way from normal.

Clearly then, our awareness that Wrong Numbers are simply the consequence of misdialing, or careless button-pushing, or some other telephonic mishap, precludes supernatural interpretation, but does not diminish the oftentimes weird and bewildering character of the Wrong Number itself. As bizarre as it is commonplace, it remains a phenomenon like no other.

Lautréamont, who reminded us more than once that he, too, was a scientist as well as a poet, also had occasion to insist that "Nothing is incomprehensible." Everything leads us to believe that Wrong Numbers will illuminate the "occult" and "paranormal," rather than the other way around. Many occult treatises, however, and even some studies of the "paranormal"—particularly those which can be said to be under the influence of poetry—are bubbling with hints and hypotheses that we are free to adapt to our own purposes. From the Elizabethans through the most recent developments in surrealism, poets have demonstrated time and again that the recovery of latent, lost or hidden powers is most effectively achieved by rigorously *poetic* means, *via* the magic of *word* and *image*. The lessons of "pure psychic automatism," as expounded in the first *Surrealist Manifesto* in 1924, proved decisive in this regard. And in his last major theoretical work, *Magic Art* (*L'Art magique,* 1957), Breton emphasized the contemporary urgency of Novalis's broad conception of magic and its relation to poetry and art, and furthermore upheld the German poet's "brilliant apprehension of a need for extrarationalist investigation and intervention" in these realms.

Misdialing the phone can open still other doors to the hiding-places of the mind. The Wrong Number's capacity for fogging up ego boundaries, its sometimes divisive effects on the ordinarily unified self, its instigation of a sense of unreality: All these (and the list could easily be extended) belong to the praxis of every poet-magician. Harbingers of the unexpected and improbable, Wrong Numbers naturally become precipitators of inspiration, and as such, transmitters of revelations or levers of the actualization of poetry. As Joyce Mansour once pointed out: "Every object can be used magically."

Similarly, although there is nothing mystical about Wrong Numbers, a Wrong Number can, like anything else, spur a "mystical" experience. Because of its suddenness, oddity, and chance quality, a Wrong Number might be expected to serve in this capacity more frequently than most things. Many Wrong Numbers, for example, hit us with the surprise punch of a Zen koan, and it is not hard to imagine a Wrong Number triggering the experience of *satori.*

Verily it can be said of the Wrong Number, as Basilius Valentinus wrote of Antimony: "The manifold variations which it undergoes might puzzle the oracle of Delphi."

This does not mean that the Wrong Number is all things to all people. It would be more accurate to say that its masks are infinite, and that it enjoys disguising itself as unknowable. Neither friendly nor hostile, true or false, right or wrong, its intrusive dynamism is such that the Wrong Number is always Something Else.

Like poetry, moreover, the Wrong Number is always fiercely antidogmatic. To the perpetually recurring question, "What next?" it proposes, not precise answers, but random suggestions, which invite imaginative and tentative interpretation as well as development.

Fundamentally, the Wrong Number is not a mystery but a unique, rich and many-sided *experience*. However "unbelievable" it may appear, it's here and it's ours, to have and to let go. Like all experiences worthy of the name, it contributes to knowledge. And isn't everything that is worth knowing *beyond belief*?

## A Voice and a Name: The Gnostic Connection

Far from providing what experts in pertinence call "pertinent data," Wrong Numbers offer data only of the utmost *im*pertinence. They convey nothing of what is ordinarily regarded as "useful information," and seem to bear no relation to what men of affairs designate as the "problems at hand," or any other problems, for that matter. Precisely because of their emphatically non-utilitarian character, Wrong Numbers have been "factored out" of the field of consideration, and put beyond the pale as utterly *alien*.

Consciousness of alienation—especially one's own—was a prime component in the outlook of the Gnostics of the pre-christian and early christian era. Unrelenting both as an *example* of the alien and as a force to provoke a philosophical awareness of it, the Wrong Number could be described as the Gnostic element of telecommunications.

The only known work by the itinerant Gnostic agitator Simon Magus had for its title *The Revelation of a Voice and a Name*—the very substance of every Wrong Number. Like other Gnostic stump-speakers on the road in ancient Palestine, Samaria and Anatolia, Simon Magus boldly posed the questions: "Who are you?" and "Who am I?"—the classic Wrong Number questions. A key phrase in his *Revelation* declares: "Thou and I are but one"—a veritable Gnostic watchword that also applies to the mystery of misdialed numbers. For in the Wrong Number, "You" and "I" are practically an encyclopedia of All and Everyone. In this light, it is hard to tell us apart.

The Gnostics regarded all existing institutions—religious, political, and economic—as shams, irredeemably compromised by corruption, hypocrisy, and oppression. Toward all forms of established authority, they maintained an attitude of doubt, insubordination, refusal and revolt. Recognizing themselves as *outsiders* who, having broken through the distorted looking-glass of official "reality," they chose to live a radical counter-life in oppositional anarcho-communist communities.

Through *gnosis* (knowledge), they strove not only to make us aware of the *spark* latent in each of us (Blake's "Poetic Genius"), but also to strengthen and expand it, and to unite it to the sparks of others (Lautréamont's "poetry made by all"). Moreover, as properly emphasized by the late-blooming Gnostic philosopher Hoene Wronski, writing in the first half of the nineteenth century, *all real knowledge is by nature ecstatic.* The early Gnostics made no secret of their aim; like their descendants—Blake, Wronski, Fourier, and more recently the surrealists—they sought to awaken the combined consciousness of a liberated humankind, so that I, Thou, He, She, and They would evolve into We: a new human solidarity.

A way of talking out of turn, the Wrong Number can help us *return to the source*—that is, to discover our own originality. "*In* the world but not *of* the world," as the Gnostics thought of themselves, Wrong Numbers are poetic evidence that Desire is the root not only of redemption, but also of revolutionary social transformation.

These echoes of a Voice and a Name recall deserted ruins of the long ago and far away, and yet they are just around the corner—ready or not!

It takes all kinds to make a world, and you can find them all in Wrong Numbers.

## A Call While Reading the *Archeometer*

On the evening of May 12, 1995 I was seated at an eight-sided table studying a large volume titled *L'Archéometre* by Joseph Alexandre Saint-Yves d'Alveydre. A major figure of European occultist philosophy, Saint-Yves (1842–1909) is generally considered the philosophical heir of Fabre d'Olivet, and his work also has more than a slight kinship with the ideas of the Polish Romantic philosopher Hoene Wronski.

Saint-Yves is best known for his writings on the hidden city of Agarttha—an invisible utopia "somewhere in the Himalayas," and the locus of an immemorial university of traditional sciences which, so Saint-Yves himself tells us, was the source of most of his own special knowledge. His invention, the Archeometer, was patented in 1903. According to the subtitle of his book on the subject, it provided "Keys to All the Religions and Sciences of Antiquity" as well as a plan for the "Synthetic Reform of All Contemporary Arts." Impossible to describe in a few words, the Archeometer is a complex instrument for the precise analogical calculation of humankind's social, intellectual, esthetic, architectural, musical and poetic possibilities.

As it happens, I was searching through this impressive tome for any "correspondences" it might suggest regarding the life and work of the distinguished nineteenth-century African-American crystal-gazer, trance-author, master of erotic magic, and proto-hipster: Paschal Beverly Randolph. This research, pursued in a state of mind not far from the borders of stupefaction—I was in fact feverishly ill with bronchitis at the time—was interrupted by the ringing of the telephone, a Wrong Number. It was a call for Albert, pronounced as in French, with the accent on the second syllable.

The name provoked several immediate associations: Albert Ayler, Albert R. Parsons, Albert the Alligator (from the *Pogo* comics), Albert Einstein, Albert Weisbord (Communist leader of the 1926 Passaic Strike, with whom Penelope and I had some acquaintance in the 1970s), and the bush-league baseball player featured in Ring Lardner's *You Know Me Al*, which I had recently reread. I did not, however, linger long on these detours, preferring—in a state of free-floating single-mindedness—to complete my journey through the 580 large pages of the *Archeometer*. A few minutes later, having turned to Jean Saunier's *La Synarchie* (which contains several chapters on Saint-Yves) to confirm a detail, I came across a reference to F.-Ch. Barlet, the first biographer of the author of the *Archeometer*, explaining that his real name was Albert Faucheux, and that his *nom de plume* Barlet is in fact an anagram of Albert. Moreover, he was a leading representative in Europe of the Hermetic Brotherhood of Luxor, the occult secret society that was so deeply influenced by Paschal Beverly Randolph. An amusing personal link: Barlet is described in a note as the "librarian of the Arsenal" (acquaintances not infrequently introduce me to others as the "editor of *Arsenal*").

## An Open Entrance to a Shut Palace

Alchemy has always been the most materialist of the traditional sciences, but not because it offers any material reward. "Who lucre coveteth," as Thomas Norton put it in his *Ordinall of Alchimie*, first published in 1618, "this *Science* shall not finde." Rather, alchemy's materialist groundedness lies in the fact that its praxis is closest to the real substances and processes of nature. The whole world of matter and its infinite transformations are the focus of its research, and of the reveries it inspires. Not incidentally, alchemy was and remains the traditional science closest to the practice of poetry—and of course the one that true poets have always loved best.

Ancient though it is, it is still full of meaning for us: a supreme adventure, a source of knowledge. As Ethan Allen Hitchcock argued in his1857 *Remarks*, "the questions about which the Alchemists employed themselves have not passed away" because "they are the most interesting questions which the heart can propose."

Alchemical writers enjoyed using the most luxurious metaphors and images to describe the scope of their science, their implements, principles and procedures. The names of the alchemists' "matter" are legion. Stormy Water, Incombustible Ash, Sun's Brightness, Peacock's Tail, Virgin's Milk, Ostrich's Stomach, Fish's Eye, Egg's Yolk, Eagle's Tears, Mushroom's Saliva, and Black Blacker Than Black are just a few of its countless aliases. Dom Pernety's *Dictionnaire Mytho-Hermetique* (1787) includes more than six hundred names, and his list is far from complete.

What is especially interesting is that *prime matter*, the state in which the Philosopher's Stone originally appears to the student of alchemy, is invariably described in the most disparaging terms: despicable and repulsive, "worthless and rejected," "the vilest of the vile." Only when purified by alchemical art—only, that is, when it is freed of its "superfluous matter" and thereby allowed to develop according to its own internal dynamic—does it become the instrument of wonder-working transmutation. As the *Turba Philosophorum* tells us, the Stone is a thing "found everywhere . . . contemptible and precious, hidden, concealed, and yet known to everyone." Nicolas Flamel, in his *Desire Desired*, drove home the point with a statement he attributed to Pythagoras: "This stone known by all names nonetheless has only one name."

Is there a better name for the Philosophers' Stone today than *Wrong Number*?

The critic Jean Ferry, some years after his departure from the Surrealist Group in Paris, made light of what he regarded as André Breton's tendency to perceive hermetic significance in texts that seemed to give no outward sign of it. The author of *Arcanum 17*, Ferry went on to say, would find alchemy in anything—even in the telephone directory.

When I mentioned this a few years ago to my friend Leonora Carrington, whose knowledge of alchemical literature and lore is prodigious, she asked: "Is that supposed to be a criticism? The telephone book *is* full of alchemical evidence. How could it *not* be, with all those names and numbers? On that point," she concluded, "I would certainly agree with Breton."

This calls to mind an old gag in which a playwright describes the telephone book as having "a hell of a cast, but a lousy plot."

For my part, I have come to think of the Wrong Number as the heretofore undiscerned plot—the poetic *raison d'être*—of the telephone itself.

Gold is where you find it!

## A Brief Message From the World's Greatest Rabbit

Sometimes, when telephoning friends, I have been known to start with the words, "What's up, Doc?"—a greeting popularized in the early 1940s by a film- and comic-book star who happens to be one of the very few world-class celebrities I admire.

Occasionally I have used this opening in calls that turned out to be Wrong Numbers. In every case I was able to tell that it was a Wrong Number well before the recipient uttered a sound, for my three-word question was invariably followed by at least five and sometimes fifteen or twenty seconds of silence. Long by Wrong Number standards, this silence was always broken by another question, asked in such a way as to convey indignation or mistrust, such as: "I beg your pardon?" or "Is this some kind of joke?" or "Who is this and what do you want?"

Not once, it is my sad duty to report, has a recipient of one of these calls ever answered in the voice or manner of Daffy Duck, Sylvester Q. Pussycat, Yosemite Sam, or any of the other characters who inhabit the world of the old *Looney Tunes & Merrie Melodies* cartoons. Could it be that the U.S. phonotariat suffers from an overdose of seriousness?

For a dismaying number of people, it is evidently bad enough to get a Wrong Number, but to get one from someone quoting Bugs Bunny is really too much for their minds to bear.

Fortunately, the World's Greatest Rabbit has also left us just the right response for these stuffed shirts. After saying, "I guess this is a Wrong Number, Doc," I often add another direct quotation from Bugs himself:

"Don't think it hasn't been lovely—because it hasn't!"

## Spilling Soup on Tuxedoes

An unwanted child of telecommunications technology, the Wrong Number was abandoned at the intersection of Carelessness and Indifference. Despised and disowned by all, it was sent hastily on its way with nothing more than a few emotionless phrases that could serve as models of calculated insincerity. And yet, with all the chips and microchips stacked against it, the Wrong Number has not only survived, but has reserved the last and best laughs for itself.

It's a rewrite of *Oliver Twist*, with a lot of new twists.

To put this admittedly out-of-the-ordinary way of looking at it into better perspective, I must point out that young Twist haunted my childhood. All through my grade-school years the works of Charles Dickens were a central reference in the ever-restless Rosemont residence (by the time I started eighth grade we had moved five times and I had attended four schools). Not until high school did I read books of 400 or more pages, but my father's stories—he could recite whole pages of Dickens from memory—as well as old movies, radio and TV plays, and *Classics Illustrated* comics enabled me to perceive the world through a dark Dickensian lens. Such characters as Twist, Copperfield, and Mister Micawber appeared much more real—more *alive*—than the dull-witted teachers at school, or the droning newsmen on TV. Full of upheavals, disappointments, downfalls and disasters, as well as resistance and revolt, Dickens's furious tales approximated a lot of what I saw of life in Chicago's workingclass western suburbs in the 1950s. *David Copperfield*, that amazing child's view of childhood terror, was especially vivid (and, incidentally, Freud's favorite novel), but I also felt akin to the indefatigable Twist and the crippled Tiny Tim (I was on crutches myself for a few months at the age of nine).

Just for the record: On August 26, 1995, I received a call for Oliver—a *collect* call, from the Philippines. I did not know anyone named Oliver, in the Philippines or elsewhere, so I asked the Operator for further information. Following some loud crackling on the line, the Operator said: "I'm sorry, sir, there seems to have been a mistake." *Click!*

But now, back to our story: The rejected and recalcitrant orphan known as the Wrong Number "jes grew" until it became ubiquitous and even Ubuesque: a formidable projection of something that somehow manages to avoid seeming real at all. This unsettling "something," moreover, not only elected to remain aloof but also chose (and chooses still) to go forth and multiply. The sheer *number* of Wrong Numbers that have been unloosed on the world is astounding to contemplate. No one knows when or where the Wrong Number first arrived on the scene; no one could even begin to calculate the grand total of its subsequent appearances.

Quantity and frequency notwithstanding, most people continue to act as if they don't exist. The Wrong Number is thus treated like sneezing at a wedding, or spilling soup on tuxedoes: moments of embarrassment people do not care to acknowledge, much less to discuss in public.

For some people, on the other hand, the Wrong Number's *intrusive* aspect surely recalls other unwanted "intruders": all those whom elitist "Society" wishes to keep at a distance. (In Dickens's day, Lord Melbourne found *Oliver Twist* offensive because it portrayed child labor, poverty, and other "unpleasant" subjects which, in his opinion, were better left unmentioned.)

It does not seem too far-fetched to suggest that the persistence and multiplication of Wrong Numbers in the dominant culture exemplify the vertiginous process by which the "excluded" (alias *workers, foreigners, homeless, "illegal" aliens*, etc.) struggle to make a place for themselves in existing patterns of thought and behavior, thereby not only changing these patterns, but also evolving new and rebellious patterns of their own.

In its hide-and-seek with "seriousness," meanwhile, the Wrong Number always seems to have new tricks to play on us. What at first may have seemed merely a crude but unostentatious sort of vocal jostling, a telephonic equivalent of bumping into a fellow passenger on the bus, eventually metamorphosed into an elaborate dialogical tango—for it takes two to make a Wrong Number, and their variations must be close to infinite. As for their future, anything is possible. In these green and magnetic fields, where the paranoiac-critical method frolics with phonetic cabala, Vico's idea of the importance of unintended consequences in history—how seemingly narrow aims are made to serve wider ends—serves well both as point of departure and point of return.

Against all odds, the Wrong Number is here to stay, but always refuses to stay put.

The irrepressible quality of the self-multiplying orphan makes the Wrong Number a symbol not only of the return (and revenge) of the repressed, but also of the eventual overcoming of repression. Disconnecting us momentarily from the reassuringly familiar but restrictive matrices of conventional life, it offers us unexpected connections with the infinitely larger and freer family known as the *unfamiliar*.

A well known ideological oversimplification pretends that the best things in life are free. In truth, the best things in life are *concrete manifestations of freedom*, and they are always the outcome of struggle.

Oliver Twist asks for more!

Like the proletariat and the imagination, the Wrong Number is revolutionary or it is nothing.

## Toward a Methodology of the Inadvertent

Once I resolved to explore the *terra incognita* of Wrong Numbers and actually took the plunge, I wondered how best to proceed. I had nothing in the way of maps, guideposts, landmarks, or frame of reference. For some years I had been slowly gathering notes on the calls I received, and puzzling over them—looking at them this way and that, trying to piece them together and above all to follow where they seemed to beckon. My preliminary aim was to get "inside" them, to learn to "read" them, to tease out their secrets (i.e., their "meanings"), and to see where they were heading. Alas, in the swirling fog of non-information at my disposal, each new Wrong Number came as a flicker of light that vanished as fast as it appeared; no clear image emerged.

Spread out before me were all the scraps of paper on which I had made notes of these calls. In this mass of jottings I searched for patterns, correspondences, connecting links. The result was easy to sum up: *Nothing*.

Undaunted, I arranged the data in columns and rows, comparing such variables as the time the calls were made (morning, afternoon, evening, late at night), the day of the week and month, and the sex of the caller as well as of the hoped-for recipient. I made charts, diagrams, mathematical calculations. This time the result was—*Nothing*.

So then I tried a series of rearrangements of varying degrees of complexity. The one that seemed most promising—and this should convey something of my state of mind at the time—consisted of *shuffling* the data, in the hope that some common and cohering element would spring to view. The result of course was only to return to the starting-point—in other words: *Nothing*.

Here I was, confronted by some threescore cryptic messages that could point in any direction, in several directions, in all directions, or no direction at all, and I could not figure out what to do next. Even the most elementary criteria seemed to be lacking.

Thus far I had succeeded only in confusing myself again and again, albeit each time in a different way. Isn't that how most history is written, and practically all philosophy? In intellectual funhouses such as these, new myths and old run into us at every turn, and we run into them, or at least jostle them a little, and none of us—the myths or us—are quite the same afterward. Wandering in the dark, you can't really see what lies ahead, but by sheer dogged persistence we find the way, or stumble upon it—or the way finds or stumbles upon us—and when that happens we realize that the game is worth the candle after all.

In the midst of these nocturnal broodings I chanced on a copy of the *Hermeneutic Interpretation of the Origin of the Social State of Man* by Antoine Fabre d'Olivet, whose name I knew from André Breton's splendid poem, *Les Etats Généraux*, and whose books my friend Philip Lamantia had highly recommended. The *Hermeneutic Interpretation* is an esoteric "philosophical history" of humankind, covering some 12,000 years. Leafing through its 548 pages, my eyes fell upon this bold advice: "As to the details, it is necessary to avoid them as much as one can in a subject where they are infinite."

I recognized at once that the secrets of Wrong Numbers would never reveal themselves in mere details; that the Wrong Number, as a universal social phenomenon, is vastly more than the sum of its parts; that the individual Wrong Number, or even a selection of Wrong Numbers, was only a fragment, a hint, a beginning.

Or rather, a fragment of a hint of a beginning.

Or perhaps: fragments of hints of *many* beginnings.

I was convinced that the Wrong Number was not a "thing," and certainly not a "thing apart," but rather a special kind of action, gesture, energy, or natural occurrence, with it own peculiar laws and dynamics. Increasingly, as evidenced in the foregoing chapters, I let my attention slide from mere facts and lists, and began to consider the Wrong Number's sundry relations to such matters as language, the problem of identity, dreams, psychological disorders, theater, sexuality, magic, heresy, alchemy, and humor. Once the "details" no longer dominated the scene, other possibilities emerged, as big as life.

The time had come to step back and take in the larger picture.

## In the Light of Analogy

Desperate situations often call for playful measures. Fabre d'Olivet's advice about details came to me like a treasure-map in a bottle tossed in the sea. It arrived at *just the right moment* and radiated the magic immediacy of poetry as it threw all the mind's doors and windows wide open. It was one of those wonderful things you sometimes find when you are frantically looking for something else that really didn't matter after all. Most importantly, Fabre d'Olivet's message led me directly to a sure-fire method: *Analogy*—the unbreakable thread that enables us to find our way through the labyrinth of Wrong Numbers.

The foundation and pivot of all knowledge, analogy is as old as language itself, rooted in metaphor, *symbolique*, the play of words, the development of the human passions. Its premise is as simple as it is profound: Everything "outside" or "external" to us—the starry heavens, the whole Earth, mountains, rivers, trees, flowers, birds, other creatures, mathematics, music, alphabets—is also *within*, as double, reflection, echo, or in some other way, *by analogy.* As Gérard Legrand wrote of Hegel's Absolute Knowledge, "analogy changes all problems into *emblems.*"

Hegel himself regarded analogy as "the instinct of reason," and in the lesser *Logic* he emphasized that it "deservedly occupies a high place, and has led to results of the highest importance" in what he called the "experiential sciences." The mainstream Hegelian tradition, however, has been deplorably weak in analogical insight. Here as elsewhere, surrealism has continued to raise the stakes: Only when reason is developed in the wildest flights of analogy can it be said to add to the sum total of human happiness.

Universal Analogy is of course not merely a method, but a *force*—a radical force for poetry and the realization of poetry in daily life. A live mirror that makes intuition *active*, analogy is also an inspirer of audacity and a lever of social change. The chief avatars of this boundless and subversive science have distinguished themselves by their fierce opposition to the existing order, and as exemplars of the negation and/or supersession of that order. In their view, analogy was the best way to reconstitute the innocence of Eden—humankind's original unity with itself and the world. Gnostics, heretics, alchemists, Ranters, the socialist visionary Charles Fourier, the Wronskian philosopher Ange Pechméja, author of *L'Oeuf de Kneph* ("The Secret History of Zero"), the maverick metaphysician/etymologist Jean-Pierre Brisset, and the most uncompromisingly free-spirited poets—from Shakespeare, Blake, Novalis, Emily Brontë, Emily Dickinson, Lautréamont and Saint-Pol-Roux to André Breton, Aimé Césaire, Malcolm de Chazal, Philip Lamantia, Claude Tarnaud, Joyce Mansour, Guy Cabanel and Joseph Jablonski: That's the kind of company analogy keeps.

My quest for the meaning of Wrong Numbers began with the naive attempt to analyze or interpret individual calls or a series of calls.

Looking backward, it is easy to see now that I was going about it all in the wrong way, but how could it have been otherwise in research that put the "wrong" at its very center? From the start, analogical thinking had sparked what little I knew—or rather sensed—about Wrong Numbers, but thus far I had applied it only tentatively, loosely and more or less unconsciously. Now I completely changed my method. Instead of looking *at* Wrong Numbers, I was determined to *see through* them the way I would see through a window with a panoramic view—the way I see through the work of certain painters and poets, or the piano solos of Thelonious Monk: seeing—I mean really *seeing*—through the very things that have *seen me through* the vicissitudes of life.

Always receptive to the unpredictable, analogical thought simultaneously anticipates and clears the way for the serendipitous.

Thanks to analogy, and to Fourier's "Passional Analogy" in particular, we can pinpoint the Wrong Number's true purport and social destiny.

Broadly speaking, every Wrong Number corresponds to an individual desire—yours, mine, anyone's—which, for whatever reason, remains unfulfilled.

More precisely, as an unconscious attempt to speak to someone "different"—an Other, a stranger—every Wrong Number corresponds to the latent but unmistakable desire of the human species for a new global community and a radically non-alienated way of life.

In its narrowest definition, a Wrong Number is an opening on a moment in the life of two strangers. Symbolically and analogically, however, moving from the particular to the universal, the experience can be seen as a reflection and echo of the macrocosm in the microcosm: that is, as an opening on a new life for all, and therefore an emblem of humankind's yearning for reintegration.

Announcing a potential splendor that is ours for the taking, Wrong Numbers are also microcosmic warnings of macrocosmic disaster if we don't, so to speak, heed the call.

Although Wrong Numbers rarely get beyond a few words, they are unmistakably *attempts at communication*; no one can take that away from them. They are sometimes calls for help, and always calls from "the unknown," but they are also at the same time calls from the wildest frontiers of our own innermost yearnings, dreams and despairs.

Each Wrong Number tells the individual dialer and recipient something about themselves, but it also tells them and us something about the larger society. What any particular Wrong Number may mean to you or me is only a tiny fraction of what Wrong Numbers as a whole mean to all of us.

In all their magnificent wrongness Wrong Numbers are the most ringing challenge to the alleged "correctness" of the entire quantitative order. They are always interruptions, but they are also *invitations* to question and rethink the "real." A small, person-to-person way of reversing the established scale of values, they point the way to the remaking of human society, from top to bottom.

In these United States, particularly—a country in which violence is routinely mistaken for bravery; authoritarian brutality for justice; literary snobbishness for poetry; hypocrisy and bigotry for honor; sycophantic conformism for freedom; and nauseating sentimentality for love—the Wrong Number signals a "new moral world," the old dream of reintegration and fulfillment come true.

Here, too, are seeds that could sprout into a new radical social movement. As a kind of unconscious chance encounter "outreach program"—open to anyone, everyone, anytime—the Wrong Number implicitly rejects the false security of selfishness, self-justification, and every form of greed, exploitation, and misery. Indeed, Wrong Numbers suggest a spontaneous collective playfulness—call and response—that resolutely embraces life, liberty, the pursuit of happiness, and the possibilities of poetry in action.

Like the world of dreams and love at first sight, the Lost City of Wrong Numbers is a maelstrom in which the shape of things to come actually comes tapping at the window.

Wrong Numbers are beyond all rational answers to *why*. They cannot be grasped by grasping. Between solitude and solidarity, they are a cloud of unknowing that knows what clouds know, and are willing to share their secrets with us.

With analogy to light the way, we can at last regard Wrong Numbers *as a whole*, and in their own internal coherence, details and all.

In proportion to our awareness of our own otherness, the future speaks in voices easily recognizable as ours as well as theirs.

And the more we swim in the ocean of analogy, the more our perception of the world assumes an almost *animistic* expansiveness, so that everything becomes *alive*, and actively related to us.

Emerging from thin air and disappearing back into it, Wrong Numbers are as solid a foundation as one could hope for.

"WHEN ONE KNOWS!" as Jacques Vaché put it in one of his *War Letters*.

Reading Wrong Numbers is a little like learning to fly.

The first step is letting go.

And so, said I to myself, *let's go!*

# 5.

# THE WITHERING AWAY OF THE STATE OF ANXIETY

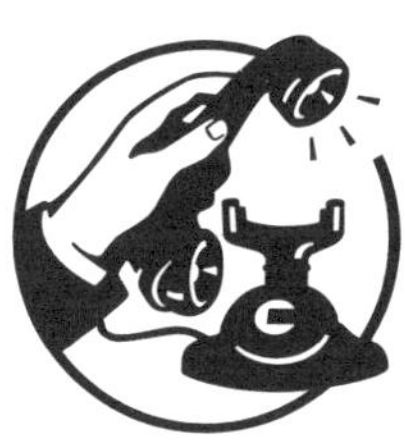

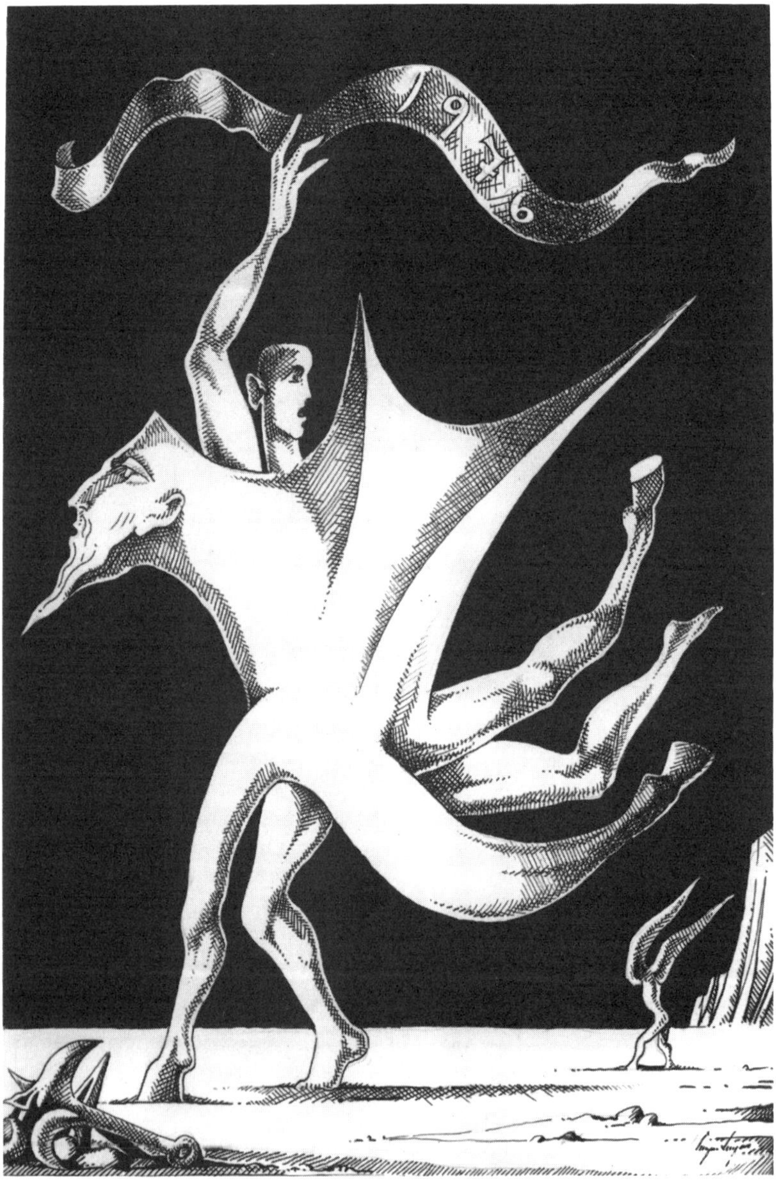

## A Wide Open Secret Society

In his *New Industrial and Societary World* (1829), Charles Fourier announced that at least a million analogies remained to be discovered. (That was twenty years before Antonio Meucci's first telephone, so the estimate clearly was much too low.) In this concluding section, I offer a modest baker's dozen plus four, each concerned with a different aspect of the Wrong Number and its social, psychological, and poetic ramifications. To these brief essays in applied analogy I have added a soapbox rant, a dream, and—instead of a conclusion—a few first principles which, for me, are also "last and always" principles.

Here, in this opening chapter—for the first time anywhere, as far as I can tell—is an analogical inquiry into the Wrong Number's *organizational* implications.

Sympathetic recipients of Wrong Numbers—the select few who actually pay attention to such calls and make no effort to suppress them from their consciousness—constitute an unusual group: a highly informal group whose "members," unaware that such a group exists, are therefore unaware of each other's existence. Far and away the most secret of all secret societies—so secret that its own adherents don't know they belong to it—it is also the freest of all free associations, based solely on spontaneous and elective affinities.

The way I see it, the "Friends of Wrong Numbers" meet the definition of a distinctive but rare variety of social organization: the *Egregore*—a word used by alchemists and other students of hermetism in the early Renaissance, and introduced into contemporary discourse by the French surrealist Pierre Mabille in 1938. Mabille defined an Egregore as "a special kind of human group endowed with a personality different from that of the individuals who form it." Such groups originate in a powerful emotive shock, embody a highly intensified consciousness, and exert an influence disproportionate to their numbers and the physical means at their disposal. P. V. Piobb, Mabille's friend and mentor in the magic arts, regarded the Egregore as a collective psychical being, a "materialization" of a group's thought as it comes to have a life of its own. This collective being assumes greater power and clarity as the group itself expands its relations to the world and acquires ever greater possibilities for action.

Among the Egregores that have changed the course of history are the German Romantics, the Young Hegelians, the New England Transcendentalists, the Chicago Anarchists of the 1880s, the founders of the Industrial Workers of the World (IWW), the Surrealist

Movement, and the world of jazz—especially bop, post-bop, and groups such as the Association for the Advancement of Creative Musicians (AACM).

As an authentic Egregore, the friendly recipients of Wrong Numbers cannot be dismissed as isolated eccentrics, for they are truly a poetic and philosophical force, exemplifying what André Breton called "the minority which is ceaselessly renewable and which acts as a lever."

Like their historic forerunners, the Friends of Wrong Numbers add up to a living and mutually reinforcing experiment in do-it-yourself utopia and anarchy—that is, a prefiguration of what is best, freest, and most exalting in the future.

In the strange not-quite-dialogues of countless pairs of unknowns, sparks of new knowledge light the way forward to a new society.

After all, as the Zohar affirms, "Words do not fall into the void."

## The Abolition of Everyday Misery

What is called everyday life is an invention of class society, and one of the worst, for it provides the social framework in which all the horrors of class society are tested and applied. The very term everyday life indicates a radical separation, for life and everyday life are clearly not the same. The old tribal societies made no such distinction. They knew *life*, and they lived. The notion of the everyday, imposed much later, signified a break with life—the setting aside of life for various activities which, taken together, offered much less than life.

The acceptance of everyday life, as such, makes further brutalization infinitely easier. In civilization as we know it, everyday life is thought of as something to be endured, a long-drawn-out ordeal of drudgery and suffering that one hopes to survive. The notion of "real" life beyond the daily grind tends to recede from consciousness. The great majority learns early to accept squalid substitutes: summer vacations, fantasies of retirement, sad projections of an afterlife.

Everyday life, then, is a product of human misery which can be said to epitomize that misery. And there is no way out short of a sweeping social transformation that would enable people *to live differently* in ways tending to resolve the contradiction between the marvelous and misery.

The abolition of everyday misery is a problem for poetry and its allies: love, humor, play, revolt, and revolution.

It is important to recognize, however, that everyday life is never monolithic. In the very contradictions it embodies we sense that a different life, many different lives, are not only possible, but actually striving for realization.

Of special urgency are the more or less isolated pockets of poetry and freedom that still persist in the world. Quietly defying the impossible, the informal networks of jazz, blues and zydeco musicians and enthusiasts; the free-spirited communities so movingly evoked in several of Les Blank's films; the growing number of people of all colors who refuse the abject protocols of "white supremacy"; the small but interconnected groups of malcontents and dissidents of all kinds who refuse to join the oppressors or to give up the struggle: All these "infrapolitical" groupings, in their own ways, are echoing and responding to David Roediger's call, in his *Towards the Abolition of Whiteness* (1994), for a "highly poetic politics"—the only kind of politics that can truly put an end to miserabilism.

Even in places where conformity is most brutally enforced—in school, prison, the armed services, the workplace, the suburbs, and large apartment complexes—rebellious outbreaks occur and recur with greater frequency than the "news" cares or dares to acknowledge. And each outbreak calls to mind the grand old dreams of Jubilee, a "New World A-Coming," of international solidarity, workingclass self-emancipation, complete equality for women, real freedom for all. Such dreams may be held in contempt by the bosses, bureaucrats, and sycophants of all countries, but that doesn't and can't prevent these dreams from rising again.

The struggle for a "poetic politics" takes place on many levels. By no means least are the small "internal disorders" of everyday life itself: outbursts of hilarity, generous gestures, impossible chance encounters, dreams that haunt one for weeks on end, fits of delirium, the unexpected discovery of authentically surrealist objects, spontaneous acts of refusal, inspired slips of the tongue, stunning coincidences that irrevocably alter the whole course of one's life.

Scandalous and exemplary, these scarcely visible individual and inward upheavals expose the rationalized rottenness of what is passed off as the "real" and "reasonable." Resistant to domestication, such exceptional disturbances cannot be "monitored." Immune to the forces of repression, they are themselves *forces of poetry* and therefore of freedom. In a multitude of ways, such mishaps revive our spirits and strengthen the anti-miserabilist cause. Extensions and reinforcements of Wrong Numbers, these parenthetical respites from the drab and dreary renew our capacity to dream, to feel, and to realize *other* impulses and other desires we didn't even know were ours. Working our way inside out from the lower depths of despair's secret hideaways, they give us recklessly new sensations of *ascent*, and inspire individual and collective motion and emotion.

Abolishing alienation, fear, and other forms of everyday misery inevitably also involves overcoming the infamous "language barrier." An audacious direct-actionist approach to this age-old problem was proposed a few years ago by the poet Gellu Naum. In one of my letters I told Naum that there were matters I was so eager to discuss with him that I was almost tempted to telephone him, despite the fact that I hardly knew a word of Romanian. On December 22, 1992, he replied:

> I assure you that if you, who do not speak Romanian, would phone me, who does not speak English, we would have the chance—in a unique moment, at two ends of the world, stuttering in languages unknown to the other—to understand each other better than ever, and also a chance of finding the solution to the problem of breaking out of Hell, at least for a moment.

Meanwhile, everywhere and at all times, the struggle against everyday misery goes on.

Some would-be revolutionists, including many who think of themselves as Marxists or anarchists, have shared a misplaced confidence that "numbers" are on their side. An old-left reflection of bourgeois positivism's exaggerated faith in the quantitative, such naivete also manifests a fear of the individual, the personal, the subjective, the exceptional. In the revolution of everyday life, however, the exceptional is the rule. Numbers count, but in transforming everyday life, Wrong Numbers count, too.

No strategy for social emancipation can afford to ignore the individual and local heartbeats of the world's topsy-turviness. The transformation of daily life spells the end of the war of each against all and the beginning of new chapters of *Mutual Aid*, *Black Reconstruction*, *Mad Love*, and *Freedom Dreams.* As far as the "everyday" is concerned, the living, breathing magic of the irreconcilably imaginary *is* the Revolution.

# The Anti-Political Anti-Economy of Misdialing

Not least of the virtues of Wrong Numbers is that they are regarded as definitively *useless*. In our acquisitive, property-obsessed society, the fact that the Wrong Number is not a marketable commodity would alone suffice to condemn it irretrievably. Wholly outside the framework of political economy, the Wrong Number can be neither bought nor sold; its utility, so to speak, is so defiantly and preposterously marginal that it remains, in strict economic terms, absolutely devoid of value. In other words, it is not convertible into cash, and therefore, in a capitalist society, it is beneath contempt.

As such, it is in good company. The use-value of Wrong Numbers is the use-value of dreams, trances, slips of the tongue, found objects, chance encounters, the sound of the sea in a shell, and indeed, of poetry itself, which, as Marx pointed out in his *Theories of Surplus Value*, is fundamentally incompatible with capitalism. Like Blake's wild flower and grain of sand, the Wrong Number remains outside, unique and priceless.

Although the Wrong Number cuts across class lines, the lion's share of such calls are doubtless worker-to-worker. Wrong Numbers therefore foster links between individual members of the producing class who otherwise have little opportunity for fraternization outside their workplaces or communities.

My own experience, moreover, indicates that working people are much more likely than others to pursue Wrong Number dialogues beyond the usual five to ten seconds.

"Chicago! I'll be damned! I wonder how *that* happened! I'm in West Virginia, tryin' to call my daughter in Texas! She's goin' to college there, and she called a while ago when I was out, so I'm callin' her back—or at least tryin' to!"

"Well, I hope you get through to her."

"Yeah, if at first you don't succeed. . . How's the weather in Chicago?"

"Oh, pretty cool today—cool for July in Chicago."

"Oh yeah? You want to see what cool is like in July, come to West Virginia sometime."

"Actually, I've been through West Virginia more than once, and I liked it. I like hills and mountains."

"Hey, if you like hills and mountains, this is the place! Myself, I never been to Chicago—don't care for big cities all that much. Anyway, I guess I should try my daughter again. Nice talkin' to ya!"

Another time, researching soapboxers at Chicago's old-time outdoor free-speech forum, Bughouse Square, I was checking a 1950s list of speakers to see whether any of the names were still in the current phone book. Out of thirty-six names, only one was listed: a woman speaker. When I dialed, it was answered by another woman of the same name—a softspoken African American who, it so happens, was quite interested in the old soapbox culture. "I remember Bughouse Square," she told me, "but I never spoke there." She recalled that "all kinds of people" spoke at the Square, "on all kinds of subjects." Although she did not remember any particular speakers by name, she emphasized that there were "a great many" of them, and that often, especially on weekends during the summer, the audience numbered in the hundreds or even more.

When I apologized for disturbing her, she said, "Oh, no, not at all, I'm very glad you called. I'm in my eighties now and I don't get many calls any more. I only wish I had more to tell you."

I thanked her and she added: "Thank *you* for calling—and good luck on your research!"

In bourgeois Wrong Numbers, such conversations just don't happen.

I am not pretending that this is what Marx and Engels meant by the watchword, "Workers of the world, unite!" It is nonetheless notable that the Wrong Number, an accidental byproduct of a technology devised, like all modern technology, to serve the exploitative needs of business and government, is also used effectively, for pleasurable purposes, by the only class capable of bringing class oppression to an end.

Chance may be an erratic organizer, but it appears to be more effective at bringing workers together, even if only on a one-to-one basis, than most others in the field today. Callers and recipients of Wrong Numbers may be unorganized, but they're out there talking, getting acquainted, and that's a good way to start. Along with singing Wobbly songs, striking on the job, and making fun of the boss, the Wrong Number can be considered one of the more playful forms of workers' self-activity.

## Nobody Here by That Name

Contemporary capitalist society is drowning in celebrities. Celebration of the overcelebrated is the ludicrous and sole theme of hundreds of glossy supermarket magazines and countless best-selling books. Celebrity worship is not only a major industry but also America's, and perhaps the world's, dominant religion.

Like other cultural commodities, celebrities are designed, manufactured, and marketed. Though little more than mannequins or robots, they are promoted and sold to a gullible public as a kind of pseudo-aristocracy. Their principal social function, of course, is to show up everyone else's alleged insignificance. Celebrities are touted as the official Somebodies: *They* perform, pose, pontificate, put in appearances, and get richer and richer in the process. All the rest of us are supposed to do is gawk at them, listen to them, applaud them, read about them, and pay for the "privilege."

The antithesis of the celebrity is the nobody—that is, everybody who is not a celebrity. And nobody epitomizes the nobody better than Nobody-Here-By-That-Name, the invisible and silent "star" of every Wrong Number.

Langston Hughes's famous line, "We're all in the telephone book," resonates with the spirit of universal solidarity. As it happens, however, most celebrities insist on *unlisted* numbers, and therefore are *not* in the book. In other words, the telephone directory—the single most consulted book of the past hundred years—is a Who's Who of Nobodies.

How often we hear it said that "It's not *what* you know but *who* you know that counts"! I would argue that the people who really count are not the few "important" and "influential" individuals we know, but rather the multitudes we *don't* know and are afraid to know: the strangers, outsiders, and nobodies whom we *might* get to know if we were not afraid of being ourselves.

It is the historic mission of the nobodies of the world to abolish their nobodiness. As each and every nobody, each in his/her own individual way, becomes the somebody he/she really is, the mass addiction to celebrities will come to an end. Only nobodies can accomplish this greatest of all revolutions. Nobody else can do it.

# A Calculus of Desirable Improbabilities

Miraculous encounters, startling coincidences, unexpected apparitions, chance discoveries, the experience of love at first sight, undreamed-of free unions of all kinds: These are the substance, shadow and vital spark of life's best, most exalted and exalting moments, the essence of all originality and invention, the root of all that we call inspiration and genius. Here in the living core of Vico's "small things which have great consequences" we trace the ceaseless patterns and rhythms in what he called the "heterogenesis of ends"—the countless cunning ways in which, as popular speech has it, "one thing leads to another."

In the discontinuous yet non-stop crisscrossings of thought and action that make up the contradictions of daily life, the clash of opposed intentions, and the oftentimes greater clash of absences of (conscious) intention are not the only contenders. For there is also the all-important factor of *randomness*, especially as it intersects with (unconscious) desire. Rationalist and *fideist* prejudices notwithstanding, actions and consequences neither planned nor foreseen seem to be what has made the world go round.

Navigators of these endlessly meandering corridors should take care, therefore, to leave behind the burden of determinism as well as the many duplicitous (*i.e.*, non-dialectical) notions of Necessity that make it even more unbearable. The truth is, verifiable knowledge in this realm is inaccessible to the deterministic inquirer. It is precisely the concept of the *aleatory*, rather than determinism, which makes human beings scientifically intelligible. Pierre Vendryès, one of the most inspired researchers in this field, posed the problem and drew the line:

> Although we are able to know, several centuries in advance, where Jupiter will be in the solar system, we are unable to know ten minutes in advance where a cabdriver will be in the city of Paris. Between the two examples, there is a fundamental difference in nature. The cabdriver is autonomous in relation to his system of reference, but the planet is not.

Vendryès was no vulgar anti-determinist; he simply recognized the narrow limits in which determinism applies. In his physiological studies, he traced the biological origins of individual autonomy—the human's ability to stand and walk, for example, and the movement of the elbow and hand. It is precisely "in acquiring autonomy in relation to the external milieu," he argues, that "the human being acquires the possibility of entering into aleatory relations with it."

No contradiction exists between Freud's scrupulously defined "psychic determinism" and Vendryès' concept of "intellectual autonomy." In Vendryès' writings, however, one discerns a strong element of utopian dreaming—in the best sense—that is rare in Freud. Perceiving the connection between humankind's physiological autonomy and our still developing intellectual and social autonomy, Vendryès also recognized the possibility that so-called chance interruptions in the existing scheme of things might turn out to be forecasts of new and more desirable schemes of things. His letters, even more than his books, reflect a sense of urgency, a conviction that his theories were not merely objectively valid, but also morally and even politically of the greatest importance as harbingers of a better world. His probabilistic speculations can easily be read as an elaboration of Fourier's vision of Universal Harmony and of the surrealist conception of *objective chance*: the astonishing occurrences in which the real and the imaginary seem to coincide perfectly, and which André Breton identified as the "center of conciliation for natural and human necessity—point of revelation, pivot of liberty." In his article, "Surrealism and Probability," published in the journal *Médium: Communication Surréaliste* in 1954, Vendryès explicitly related his scientific findings to the field of surrealist research.

The perspectives advanced by Pierre Vendryès, the man who put the Brownian Movement at the service of surrealism, bubble over with the most hilariously liberating kind of revolutionary implications.

The extent to which his expanded probability theory in turn expands the scope of the possible was brought home to me forcefully in the wake of the San Francisco Earthquake of October 1989. Concerned about our closest San Francisco friends, Philip Lamantia and Nancy Joyce Peters, Penelope and I made repeated attempts to reach them by telephone. These efforts, however, proved unavailing; a recorded message informed us that the telephone company was sorry, but because of the unusual volume of calls, ours could not go through. Day after day we were subjected to this gloomy recording. And then one morning the mail brought us a postcard from Philip and Nancy, safe and sound—in Egypt! Immediately after the earthquake, they explained, they had taken the next plane out.

That same morning's mail brought yet another surprise from afar: a parcel, sent to us by a Belgian friend of Vendryès who happened to be living in Argentina. It contained one of Vendryès's older books (Paris, 1952): *De la probabilité en histoire: l'exemple de l'expedition d'Egypte.*

A greater grasp of the implications of the aleatory, as Vendryès put it in one of the letters he wrote me, "could help humanity find the *equilibrium* it needs so absolutely."

Our relation to the Wrong Number is fundamentally aleatory, whether we like it or not. However, the more we know about the aleatory, the more we like it.

A misdialing of the phone never will abolish chance, but it can multiply its *adorability*, and therefore its *poetic use-value* in the revelation and realization of the Marvelous.

Etymologically, we do well to remember, *error* is derived from the Latin *errare*, to wander.

"To err is human" is one way of saying "wandering with freedom in mind."

*Rrose Selavy. Errors: C'est la vie. Erode slavery.* Certainly Marcel Duchamp knew that the doorway to freedom is open and closed at the same time.

In randomness lies the preservation of autonomy.

For Those Who Know, distractions are proportional to possibilities.

## Revolutionizing Time Out of Time

All Wrong Numbers are up-to-the-minute when they happen, and no matter how many one receives, they never seem to grow old. In every country of the world, the Wrong Number is still as young as it used to be. Is its agelessness a consequence of its time-annihilating nature? The question, as far as I have been able to ascertain, is not often asked. The fact remains that, since telephones began to be widely used in the late nineteenth century, Wrong Numbers have been as common as weeds, beer cans, and police corruption. In the U.S. alone, the Wrong Numbers of yesteryear must figure in the octillions or higher. Where are they now? And where are we now, especially with respect to time?

Time as we sense it—that is, time as it has been imposed upon us in the particular form of social disorder that surrounds us—is the inveterate enemy of the free spirit. Quantified, linear, homogeneous, cumulative and insatiably empty, its primary relation to living human experience is that of a devouring parasite. Robbing us of freedom and joy, time is the deadly measure of the poverty and unfreedom of life today.

By challenging the dictatorship of time, the Wrong Number intervenes in its very structure, and opens up possibilities for us to break out of the temporal prison, at least "for the moment." In every Wrong Number, the *present moment* is not only isolated but also intensified by the unexpected; while it lasts, it is the sole focus, the whole reality. Like poetry and love, the Wrong Number recognizes the present moment—the magical *now*—as the "open sesame" of freedom, the Marvelous, the fulfillment of our wildest dreams. Here, in the "now," is the starting-point for abolishing the slavery of chronology in its fetishized commodity form.

For the Gnostics, the passage and measurement of time were the surest proofs of humankind's alienation from the true life of the Eternal. In their view, reverence for the past and self-sacrificing concern for a future life were unnatural delusions that merited only laughter and scorn. Their principal self-assigned task was to rescue as many as possible from that sort of slavery.

In "our" time, in which "time is money," and money equals dead labor, time itself is dead and stifles the living. "Boredom invented the clock," Malcolm de Chazal wrote in *Sens-Plastique*, "and the clock increased boredom." What we call time is above all an ideological mechanism—a small but crucial component of the larger repressive apparatus. Clocks, timetables, schedules, the "speed-up" process, the "fast track," and related miseries are infernal devices to divide us and keep us divided. Today, under such tyranny, it is hard to regard time as anything other than a sorry symbol of our fragmentation, our *separation* from ourselves, from other human beings, from other creatures, from the entire planet, from life itself.

The Wrong Number is a call for desertion, and especially desertion from the dominant time-scheme—the sort of "time" that "keeps us from the light," as Meister Eckhart warned. But it is also a call to participate in the realization of a new collective dream, and therefore of a new collective dreamtime. Everything about it implies an attitude toward past and future based on radically different assumptions concerning time.

This desertion involves a willing suspension not of disbelief, but of belief, and first of all the belief in the rightness of what is too casually called "reality." By welcoming the unknown, breaking down frontiers, upsetting dogmas, removing straitjackets, the Wrong Number promotes originality, spontaneity, synthesis, and a politics rooted in pleasure and play.

Among much else, the Wrong Number can be considered a way of establishing reciprocal relations with a multitude of unknown other people's "heres" and "nows." However tentatively, therefore, it allows us—in the wink of an eye—to bridge the abyss that distances every individual from every other, and all of humankind from wild nature. It is, in other words, an adventure beyond time as we are used to enduring it—an aid in the apprehension of an immeasurably expanded reality whose structure is so alien to Western culture's inhibited understanding that it can be approached only by those who have experienced the most radical deconditioning, and who are prepared to rethink all of this culture's presuppositions.

In passing, Wrong Numbers offer us unscheduled flights into a *different* time—or what a latter-day Gnostic, Louis Claude de Saint-Martin, in his extraordinary book *The Crocodile* (1799), called "other forms that time could assume." It is too easily forgotten that the concept of time has changed, and changed often, and is still changing, with the passage of time. During the so-called Middle Ages, for example, when prophecy was as much a factor in the course of life as hockey and soap operas are today, "time" was not at all what it is in "our" time. In those distant times, the "present" was regarded as having taken place long ago in the "future," and the "past" was looked on as occurring right now.

Like poetry, love, play, revolt, and revolution, the Wrong Number is always an *interruption* in complacent continuity: a way of calling "Time Out" from time as we know it. What is involved here is not so much a question of "making" history as of *breaking* with it, creating new spaces and a new, liberating sense of time.

Moreover, in keeping with the principle of Poe's "Purloined Letter," the Wrong Number demonstrates that the best-hidden treasures are not secreted away in some remote corner where anyone can find them, but are left out in the open where nobody would even dream of looking for them.

In English, the most frequently used letter of the alphabet is *e*—the beginning of Eternity and the end of Time!

Starting from zero, with no help from the Operator (live or robotic), nobody knows where a Wrong Number will end. Like poetry and love, they follow a logic of their own in which one and one can add up to anything.

Beautiful as the prognostic, galloping silences, the delicious non-Euclidean horizons, and the true-blue fanatics of love who dance the night away on the edge of the world in the drawings of Artur do Cruzeiro Seixas!

## Love Above All

The supersession of a narrow, rigidly measured and one-way-only Cartesian time by an expansive, non-linear, multidirectional, post-industrial and post-historical time also involves—to use the charming term proposed in the 1940s by the Romanian surrealist Gherasim Luca—a "non-Oedipal" outlook on life and the world as well as a "non-Oedipal" sense of time. In the course of this long emancipatory process, humankind will evolve a fluid, dynamic, never-a-dull-moment *timeless present* in which time and timelessness are one and the same.

Writing in the Spring 1957 issue of *Le Surréalisme, même*, André Breton emphasized that this "new structure of time" will reveal itself only by means of "*new affective states.*" In this little-known text, titled "Magirama 1957," Breton cited several major contributions toward that development: the work of Marcel Duchamp and John W. Dunne, and the "polyvision" elaborated by film-makers Nelly Kaplan and Abel Gance. As I hope to have shown in the preceding pages, the Wrong Number is also a harbinger and progenitor of such new states.

The abolition of wage-slavery, however—and the accompanying radical decline of anxiety, fear, disappointment, depression and other consequences of class exploitation—also implies the liberation, expansion, and transformation of "traditional" affective states as well: enthusiasm, for example, and elation, and generosity, and love above all. "Our consciousness," Nicole Mitchell affirms, "evolves through love of another [and] our understanding of love has to grow as we evolve."

As cathectic energy is no longer wasted on work, making money, war, government, punishment, and other authoritarian miseries, that energy—renewed on a massive scale—will naturally turn to playful, creative, pleasurable pursuits, and the human emotions will blossom anew in many directions. "The miraculous healing power of love," invoked by the psychoanalyst Sandor Ferenczi in his *Thalassa*, applies not only to individuals but also to society as a whole. In the collective re-creation of humankind's individual and social being, there is every reason to expect that love, and lovers, will lead the way forward.

Unlike the bourgeois couple, which, as Fourier noted, tends to be a selfish, hate-filled conspiracy against everybody else, and is therefore a miserable prop of the incoherent and competitive social regime, true lovers are always a challenge to arbitrary power and all injustice, and thus a revolutionary nucleus of a free society. Embracing, as it does, "not only trust but also true knowledge and unshakeable certainty"—I am quoting Meister Eckhart—love becomes a *social force.* By creating tentative, open-ended anything-is-possible "space-times" of its own, rooted in the free play of elective affinities, true love—reciprocal, sexual, mad, and sublime—is always the active principle in anarchy at its best.

The secret—or at least one of the secrets—of this active principle is a special kind of telepathy. In his extraordinary study, *Human Personality*, F. W. H. Myers—who coined the word "telepathy"—went so far as to define love itself as "an exalted but unspecialized telepathy . . . the simplest and most universal experience of [the] mutual gravitation or kinship of spirits." All lovers know this, and it is surely in part because of this lovers' common knowledge that Luca and his friend Dolfi Trost, in their *Dialectic of Dialectic* (1945), came to recognize love as "the general revolutionary method proper to surrealism."

This highly specific telepathy—a "subliminal uprush" for two—is essentially a conscious sharing of what is already shared sur- and subconsciously. Not surprisingly, these manifestations of objective chance often assume playful forms, and are sometimes rather like games. For Penelope and me, the occurrences have always been so numerous that we long ago gave up the attempt to record them all. Some particularly striking exceptions, however, have continued to reverberate for us through the years.

Out of hundreds of examples of this reciprocal clairvoyance, here are two:

### The Multiplication of Poe

> Late at night on the10th or 11th of September 1976, after reading several pages of *The Complete Tales and Poems of Edgar Allen Poe*, I made a few notes, among them the cryptic phrase: "the multiplication of Poe." The words puzzled me, but my mind's eye looked out on a vast expanse in which a greatly enlarged photograph of Poe appeared in a hundred places.
>
> The following morning, Penelope and I happened to be reading different volumes by Poe. As I laid my book aside, Penelope quite spontaneously remarked that some of Poe's stories were so unlike the others that they almost seem to have been written by different people, "or perhaps there was more than one Poe." When I mentioned "the multiplication of Poe," we both laughed.
>
> Late that same day we decided to go for a ride in the country, and set out for Lake County, some fifty miles or so northwest of Chicago. We had not been out there for over a year, perhaps two, and we were surprised to be confronted by something new on the horizon: Protruding from the fields on all sides, mile after mile,

were dozens of large signs bearing the words POE & POE. The fact that these names signified a local real estate agency did not diminish the impact of these multiplied Poes.

### Playing While Dreaming

As lovers have done since long before time began, Penelope and I often start the day by telling each other our dreams. On the 24th of May, 1989, I awakened with a clear memory of a dream in which I announced that an "urn full of ashes" was a near-homonym of "Earn, fool! Love cash!"—and that together these two four-word phrases were a perfect symbol and motto of contemporary capitalist society.

Penelope, meanwhile, had dreamed a new proverb: "You can study Berkeley at Berkeley, but you have to study Hume at home."

Side by side in deepest slumber, each of us had engaged in humorous word-play—word-play with political and/or philosophical implications.

In the language of sleep, words dream and dreams speak. And isn't waking up with word-dreams a good way of staying in dreamland a little longer?

Such experiences—and the lives of all lovers are full of them—seem to me to be psychical flights to what Malcolm de Chazal called the "land of innocence"—refreshing escapes from chores, stress, news, social obligations, and other "business." I am convinced that these leaps beyond the ordinary hold the secrets of the universe and the keys to utopia. It simply won't do to make light of them as foolish or childish. William Blake insisted that "The fool who persists in his folly shall become wise." And André Breton declared in the first *Surrealist Manifesto* that "It is perhaps childhood that comes closest to 'real life.'" These burning truths from out of the past are still burning brightly today.

"All the same! All the same!" cried Jacques Vaché.

## The Call of the Wild

Can a society gone hopelessly wrong be righted by the right use of Wrong Numbers? The answer, of course, is no, but an appreciation of Wrong Numbers and their multifarious implications can help us take a fresh look at our corrupt, polluted, unfree, overmanaged, and overpopulated society, and thus could also help us create a truly free society—a society worth living in.

Appreciation of Wrong Numbers would not only expand people's awareness of their own autonomy and solidarity, but also, by natural extension, could be expected to awaken in them a sense of how *urgent* it is to establish new relations with other individuals—including total strangers—and the entire larger society as well as with the other animals and the planet we share with them.

In the degraded state of affairs known as "social reality" today, animals are living, breathing, visible Wrong Numbers. Their very being contradicts and blows away the most cherished rules and assumptions of our civilization. Animals are not at home in any Western philosophical system. They have no place of their own in the virtual mirage known as "the American Way of Life." At best they are pets, or performers to be viewed in the circus-ring or behind bars at the zoo, or colorful pin-ups on glossy "nature" calendars. More typically, alas, they are food, or articles of apparel, or victims of torture by the pharmaceutical and cosmetic industries, or "problems" to be "dealt with" by fiendish "Animal Control Units."

Symbolically, animals—especially wild animals—are the *furthest outside* of all that is outside our hyperurbanized culture. For most people, they have only the vaguest sort of "presence"—fleeting, disturbing, scary, distant. In truth, though few humans seem to be aware of it, animals are infinitely precious—to all of us and to the world.

Knowing what the wild creatures of the Earth want and need should help us solve the riddle of what humankind wants and needs, for a world worth living in is a world in which happiness is possible for animals, too. Every emancipatory movement today needs not only the preservation of wilderness, but the *expansion* of wilderness.

As I see it and hear it, Wrong Numbers constitute a kind of imaginal flyway between a technology in disarray and the wild places of the Earth. In this non-dimensional space, surrounded by doors that might well be death's, we realize the acute precariousness of all and everything.

I don't know if I am a voice crying in the wilderness but I know that the wilderness is crying in my voice.

To work wonders, the imagination must be left to its own devices. I envision the playful science of Wrong Numbers as part of a larger science of neglected phenomena of all kinds, and more particularly of the neglected relations between neglected phenomena. Assisting in the recovery of lost or suppressed emotions, the discovery of new emotions, awakening the mind's latent powers, and stimulating other forms of research in which poetry and science work hand in hand, this ecology of the disregarded is in turn the front door of the ecology of the Marvelous.

Unless it is rooted in the practice of poetry—the experience of the "outside" *from within*—even the deepest "deep ecology" barely scratches the surface.

Surely the ludic process by which one human imagination responds imaginatively to another—a process which, during life's most exalting moments, enables masses of people to surge forth in grand, joyous, free-spirited festivals of all kinds—provides the soundest basis for a new human community which, true to the promise of poetry, would be thoroughly non-exploitative and therefore non-anthropocentric as well.

Isn't it obvious that if people were not forced to "earn" (?) a "living" (?) *via* the meaningless degradation called work, they would have all the time they need for admiring snowflakes, walking in the woods, climbing mountains, and getting to know their bird, mammal, reptile, and insect neighbors?

As a single leaf profiles the whole tree of which it is a part, so too the Wrong Number, a leaf from the tree of knowledge, profiles our society's contradictions and possibilities.

Certainly it is high time to realize that the reality we've been dialing is no longer in service—or rather, that the "service" it pretends to render is harmful to life on this planet.

## Revolution as Play

Every Wrong Number is a problem encounter. It poses the question "What is to be done?" in the most immediate personal terms, for the Voice of the Unknown is not speaking to anyone else but the recipient. Curiously, instead of accepting this experience as a welcome stimulus to imaginative spontaneity—an invitation to join the game—it is scorned as an unpleasant occurrence. The explanation lies less in the particular phenomenon of the Wrong Number itself than in a more generalized phenomenon, of which antipathy to Wrong Numbers may be considered a part: *the fear of play*.

All children know what play is without having to look it up in the dictionary, but adults have a much harder time with it. In most people the sense of play seems to fade away long before high school. Those in power regard knocking play down as a prerequisite of growing up. In advanced industrial or postindustrial society, "responsible adults" are those who obey the biblical injunction to put "childish things" behind them.

No country in the world is as playless as the United States, and this stark playlessness is surely at the root of the deadly, aggressive cynicism which defines the sewerlike moral climate of late capitalism. And nowhere is the fear and loathing of play more horrifyingly evident than in the apalling industry known as sports.

Contrary to widespread misconception, sports are not forms of "organized" play, for nothing of the spirit of play survives in these highly aggressive, super-authoritarian and hypercommercialized corporate-bureaucratic gladiatorial spectacles. Sports in our time have even less connection with play than wage-slavery has with non-alienated labor. The so-called "players," in any case, are decidedly secondary, for sports are above all *competitive performances for spectators*. Today's athletic performances, wrongly called games, are basically fast-moving images symbolic of the permanent war economy, specially packaged in huge arenas for the most satiated and therefore most frustrated consumers on Earth. One of the most addictive forms of Capital's increasing domination of leisure, sports are the biggest and most dangerous drug on the market.

Also antithetical to play are ninety-nine percent of what is called play in U.S. schools, and by far the larger part of the activities imposed on children in the dreary playgrounds of metropolitan parks, those mini-gulags for tots. As for video and computer games, I won't even bother to comment.

In bright contrast, real play is not only a way of using up surplus energy, or a means of amusement, or an escape from reality—it is one of life's most exhilarating, pleasurable, self-developing and liberating experiences. The essence of play is *the creation of imaginary situations and active participation in them*. Spontaneous, collective, unselfconscious, dynamic, unconventional, non-competitive, uninhibited and wildly adventurous, play is a consciousness-expanding *initiation* into a real community, the vital *process* by which individuals become truly *social.*

Neva Leona Boyd was one of the outstanding theorists of play. A co-worker of Jane Addams at Chicago's Hull-House in the 1910s, she was a quiet, unpretentious individual who avoided the limelight. Her radical theory and practice, however, became highly influential through her students. Pearl Pachaco Williams, founder of the African American "little theater" movement in Chicago, acknowledged Boyd as a major inspiration. Boyd also inspired Viola Spolin's *Improvisations for the Theater*, which in turn prompted the formation of the Compass Players, Second City, and the whole still-burgeoning movement of "improv" comedy.

Boyd regarded play as "a vacation from one's everyday life," an imaginary trip as far as possible from monotony and regimentation. In her view, true play always releases the repressed elements of one's self, and is thus a natural antidote for debilitating routine: work, sports, school, church, and other morbid and alienating chores. Play, as she conceived it, is collective improvisation—a pleasurable activity in which strain and conflict are dissolved, and heretofore unknown potentialities are set free. Creative and therapeutic, play is the withering away of the state of anxiety, and therefore the best form of social education. Free play also provides the only firm basis for an eros-affirmative morality, and the most stimulating environment for creative and intellectual originality.

Although Boyd does not appear to have identified herself with the revolutionary movement, the implications of her theory and practice of play are unmistakably anarchist, and there is more than a slight touch of surrealism in them as well. The emancipation of play, as she describes it, seems to me to be synonymous with the realization of the dream of the global "festival of the oppressed" known as Revolution.

The emancipation of play, of course, can be accomplished only by players themselves. Our task, then, is clear: to overcome, by any means necessary, that fear of play which prevents the workers of the world from being players, *i.e.*, revolutionists.

Clearly Wrong Numbers have been given to humankind to make surrealist use of them—and that means first of all to *play* with them, to see how they fit into the story we happen to be telling ourselves when the Wrong Number arrives, and then to see what possibilities open up.

It was through play that my own perception of Wrong Numbers began to deviate more and more radically from the long-entrenched norm. Regarding these calls playfully, and then—albeit tentatively at first—actually playing *with* them, I found that I could no longer think of them as pestiferous interruptions, but rather as chance meetings that could, from time to time, lead to "interesting things." The more I played, the more I discovered, the more I wanted to play. My experiences led directly to my attempt at a systematic study, which in turn suggested the larger project: to rehabilitate the Wrong Number in public opinion—or more specifically: *to render Wrong Numbers attractive*. Strategically, accenting the creative and emancipatory potential of Wrong Numbers seems to be the surest step toward enlisting their aid, first in the general provoking of inspiration, then in the radical redefinition of the relations between poetry and everyday life, and henceforth in the solution of the fundamental problems of human existence.

I was encouraged to find that the alchemists of old considered play to be an essential symbolic phase in the elaboration of the Great Work. In Elias Ashmole's *Theatrum Chemicum Britannicum* (1652) we read:

> This very place is called by many names,
> As *Imbibition, Feeding, Sublimation,*
> *Clyming high Mountaines,* also *Children's Games;*
> and rightly it is termed *Exaltation.*

I was also charmed to learn that Neva Boyd described her own life's work with children in unmistakably alchemical terms: "If play is thought of as comparable to the irradiance of a brilliant jewel it will be given a truer interpretation than were a [formal] definition attempted."

With a tip of the hat to the alchemist Fulcanelli, explicator of "phonetic cabala," we can follow the transmutation of the Wrong Number from a simple *nuisance* into a veritable complex of unanticipated *nuances* which, in turn, evolve into an excitingly *new sense* of things and life, and at last into a playful *new science* of transforming the world.

"Kid stuff"? Yes, but it is also the Wisdom of the Ancients, restored and revised. The Wrong Number may open with "Hello" and close with a *click*, but it is a New Pearl of Great Price all the same.

# For a Free Society

One of the most unfortunate but also most deeply entrenched prejudices of what passes for Marxism today is its contempt and scorn for utopias and utopian thought. Karl Marx's admiration for the work of Charles Fourier was close to boundless, but in this as in so many other respects, the "Marxist" tradition has rejected Marx's emancipatory vision. In the Marxist vocabulary—as in the vocabulary of the Far Right and the liberal Center—"utopian" is always a pejorative; its synonyms include naive, chimerical, ridiculous, crazy, and impossible.

Even those who concede utopianism a place in history or literature tend to insist that it is strictly obsolete, without any possible application today, least of all in the U.S.

And yet, everyone who has given even five minutes' thought to the matter knows that the United States, despite its loud proclamations of "liberty and justice for all," is truly a land of large-scale unfreedom and injustice. White supremacist terror, genocide, ecocide, class oppression, androcentrism, homophobia, and xenophobia are glaring factors in the "American Way of Life."

How, then, can anyone pretend that utopian dreaming is obsolete?

The possibility that some other nations might be even worse is hardly consoling, and in any case is quite beside the point. During the Cold War, when the USSR was the official Number One Enemy of the U.S., an interviewer once tried to get Nelson Algren to agree that the U.S. was "more of an open society than Russia." Algren replied: "It's as though I were in a flood in Mississippi and the water is up to my waist and you're saying, 'It really isn't serious, because there are people who are drowning in the Volga.'"

A merciless critic of capitalist corruption and misery, Algren was also a utopian dreamer.

To "maintain order" in conditions of unfreedom and injustice requires a vast *system of alienation* to keep people divided, atomized, exploited, misinformed, manipulated, unequal, and at each other's throats. As my old friend Tyrone once put it: "I guess we're all trying to do the best we can—in the worst way."

Just about anywhere you look today, you can see hideous manifestations of the toxic garbage-heap of ideologies known as miserabilism. The tragic betrayal of the promise of childhood; an ever-escalating war on sleep and dreams; an all-pervasive self-destructive self-centeredness; an overweening lack of consideration for others—these are just a few symptoms of the disastrous "unconnectedness" that defines what we like to call our "communities."

Is anyone out there still pretending that utopian dreaming—dreaming of a free society—is obsolete?

No one has expressed more forcefully than Robin D. G. Kelley the vital need for this kind of revolutionary freedom-dreaming, here and *now*:

> Now more than ever, we need the strength to love and to dream. . . . Call me utopian, but I inherited my mother's belief that the map to a new world is in the imagination. . . . The conditions and very existence of social movements enable participants to imagine something different, to realize that things need not always be this way. It is *that* imagination, that effort to see the future in the present, that I call "poetry" or "poetic knowledge." . . . Now is the time to think like poets, to envision and to make visible a new society, a peaceful, cooperative, loving world without poverty and oppression, limited only by our imaginations.

As Kelley goes on to argue, such dreaming is not only very much "on the agenda," but truly a matter of life-and-death urgency for all of us.

What is the role of the Wrong Number in all this? Typically, it plays many roles simultaneously. In the face of a massive repressive system, the Wrong Number is a loose screw, an endless series of loose screws: a constantly recurring sign and signal that something is very wrong, that the system itself is out of whack.

But it is also, as we have seen, a multi-faceted symbol: a symbol of the desire to talk to someone different, a stranger—and by extension, a symbol of the universal longing for a larger solidarity, a utopia.

Wrong Numbers, moreover, automatically disregard all racial, ethnic, class, and gender prejudice and discrimination. They transcend the barriers of language, nationality, and age. The Wrong Number asks for no papers, demands no passport, checks no fingerprints, examines no I.D., cares not at all about skin-color, religious affiliation, sexual orientation, marital status, or condition of previous servitude. In a society characterized by extreme authoritarianism, injustice, bureaucracy and brutality, the Wrong Number is a bastion of innocence, anarchy, equality and nonviolence.

For many, the Wrong Number offers what is probably the only occasion in which courteous words are exchanged with people they hate or fear in "real" life. The Wrong Number is open-ended and all-inclusive: Who you dial is who you get.

In view of this universality, and in the light of Pierre Vendryès' *rapprochement* of surrealism and probability theory, it is not hard to perceive the kernel of surrational historic truth in the husk of the irrational and the accidental. Each Wrong Number regarded separately may appear meaningless and inconsequential. Viewed collectively, however, the message of Wrong Numbers is unmistakable and momentous. The revelation of this message—that *everyone in the world is trying to enter into aleatory relations with everyone else*—is truly a world-historical event. It signifies that the Wrong Number—far from being nothing but a mere nuisance—is in truth a unique unifying force, drawing together throngs of isolated individuals whose chief point in common is that they share a desire to talk to *Someone Else*. The great majority never would have had the chance to encounter each other were it not for the materialist miracle known as misdialing.

In the underground railroad of unconscious desire, the Wrong Number has turned out to be one of the most persistently effective conductors. As an undisputed master in the art of escaping through the cracks in the miserabilist system, the Wrong Number—along with its staunch allies, poetry and imagination—also helps multiply and enlarge these cracks so that others can escape through them, too, in ever greater numbers. Sooner or later, when the cracks become large enough, and numerous enough, the whole rigid wall of enforced alienation will crumble and fall, and each and all of us will be able to wander freely and do as we please.

Wrong Numbers, even the least of them, can help us dream of a "poetic politics." The best of them, however—the rare exceptions in which the insurgent imagination is uppermost throughout—project the goal of such a politics: the revolutionary transformation of several existing orders at the same time. For a Wrong Number is at once a disruptor of slavish routine, a stimulator of the (often latent) passion for diversity, difference and change (Fourier's *papillon* or Butterfly Passion), a receiver/transmitter of the magic phrases of objective chance, and a relentless agitator for an altogether different way of life rooted in love, freedom, poetry and play.

If "every little bit helps,"the Wrong Number is certainly doing its share!

Working in tandem, these diverse passions and energies may keep the mind's compass spinning for a long time, but in the end it always points to the Wrong Number's own carnivalesque version of that happy land, far, far away, where talking to strangers is a way of life, both night and day.

Building a new society in the Wrong Numbers of the old!

## Getting Nowhere Fast

As individuals, we naturally think of the Wrong Number as an individual experience, which it *is*, of course—but we too easily forget that it is also more than that: *much* more.

At any given moment countless millions of Wrong Numbers are taking place throughout the world. Wherever telephones exist, Wrong Numbers pullulate like honeybees in spring. Although no records are kept of such matters, it can be stated with certainty that every telephone user in the world is a dialer and receiver of Wrong Numbers.

The Wrong Number is therefore a *mass* phenomenon of stupendous proportions. Its impact and implications are truly *global* in scope.

As a transworld communications medium, the Wrong Number stands out—far out. All other global media are primarily used to sell commodities and spread propaganda. The Wrong Number is wonderfully free of such poisonous additives.

Unlike other media, it does not pretend to be informative, to report news, to predict the weather, to entertain us, to make us rich, or to help us in any way. It is as *radically unassuming* as a force of nature or the piece of paper I am writing on. The Wrong Number promises no salvation, offers no advice, sends no regrets, steers as clear of the absolute as of nothingness, accepts no consensus, awards no prizes, refuses to argue, has no proclamations to set forth, no positions to defend, no prejudices to uphold.

All other global media, moreover (and most national and local media), are multibillion-dollar industries run by bloated bureaucracies, shielded from the great mass of humankind by a thick web of security systems, and completely closed off to any direct involvement on the part of "the audience," who are thereby reduced to helpless passivity. The Wrong Number, in contrast, is a kind of renegade offshoot of the so-called telephone "service," an industry as bad as the others with this single happy difference: its bureaucrats and security officers are far too preoccupied with other matters to pay even the smallest attention to anything as absurd and trivial as Wrong Numbers.

Technically speaking, the Wrong Number simply provides occasions for billions of people to say whatever they want to say to billions of others—strangers, with whom they have never had a chance to talk before. As a mere accident, the Wrong Number is completely out of control: thoroughly decentralized, anti-hierarchical, uncensored, and open all day every day of the year.

Doesn't this tell us something about Wrong Numbers? Or is it simply a way of getting nowhere fast?

I answer *yes* to both questions, and hasten to add that getting nowhere fast also tells us something.

*Getting nowhere fast* is in fact a phrase commonly used to dismiss Wrong Numbers:

"Did you get through to So-and-so?"

"No, I'm getting nowhere fast. I keep getting a Wrong Number."

But *getting nowhere fast* is also another way of saying *a quick trip to utopia*. (The word *utopia* signifies *nowhere.*)

In using those words to wave Wrong Numbers away, people have been telling us more than they knew.

In the bright glare of this *nowhere* (which we are able to visit—or perhaps I should say: *which visits us*—only a few minutes a week), the Wrong Number appears as a kind of free territory, affording each and all of its participants momentary respite from the exploitative and totalitarian values that dominate the society we live in.

In short, Wrong Numbers—analogically speaking—are *glimpses* or *prefigurations* of a highly mobile, spur-of-the-moment, let's-go utopia inhabited entirely by total strangers, whose cumulative sense of the precariousness and interdependence of all life seems ready and willing to become the basis of a new global awareness and a new way of living.

## A Revolving Door on Utopia

As a kaleidoscope is turned, the larger pieces usually fall into place first, soon followed by a few of the smaller pieces, and then, quickly, by all the others, thereby forming a new, coherent pattern. It is not impossible, however, or even rare, for a seemingly modest change in the arrangement of several smaller pieces to provoke an overall transformation of image. It was precisely for such reasons, no doubt, that its inventor, Henry Brewster, regarded it as an eminently *philosophical* instrument.

No less philosophical is the curiously overlooked telephonic variant of the kaleidoscope known as the Wrong Number, whose ceaselessly changing fragments of messages arrange themselves into potentially infinite patterns that play upon the mind's ear with compelling verve and fascination. As a provoker of inspiration and fomenter of poetic *détournement*, it is always ready: a trick-or-treat bag of subversive moments waiting to happen.

By interrupting and in effect ridiculing and overthrowing (momentarily) the placidity of *what is*, the Wrong Number conjures up a sense of *what is not*, either retrospectively via memory, or prospectively, via the imagination. Its ritual questions therefore convey suggestions or implications that are not necessarily negated in the ritual replies. Like poetry and dream, the Wrong Number urges us to take *no* for a question. It sets the mind wandering in regions where, only a moment before, it had no intention of going. It automatically asks, "What next?" and hints seductively at the infinite vistas of the "could be." Wholly free of aesthetic or moralistic constraints, it liberates wonder and takes pleasure in defying the impossible. Challenging the restrictions ordinarily placed on the free play of human feelings, and of the imagination and critical faculties as well, it creates secret mental spaces—mobile hideouts for idle dreamers to rev up their idle dreams. As these infinitesimal Trojan Seahorses of the imaginary slowly impose themselves on "real" life, images of *another* life—a *desirable* life—engage the mind.

Implicit in this mass of small changes is a vast social and spiritual transformation, long ago projected—in their very different but persistently esoteric ways—by utopians (Charles Fourier, Saint-Simon, Flora Tristan, Edward Bellamy), occultists (Fabre d'Olivet, Saint-Yves d'Alveydre, Paschal B. Randolph, the Sâr Péladan), poets (Friedrich Schiller, Blake, Shelley, Isidore Ducasse, Saint-Pol-Roux, Vachel Lindsay), and, by no means least, the philosopher Hoene Wronski in his visionary, neo-Gnostic variant of Hegelian idealism. Wronski's goal of nothing less than the "absolute reform of human knowledge" is particularly interesting in the light of Wrong Numbers, for Wronski was himself a mathematician, and numbers, in great profusion—along with an ironically adversarial attitude toward chance—are central to his intricate "dialectic of heterogeneity," with its "trichotomy of the absolute" and "21 problems of the 7 fundamental realities."

Wronski's "messianic" metapolitical project—which had nothing to do with a Messiah, and abjured the formation of a cult—was posited on his recognition of a rising global consciousness, and his exuberant certainty of future splendor for all. Starting with the collective supersession of the contradiction between knowledge and action, his program, as he saw it, led directly to the spontaneous realization of "Absolute Philosophy on Earth" by an inspired and united humankind in the pleasant process of actively and consciously creating itself anew.

To confront the problems raised by Wrong Numbers is thus to step forward, backward, and sideways into a revolving door on utopia—or rather, on an incalculable number of utopias old and new.

Affectively originating from "no-one-knows-where" (as it inevitably appears to the recipient), such calls invite us to a wide variety of imaginary elsewheres. In our psychic geography, these split-second elsewheres are worthy analogues of the Japanese surrealist poet Shuzo Takiguchi's "split-second dreams." Far from the walled-in fortresses of the Reality Principle's instrumental reason, they point to the anarchic vistas of wish-fulfilling revery.

The silence after the click is not only the silence of a collapsing civilization, but also the pre-dawn silence of something better to come.

Dancers in the ruins cast long shadows, edged with a ring of flame.

## Anticipatory Echoes of the Repoetic

*The Repoetic* by Saint-Pol-Roux is the most extravagantly marvelous of all utopias. Written by a poet, it is in fact a utopia founded on poetry. It is Saint-Pol-Roux's warm response to, and vigorous correction of, Plato's cold-hearted *Republic*. The contrast between the two books could hardy be greater. All poets are rigorously excluded from Plato's prosaic, highly formal, and utterly authoritarian Republic (*res publico*). In Saint-Pol-Roux's all-inclusive and free-wheeling Repoetic (*res poetica*), all are poets.

Saint-Pol-Roux portrays a global and universal transformation, at once individual, social, biological, and cosmic. He is less interested in minor details of social structure than in the boundless creative energy of the unfettered imagination and the sheer splendor of collective life in the new conditions of Universal Harmony and freedom for all. Repoetican society, a lyrical development of Lautréamont's call for "poetry made by all," exemplifies surrealism's fundamental aspiration: *The realization of poetry in everyday life.*

In the Repoetic, poetry is no longer marginalized and debased by the enemies of poetry and their watchdogs, the false poets. On the contrary, poetry has become the wellspring, groundwork, vital center and crowning glory of all social life. Here Saint-Pol-Roux has provided the sequel to Vico's *Scienza Nuova*: Just as all humankind were poets throughout prehistory, all will be poets again in the posthistoric Repoetic.

For Saint-Pol-Roux, this radical repoeticization of life and the planet is both a natural *evolution* (*à la* Fourier), but also a *revolution*—the dialectical supersession of both civilization and History, enabling humankind at last to live in harmony with itself and Nature. War, exploitation, wage-slavery, and all other forms of human misery have therefore become impossible, for they are incompatible with poetry. The contemporary poet's task, in Saint-Pol-Roux's view, is to recognize words as living creatures, and to liberate them from the captivity of dictionaries and paralyzing prose. The way to the Repoetic is prepared by poetry, by the *activity* of poets. The process begins by developing an expanding *sense* of poetry—that is, a revolutionary poetic awareness in which action and imagination are one and the same—in ourselves and others.

*The Repoetic* draws on the works of Fourier, Hegel, Villiers de l'Isle-Adam, and on Saint-Pol-Roux's own rich experience in the vigorous anarchist and Symbolist movements in France in the 1890s. Above all it is the inspired outcome of the poet's resolutely poetic life. Saint-Pol-Roux is truly one of the supreme poets. He may be less well known than Nerval, Lautréamont, Rimbaud, Jarry, and Corbière, but he is one of their company. André Breton saluted him in 1925 as "the Master of the Image," and added: "Among the living, he is the sole precursor" of the surrealist revolution.

For true poets, according to Saint-Pol-Roux, the Repoetic is not a project to be realized in a distant future—it is always near at hand. No detailed description of it is possible, but for those who know what it's all about, it's *there*.

Please make a note of it.

## A Community of Perfect Strangers

"Tell me the person's strongest resistance," poet Jean Toomer wrote in his *Essentials*, "and I will tell you what he most wants."

Obviously the extreme resistance to Wrong Numbers, the utter scorn most people profess for them, are all out of proportion to the small amount of time they consume in a person's life, and to any and all of their other alleged "inconveniences."

It is equally obvious that the prevailing antagonism to Wrong Numbers conceals a powerful but repressed desire for a new and deliciously different society—*a community without borders or boredom*, and with equal rights for the unexpected. In this unconsciously desired community, it would be possible for anyone and everyone to talk to strangers all they liked. In the pejorative sense that the term is currently used, however, "strangers" as such would no longer exist, for all individuals everywhere would recognize each other as active participants (including those who prefer to regard themselves as nonparticipants) in the world community. "Strangeness" would remain, but no longer would it evoke fear or mistrust; on the contrary, in the new community it would be regarded as the most attractive of all qualities. Each person would be free to cultivate her/his originality in conditions of complete freedom, which would naturally encourage the most uninhibited nonconformity and eccentricity.

Such a community would involve nothing less than the supersession of everyday life as we know it.

It is also necessary to recognize that hatred of Wrong Numbers is a form of self-hatred. To cite Jean Toomer again: "Whatever stands between you and that person stands between you and yourself." This self-hatred can be overcome only by the self-realization of the strangers and outsiders within ourselves, which in turn requires freeing ourselves of whatever it is that makes us surrender to everyday misery. These may seem to be immense and even impossible aims, and perhaps they are—but compared to them, isn't everything else hopeless and inane?

At this point in history, the impossible seems to be the least we can demand of each other.

And that is precisely where poetry comes in. Only by multiplying the occasions in which poetry can infiltrate the large and small affairs of life can we begin to dismantle the miserabilist apparatus, thereby showing people that the gratification of their heart's desire is not as impossible as the self-appointed managers of Public Opinion want us to believe.

Our task, then—or rather, our pleasure—is to recharge the intellectual/spiritual atmosphere with poetic expectation, to raise the stakes in the repoeticization of life: in short, to *live* the Repoetic.

## Emancipation of the Senses

The freedom of the senses is the secret of all freedom, and as long as any sense is enslaved, none can be truly free. When something appears to make no sense, or to be "senseless," it often turns out to be the senses themselves—or the way our sense perceptions are structured, socially, psychologically, and politically—that need to be questioned.

During the past two hundred years, all through the Industrial Revolution and its techno-terrorist sequels, our senses have been invaded, insulted, and injured as never before. No wonder, then, that all our senses are (at least temporarily) out of order. That is why so large a portion of the world's population, especially in "civilized" societies, are afraid to rise from the well-cushioned coffins of convention and to see, hear, smell and touch the world for themselves.

Such is the plight of the senses in the age of mechanical and electronic reproduction. Each and every sense has repeatedly been subjected to all forms of abuse, including torture. Our natural sensory responses have been denatured, artificialized, imprisoned, exiled and otherwise disgraced. What remains are largely weak imitations, superficial, hollow, contrived.

One of the most delectable things about Wrong Numbers is that there is nothing contrived about them. Their absurd technological origin does not in the least demean their genuinely *wild* simplicity. Spontaneous, unaffected, direct, they are full of resources capable of enhancing, in their peculiar way, the pleasure of being—definitely including the pleasure of the senses.

Wrong Numbers first of all involve hearing, but hearing in such a way that seeing is also brought into play. Writ large, they allow us to see things not only from a new angle, but also in a new light, and even *with new eyes,* as when one is introduced to the marvels of peering through a microscope or telescope—or better yet, as Leonora Carrington has urged, through both simultaneously.

In a sense, or rather in two senses, it's a question of learning to see and hear *as if for the first time*. But there's more here than meets the eye and ear, for the Wrong Number, like any other phone call, also involves the sense of touch: the dialing fingertip, the phone gripped in one's hand, the earpiece pressed to the side of one's head. As an introduction to the senses' division of labor in its most troubling form, the Wrong Number makes us wonder how much Gustave Moreau might have recognized himself in the work of Thelonious Monk, and vice versa. Even while dialing, one part of you listens to the ringing while another part sees—anticipatorily—the person you think you are calling.

But what do you see when Someone Else, someone unknown, answers?

What you see in this case is not what you get; as a sensory experience, the Wrong Number is often little more than an introduction to disillusionment. Each call confronts us point-blank with the harrowing disparity between the little we know and the vastness we don't know, between reality and desire, between the familiar and the faceless. This is not what is known as sensory deprivation, but surely it involves sensory trickery, misdirection and deception.

Once in a blue moon, the few words spoken conjure dreams no disembodied voice ever let us dream before, and conquer the barrier of distance that "normally"—as is strangely said of everyday affairs in our utterly abnormal society—separates individuals. As if from nowhere, a *warm current* suddenly rises between two strangers, melting the frigid zone and carrying them along on a moment's voyage of mutual discovery. Transcending the redoubtable isolation that defines life in the age of commodities, such moments re-establish the direct, intimate, personal acquaintance with the world that children know, but which tragically disappears in the course of maturation.

Paradoxically, by disengaging people from their previous engagements, the Wrong Number is a way of *making connections*—radically *other* connections. Rimbaud's famous "systematic derangement of the senses" was a strategy designed to disrupt a sensory apparatus that had already been deranged by civilized domestication. Rimbaud's aim was not to exacerbate the existing derangement but to counter it by shifting the terrain. His "derangement," which sabotages not the senses themselves but the way they are manipulated by an exploitative order, is a kind of walkout, a strike, or an insurrection of the senses. Restoring their freedom to roam and to do as they please, it is rather like the Wrong Number itself—a step toward *reintegration*.

Moreover, as a collision of contradictory expectations, the Wrong Number at its wildest and most exhilarating has a powerful ricocheting effect. Wrong Numbers derail trains of thought, capture attention, talk their way into dreams, infiltrate moments devoted to brooding, run roughshod over revery, and hide out in the remotest outposts of memory, ready to spring forth at any moment, with or without the drop of a hat. They can snowball from whim to obsession in five moves or six. Like other unsettling episodes of daily life—especially those involving acute anxiety, lightmindedness, or love, or some combination of all three—Wrong Numbers can help rearrange our relationships as individuals to other individuals, known and unknown, and can make the unknown, and even the Unknown, a little less forbidding.

The emancipation of the senses must be the work—or rather the play—of the senses themselves, but it can be jump-started by love, revolt, or the right Wrong Number. After all, the sense of poetry has deep affinities with the sense of humor. Indeed, the former includes the latter, as it includes, refines, magnifies, multiplies and liberates all the senses.

As entirely new aspects of being and things start presenting themselves to our reawakened senses, everything begins to look, sound, smell and feel completely different. Radically altering our approach, or trying two or more approaches at once, the whole scene changes. Unforeseen and invigorating ways of re-examining the seemingly ordinary—*i.e.*, the overlooked and ignored—will make everyone realize how extraordinary everything really is.

Meanwhile, each and every one of our senses has nothing to lose, and everything to gain, from a good shower in the cold water of Wrong Numbers.

## Outsiders' International

Many of us, at one time or another, have gone fishing for the future, but how many realize that the future also goes fishing for us? The practice of poetry alone enables us to confront this basic human problem.

Like life itself, Wrong Numbers are not only stranger than fiction, but are in fact full of living, breathing strangers. It would not be going too far to say that strangers are the *sine qua non* of Wrong Numbers. By definition, you don't know who they are, but you can't have a Wrong Number without them.

If a Wrong Number without strangers is next to impossible, strangers without Wrong Numbers tend to be hopelessly sad figures, cut off from one of the rare opportunities by which they can freely interact with other strangers without the psychically and otherwise damaging intermediaries of alcohol, the army, church or prison.

What is to be done?

Look at it this way: In Wrong Numbers, people you've never

met have a chance, or at least half a chance, to meet you half way. Isn't the next step to try to create the conditions in which you can meet them all the way?

In the popular 1950s movie, *Invasion of the Body Snatchers*, which still tells us so much about everyday life in the U.S. today, one's best friends are found to be fearsome strangers, enemy aliens from "outside." The revolution hinted at in Wrong Numbers suggests just the opposite: a community in which perfect strangers turn out to be our best friends.

"A friendly stranger," T-Bone Slim advises us in a text titled "Electricity," "is half as strange as a strange friend." As a good Wobbly, T-Bone knew that the contradiction between friend and stranger can be resolved only *via* the medium of a revolutionary One Big Union of all workers. Clearly, too, an injury to one friendly stranger or strange friend is an injury to all. How they will actually go about organizing themselves is anybody's guess, but we do know this: In the world of Wrong Numbers, the call for solidarity is the one big underlying theme.

And don't forget that the world's misdialers are not only strangers, but also—one and all—*outside agitators.*

Remember, too, that the headquarters of the Outsiders' International is located *within* each of its participants, as well as in the aleatory relations between them.

And above all, keep in mind that no revolution is revolutionary enough until it is synonymous with the global efflorescence of poetic genius. In other words, at the planetary rendezvous of perfect strangers, poetry and revolution are one and indivisible.

## A Perpetual Potlatch

Wrong Numbers belong to a whole class of auditory verbal ephemera that includes, among others: (1) snatches of the conversations of passersby as we saunter along the avenues; (2) stray song-lyrics floating out of partly-open car-windows on drizzly evenings when traffic is slow; and (3) fleeting phrases heard "in passing" as we switch radio stations or distractedly watch the "coming attractions" at the movies. The chance nature of these elusive scraps of language, their troubling incompleteness and therefore their inevitably cryptic character, combine to invest them with an uncommon capacity for *haunting* us afterward.

In at least one respect, however, Wrong Numbers differ significantly from these other examples: They are personal and private, and our participation in them is active rather than passive. No matter how thoroughly I understand the plain truth that my unknown caller has reached me by mistake, the fact remains that his or her words have been spoken directly to me, and only to me. They are heard by no other ears than mine (leaving aside the possibility that my phone is tapped), and the only traces of them that linger on in the universe are in my mind. No amount of reasoning can diminish their perplexing character: quite the contrary, for—like agates and coral and birds' nests—the more we reflect upon them, the more fascinating they become.

On the surface, these few and fugitive words spoken by unknown voices hardly qualify as signals, much less as messages. At best they come to us only as the first movement of a signal, the merest outline of a message. We who are simply their modest and randomly chosen interceptors cannot be counted on to swear that any among them has any particular "meaning." They are perhaps best seen as permanently puzzling *gifts*, or rather odd pieces of gifts. They are not always received ungratefully, but they tend to be undecipherable, unexchangeable, and unapologetically lacking in ascertainable function. Each and every Wrong Number nonetheless can be regarded as a *contribution*—some obviously much more so than others—to the sum total of the kind of surrational awareness that jumps to conclusions in the form of *poetic inspiration*. Each and every one of them falls readily into place in that secret and seemingly inexhaustible reserve of magic-laden speech that we draw on, without thinking about it, when we lose or find ourselves in situations in which we have never lost or found ourselves before. In such moments we seem to stand face-to-face—and/or voice-to-voice—with the Great Invisibles.

It is not a question of putting these momentary verbal intrusions to work, but simply of recognizing that they play a part in the desperate game of language and life, and that it is possible for them to play *on our side*. Wrong Numbers seem to me to be among the few authentic contemporary equivalents of that great spiritual trash-heap of "old operas, inane refrains and artless rhythms" saluted by Rimbaud in his "Alchemy of the Word" as major sources of his poetic praxis. Like the fragments of 7-Up bottles that Sam Rodia integrated into the architectural jewelry of his glorious Watts Towers, and the colorful rubble with which Tyree Guyton has transformed so many abandoned houses in Detroit, the Wrong Number is part of modern technology's incidentally transcendental flotsam and jetsam, universally despised but nonetheless, in distinctively wayward ways, capable of sharpening the crisis of consciousness by demonstrating the *necessity* of poetry.

As "objects," Wrong Numbers are the merest odds and ends, and loose ends at that, but their elasticity and shapelessness are such that no two people will interpret them the same way. The question, "What do you make of it?" in reference to a Wrong Number, can readily be answered: "Whatever you like."

Their "function," then—to the extent that they can be said to have one at all—is purely *symbolic*, with occasional hints tending in the direction of the *mythic*.

The fact that, epistemologically and otherwise, they tend to be found wanting, is not, from the perspective of poetry and the Marvelous, an argument against them, but rather a decisive argument in their favor. That they reach us in fragments is among their brightest virtues. Their very incompleteness is an open invitation for us to lend a hand—to take part in a free exchange which need not come to an end with a couple of clicks. Wrong Numbers are infinitely recyclable, and generous to a fault. It is their nature to leave room for the imagination and to leave something to be desired. Who could ask for more? As foregleams of revolution and a free society, are they not among the best gifts of all?

Besides, as Meister Eckhart urged, "Every gift demands that we become receptive to a further and greater gift."

A mutual exchange without limits: a perpetual potlatch.

Everyone is welcome! Free admission! Come one, come all!

## Wrong Number Day (April 1): A Soapbox Rant

Everyone knows that Wrong Numbers did not help make this or any other country a Great Nation. But that is only one of their many admirable qualities. When we contemplate all that Wrong Numbers have done to ennoble life, to exalt what is best in each and all of us, and to hold out the promise of a better tomorrow—it is enough to bring tears to the eyes of even the most hard-hearted among us.

The mind reels at the magnitude of the achievements of the Wrong Numbers of the world—at the richness and many-sidedness of their contributions to the betterment of humankind and the planet.

Just think of it:

Wrong Numbers slow down the march of business, and could not care a whit about productivity or Progress. They do not add so much as a millionth of a millimeter to the long arm of the law. They are especially troublesome to parasites: bosses, bureaucrats, cops and politicians. They contribute nothing whatever to national security. They respect no flags. They are of absolutely no help in war. They are indifferent to all religions.

Wrong Numbers laugh at the stupid notion of the "White Race," and for that matter, of the whole divisive category of "race."

Is it not frightfully evident that, in matters most urgent and vital, hardly one among us can hold a candle to a Wrong Number?

And yet, in spite of the Wrong Number's impeccable record, all of us know what Wrong Numbers have had to endure lo these many years: hatred, scorn, derision, a thousand forms of vilification.

But we know, too, that "all things come to those who know how to wait." And we know that the Wrong Number has never given up.

And now, at last, the Wrong Number's day is upon us!

The struggle is far from over, but victory is in sight!

The vilest epithets hurled at us by the enemies of Wrong Numbers are now blowing back in their faces.

"Listen to the fool's reproach," said Blake. "It is a kingly title."

Like all of us who are not part of the capitalist economy, Wrong Numbers are *worthless*, but their value is immense to those who are prepared to recognize it.

Like all of us who have no place in the machinery of power, Wrong Numbers are *powerless*, but they have the power to inspire, to expand awareness, to provoke dreams.

Like all of us who have no use for militarism, Wrong Numbers are *defenseless*, but they protect us from the horror of boredom, they shield us from monotony, and they show us heretofore hidden *possibilities* of a new life.

Never forget this: Every Wrong Number is a holiday from the habitual, a break from hidebound drudgery and duty, an escape from slavery, a moment of the Marvelous, a chance to help reinvent life.

But keep this in mind as well: Of themselves, Wrong Numbers can do nothing.

What Wrong Numbers *are* depends on you.

What Wrong Numbers *can be* depends on us all.

Like all of us, they are the accidents of a moment, the chance of a lifetime, in search of poetry, freedom and love.

Let the festival begin!

## DREAM OF JULY 5, 1994

I was hurrying northward along Michigan Boulevard to the Art Institute, knowing that André Breton was in town and that I was to meet him there. He had some business with a high-ranking functionary of the Institute, whose name I do not recall, but it was evidently he who had invited André to the city and had arranged to pay his travel expenses. Out of the blue, André had phoned me and we had set a *rendez-vous* to meet in the foyer, around noon.

And there he was! He looked exactly as he had when I last saw him in 1966 in Paris, at the café La Promenade de Vénus in Les Halles, except that he seemed rather more haggard and his suit was a bit rumpled. I do not know where he had been living in the meantime, and did not ask, but it was definitely not in Paris, and probably not in Europe. Wherever it may have been, he evidently had left in a hurry, and was still in the clothes he had worn while traveling. I feel sure he was *in hiding*, though we did not discuss it. I had the impression that he had brought no luggage with him.

We shook hands and exchanged warm words of greeting. I remarked that the Art Institute seemed an odd place to meet, but he explained, with a smile: "No one would ever think to look for us here." (I am sure, too, that he also wanted to see Seurat's "Sunday Afternoon on the Island of Grande Jatte.") In his eyes a great wind made me think of the prairie at dusk, a party of Pottawatomie not far off. Yes, he said, it has been too long since we last saw each other, and yes, yes, we *must* stay closer in touch in the future.

We did not, however, dwell long on these formalities. We had plans to discuss, projects to complete, ideas to consider. I cannot say how long we spoke together, but this was no brief encounter. André had no immediate plans to leave Chicago; I am not sure that he had even decided yet where he would go next. He asked me many questions, listened attentively to all that I had to say, and commented freely, sometimes at length. Although the particulars of this conversation are beyond recall, I know we did discuss, albeit summarily, the Chicago Surrealist Group's proposal for an international surrealist exhibition on the theme of wildlife and wilderness, which he heartily approved.

Most of his friends, he said, had passed away, and his contacts with the widely scattered movement today were not extensive. The times, he added, were "very difficult," but he perceived hopeful signs. He was eager to see Penelope again, and to meet our friends in the Chicago group. I remember asking him in turn about various comrades around the world (the only name I recall here is that of Sergio Lima in São

Paulo). We agreed to exchange addresses of friends later in the day.

Then, suddenly, some invasive sound in the "real" world awakened me, and André was gone. Still more asleep than awake, I suddenly realized that *I did not have his current phone number*. My first thought, on opening my eyes, was a question addressed to him, and in fact whispered aloud: "How am I going to get in touch with you in the future?"

## Only the Marvelous is Beautiful

At the intersection of reason and delirium, theory and ecstasy, the Uncertainty Principle and the Pleasure Principle, poetry gathers momentum, the possible expands in all directions, freedom is realized, life renews itself, love conquers all.

In other words, imagination exists precisely so that we can let it run away with us.

This is *not* a conclusion. As Benjamin Paul Blood once put it: "What has concluded, that we might conclude in regard to it?"

What we want, what everyone wants, can be summed up in seven words: Freedom and the Marvelous, Now and Forever!

Always and everywhere, poetry is the best policy.

After all, it is in the nature of poetry to transform stumbling-blocks into stepping-stones.

When all is said and done, all that is worth saying and doing still needs to be said and done.

And what goes *without* saying always has to be invented all over again, from scratch.

Hello?

# P.S. / RSVP

*San Francisco, 1924*

Rosemont Apartments 214 Haight
" Aug L (Rosemont Press) r21 Rosemont pl
" Edmund (Margt) carp r176 Duboce av
" Gustave (Bertha) lithog r3748 24th
" Henry copyholder r270 McAllister
" John F (Rosemont Press) r21 Rosemont pl
" L Budd (Helen P) pub r20 Rosemont pl
**ROSEMONT PRESS THE (L B Rosemont), Book and Commercial Printing 21 Rosemont pl, Tel Market 1587**

*Twenty Years After*

Rosemont Bernard N dntst Flood Bldg..SU tter-2286
Rosemont Ed carpenter 176 Duboce..HE mlock-0817
Rosemont G Mrs r 1725 Van Ness Av.PR ospct-4241
Rosemont Helen 2nd r 275 Bright...RA ndlph-2300
Rosemont Helen P r 21 Rosemont Pl...MA rket-1500
Rosemont Letter Shop 176 Duboce...HE mlock-0817
Rosemont Press prntng 20 Sycamore..MA rket-5060
Rosemont Restaurant 3432-20th.......MI ssn-9268

*Chicago, 2003*

**Rosemont Apartments** 1061 W Rosemont Av
----------------------------------------**764-3270**
**Rosemont Cleaners** 6252 N California Av **-465-6179**
**Rosemont Convention Center**
------**See Donald E Stephens Convention Center**
**Rosemont Foreign & Domestic Auto Repair Inc**
1125 W Rosemont Av --------------------------**274-5454**
**Rosemont Gardens Inc** 3320 River Rd
Frnkln Pk-----------------------------------**800 244-4087**
**Rosemont Korean Congregation Of Jehovah's Witnesses** 6560 N Harlem Av---------------**763-2668**
**Rosemont Park Cemetery**
6758 W Addison---------------------------------**736-2553**
**Rosemont Stucco** 4800 W Armitage Av----**637-0090**

*Rosemont (Franklin).*

# Index

## SURREALIST EDITIONS
# Black Swan Press

***SURREALIST EXPERIENCES: 1001 Dawns, 221 Midnights***. Essays by Penelope Rosemont on Landscapades, Prehensilhouettes, Alchemigrams, Maxwell Street blues, Love, Anarchy, Humor, the Future of Surrealism, and "A Brief Rant Against Work." Foreword by Rikki Ducornet, and a Note by Leonora Carrington. *"Embodies art, action & vision, in playful yet precise language . . . daily experience as an experiment in revolution"—**Fifth Estate.*** 204 pp. 40 illus. Cloth $24 / paper $12.

***THE FORECAST IS HOT! Tracts & Other Collective Declarations of the Surrealist Movement in the U.S., 1966–1976***, edited with introduction & notes by Franklin Rosemont, Penelope Rosemont & Paul Garon. 320 pages of essential documents from the first ten years of U.S. Surrealism, with an introduction which is in truth a Surrealist Manifesto for our time. 276 pp. 87 Illus. Index. Cloth $30 / paper $15.

***ARSENAL/Surrealist Subversion 4***. Lavishly illustrated oversize international anthology: a must for anyone interested in the theory & practice of surrealist revolution today. Texts by Luis Buñuel, Leonora Carrington, M.de Chazal, Jayne Cortez, Marcel Duchamp, Paul Garon, Jan Hathaway, Joseph Jablonski, C.L.R. James, Ted Joans, Nelly Kaplan, Philip Lamantia, Mary Low, Nancy Peters, Herbert Marcuse, Dave Roediger, F. Rosemont, P. Rosemont, Karel Teige & many more. 224 pp. Paper $15

***DOWN BELOW*** by Leonora Carrington. A surrealist classic: a brave woman's harrowing adventures on the other side of the mirror on the eve of World War II, after being declared "incurably insane." With the original map, and new collages by Debra Taub. 48 pp. Paper $12

***MARVELOUS FREEDOM /VIGILANCE OF DESIRE***. Large-format catalog of the 1976 World Surrealist Exhibition. Scores of articles, poems & reproductions by surrealists from 31 countries. Cover by E. F.Granell. Original blueprint pasted in. 56 large pages. *Supply limited!* Paper, $25

***THE POETICAL ALPHABET*** by Benjamin Paul Blood. A short treatise on poetic language by the 19th-century poet/philosopher of "Anaesthetic Revelation." Introduction by Franklin Rosemont. 24 pp. $5.00

## SURREALIST POETRY

Paul Garon. **RANA MOZELLE**. Authentically amphibious surrealist texts, preceded by a short treatise on the "Fate of the Obsessive Image." Surrealist Research & Development Monograph Series. 16 pp. $5

Robert Green. **SEDITIOUS MANDIBLES.** Drawings & poems of scandalous laughter, dedicated to Mass Uprising. 24 pp. $6

Joseph Jablonski. **IN A MOTH'S WING**. Poems of alchemical and utopian fervor, with a preface: "Dream Bait, or, Dr. Faust, Your Hair Is on Fire." Surrealist Research & Development Monograph Series. 28 pp. $5

Joseph Jablonski. **THE DUST ON MY EYES IS THE BLOOD OF YOUR HAIR**. Poems to increase the velocity of evil thoughts. 24 pp. $5

Mary Low. **A VOICE IN THREE MIRRORS**. Poems of Delight, Darkness, and Defiance, with collages by the author—a lifelong surrealist activist who helped co-organize the women's militia in revolutionary Spain in 1936. 48 pp. $6

Mary Low. **WHERE THE WOLF SINGS**. New poems and collages of the enchanted life, anguish, combats and diversions, by one of the stalwarts of the Surrealist Movement in the U.S. 64 pp. $7

Nancy Joyce Peters. **IT'S IN THE WIND**. Poems of love, the death of mirrors and the General Strike, with papercuts by Mado. Surrealist Research & Development Monograph Series. 16 pp. $5

Franklin Rosemont. **THE APPLE OF THE AUTOMATIC ZEBRA'S EYE**. With ten positive & negative drawings by Schlechter Duvall. Surrealist Research & Development Monograph Series. 28 pp. $5

Franklin Rosemont. **LAMPS HURLED AT THE STUNNING ALGEBRA OF ANTS**. Twenty-seven poems of humor and delirium by a poet officially declared "morally disqualified for military service" by the U.S. government. With twelve radiantly magical drawings by Karol Baron, from the Surrealist Group in the Czech Republic. 48 pp. $5

Franklin Rosemont. **PENELOPE: A POEM.** A vertiginous epic of mad love and revolution, direct from the Elixir Amyranth, open all night all ways always! With six drawings by Jacques Lacomblez. 64 pp. $7

Penelope Rosemont. **ATHANOR**. Seventeen hermetically open, all-or-nothing, anything-is-possible poems, illustrated with wondrous alchemical engravings from Abraham Lambsprinck's *On the Philosophers's Stone* (1741) and other ancient works . . . 16 pages. $5

Penelope Rosemont. **BEWARE OF THE ICE & OTHER POEMS.** The language of birds joins the revolt of the unexpected! No-Compromise Poetry in Defense of the Marvelous! Drawings by Enrico Baj. 64 pp. $6

## SURREALIST BOOKS from OTHER PUBLISHERS

***SURREALIST WOMEN: An International Anthology***, edited and introduced by Penelope Rosemont. A breakthrough compilation! Hundreds of texts by 97 women active in surrealism in dozens of countries from the 1920s through the present. The superb introductions to each of the book's six beautifully illustrated sections tell the hidden story of surrealist women & their wide-ranging impact. University of Texas Press. No. 1 in the "Surrealist Revolution Series." 576 pp. Cloth $50 / paper $25.

***MAX ERNST & ALCHEMY: A Magician in Search of Myth*** by M. E. Warlick, with a Foreword by Franklin Rosemont. 309 plus xxiv pages. A passionate, thoroughly researched & profusely illustrated account of an exceptionally important but too-little-known facet of Ernst's life & work. The Foreword is a veritable mini-manifesto on the past, present, and future of surrealist scholarship. University of Texas Press. No. 2 in the "Surrealist Revolution Series." 333 pp. Paper $25

***WHAT IS SURREALISM? Selected Writings of André Breton***, edited & introduced by Franklin Rosemont. First published in 1978, this book has long been acknowledged as the standard collection of Breton's shorter writings, and a selection of surrealist documents. This book has been kept uninterruptedly in print through numerous printings here and in England. This new edition features larger type, and hence is a larger book: two volumes in one. Pathfinder Press. 212 + 529 pp. Illus. Paper $35

***DISCOURSE ON COLONIALISM,*** by Aimé Césaire. This major work of surrealist social criticism was first published in 1950. The new edition includes a brilliant 50th Anniversary introduction ("A Poetics of Anti-colonialism") by Robin D. G. Kelley. Monthly Review. 102 pp. $14.00

***BLUES & THE POETIC SPIRIT***, by Paul Garon. New, expanded edition of the pioneering and influential surrealist study of the African American blues tradition. *"Absolutely the best book on the blues"*—Robin D. G. Kelley. City Lights. 252 pp. Illus. $15.00

***WOMAN WITH GUITAR: Memphis Minnie's Blues,*** by Paul and Beth Garon. The first full-length biographical/critical study of one of the all-time greatest blues artists, noted for her hard-hitting highly imaginative original lyrics. *"A delight . . . both thorough and brilliant, a rare combination these days"*—David Roediger. DaCapo. 332 pp. Illus. Paper $15.00

***THE DEVIL'S SON-IN-LAW: The Story of Peetie Wheatstraw & His Songs*** by Paul Garon. Lavishly illustrated life & times of a legendary Depression-era blues-singer, with eight newly transcribed songs & a 24-track CD. Charles H. Kerr. 156 pp. Cloth $21; paper $15.00

***JOE HILL: The IWW & the Making of a Revolutionary Workingclass Counterculture***, by Franklin Rosemont. An in-depth study of U.S. labor's most renowned bard and martyr, and of the Wobbly movement he continues to exemplify. *"The best book ever written on Joe Hill"*—Utah Phillips. 639 pp. Profusely illus. Charles H. Kerr. Cloth $35; paper $18.00.

***VIVA POSADA! A Salute to the Great Printmaker of the Mexican Revolution***, edited & introduced by Carlos Cortez. Includes short texts by Diego Rivera, André Breton, Dennis Brutus, Lawrence Ferlinghetti, Frida Kahlo, José Clemente Orozco, Octavio Paz, and by 32 participants in the Surrealist Movement in the U.S. Charles H. Kerr. 94 pp.121 illus. $10.00

***SURREALISM: REVOLUTION AGAINST WHITENESS***, edited & introduced by Franklin Rosemont. This special issue of the anti-white-supremacist journal *Race Traitor* explores, for the first time, the role of surrealism in the struggle against white supremacy. Starting with a mini-anthology of "Surrealists on Whiteness, from 1925 to the Present," the book includes articles by Ronnie Burk, René Crevel, Artur do Cruzeiro Seixas, Nancy Cunard, Paul Garon, Joseph Jablonski, Charles Radcliffe, Myrna Bell Rochester, David Roediger, Penelope Rosemont, Ron Sakolsky, Peter Lamborn Wilson and many more. 144 pp. Illus. $5.00

**SURREALISM IN THE U.S.A.*: The Complete Contents of the Suppressed Surrealist Issue of* Socialist Review**, edited & introduced by Ron Sakolsky. This special double issue of *Race Traitor* (No. 13–14, Summer 2001) develops many of the themes taken up in the earlier (1998) Surrealist issue. Includes texts by Gale Ahrens, Paul Garon, Joseph Jablonski, Robin D. G. Kelley, Don LaCoss, Anne Olson, David Roediger, Mari Jo Marchnight, and Franklin Rosemont; an interview with Penelope Rosemont by Danny Postel; a section on "Surrealist Subversion in Everyday Life," and poems by Ronnie Burk, Jayne Cortez, Ted Joans, Casandra Stark Mele & others. Aside from a few short texts, **all the material in this issue is unavailable in any other publication.** 256 pages. $12.00.

*The biggest and best book yet on Surrealism in the U.S.!*

**SURREALIST SUBVERSIONS: Rants, Writings & Images by the Surrealist Movement in the United States**, edited and introduced by Ron Sakolsky, with a Foreword by Franklin Rosemont. Contains over 200 texts (*more than two dozen appearing here for the first time*) by more than *fifty* participants in the Surrealist Movement, making this the largest, most comprehensive and lavishly illustrated compilation of surrealist writings ever published anywhere. Long sections are devoted to play, popular culture, Black music, outsiders, contemporary surrealism in the arts, surrealist games, and "Subverting the Institutions of Unfreedom." Editor Ron Sakolsky's provocative and far-ranging 86-page introduction explores the historical development of "Chicago Idea" surrealism as well as its current cultural/political actuality in the U.S. and the world today.

Texts and/or images by Gale Ahrens, Jennifer Bean, Jen Besemer, Daniel C. Boyer, Paul Buhle, Ronnie Burk, Leonora Carrington, Laura Corsigilia, Jayne Cortez, Guy Ducornet, Rikki Ducornet, Jan Schlechter Duvall, Alice Farley, J. Allen Fees, Beth Garon, Paul Garon, Eugenio F. Granell, Robert Green, Miriam Hansen, Diedra Harris-Kelley, Jan Hathaway, Corinna Jablonski, Joseph Jablonski, Ted Joans, Gerome Kamrowski, Robin D. G. Kelley, Don LaCoss, Philip Lamantia, Clarence John Laughlin, Mary Low, Herbert Marcuse, Tristan Meinecke, Casandra Stark Mele, Anne Olson, Nancy Joyce Peters, Myrna Bell Rochester, David Roediger, Franklin Rosemont, Penelope Rosemont, Ody Saban,

Louise Simons, Martha Sonnenberg, Christopher Starr, Ivan Svitak, Cheikh Tidiane Sylla, Claude Tarnaud, Debra Taub, Dale Tomich, Patrick Turner, Darryl Lorenzo Wellington, Jordan West, Joel Williams, Haifa Zangana **& many more!** Published by Autonomedia. 144 illus; bibliography; index. 742 pp. Paper, $23.00

## SPECIAL IMPORTS

***ÇA VA CHAUFFER! Situation du Surréalisme aux U.S.A., 1966–2001***, by Guy Ducornet. The first full-length French-language study of the Chicago Surrealist Group & the Surrealist Movement in the U.S. (Mons: Editions Talus d'approche), 125 pp. Illus. Paper, $12.50

***ANTHOLOGIE des poètes surréalistes américaines***, presented and translated by Jean-Jacques Celly, with a Preface by Franklin Rosemont. The first major compilation exclusively devoted to U.S. surrealist poetry. Poems (in English and French translation) by Gale Ahrens, Jennifer Bean, Ronnie Burk, Jayne Cortez, Rikki Ducornet, Joseph Allen Fees, Paul Garon, Joseph Jablonski, Ted Joans, Philip Lamantia, Mary Low, Casandra Stark Mele, Anne Olson, Nancy Joyce Peters, Larry Romano, Penelope Rosemont, Franklin Rosemont, Pete Winslow. Remoulins sur Gardon: Editions Jacques Brémond. 143 pp. Paper, $35

***CRUZEIRO SEIXAS: Other Forms of Dancing, Flying, Dreaming and Wandering***. A large & lovely book on one of the greatest surrealist painters and poets of our time, the catalog of a recent major exhibition. Essays by André Coyné, Edouard Jaguer, Franklin Rosemont, and Luis de Moura Sobral. All texts are in English, Spanish, Portuguese, and Galego. Published by the Fundación Eugenio Granell in Spain. 151 pp. 93 reproductions, mostly in color. *Supply limited!* Paper $30

## ORDERING INFORMATION

All Surrealist Editions/Black Swan Press titles, plus the Books from Other Publishers and Special Imports listed above, can be ordered from the **Charles H. Kerr Publishing Company,** 1740 West Greenleaf Avenue, Chicago, IL 60626. *Please add $2.00 shipping for the first title, and fifty cents for each additional title.* **Make checks payable to Charles H. Kerr Publishing Company.**

*Or, for online service & credit card acceptance ($25 minimum), order from:*

**Chicago Rare Book Center**, 56 West Maple, Chicago, IL. 60610 (312-988-7246 / Fax 312-988-7247 / email chicagorare@attglobal.net

**For further information on surrealist activity today visit the web-site of the SURREALIST MOVEMENT IN THE U.S.**
**www.surrealism-usa.org**